D0364012

Auto da Fay

Also by Fay Weldon

Fiction

THE FAT WOMAN'S JOKE
DOWN AMONG THE
  WOMEN
FEMALE FRIENDS
REMEMBER ME
LITTLE SISTERS
PRAXIS
PUFFBALL
THE PRESIDENT'S CHILD
THE LIFE AND LOVES
  OF A SHE-DEVIL
THE SHRAPNEL ACADEMY
THE HEART OF THE
  COUNTRY
THE HEARTS AND LIVES
  OF MEN
THE RULES OF LIFE
LEADER OF THE BAND
THE CLONING OF JOANNA
  MAY
DARCY'S UTOPIA
GROWING RICH
LIFE FORCE
AFFLICTION
SPLITTING
WORST FEARS
BIG WOMEN
RHODE ISLAND BLUES
THE BULGARI CONNECTION

Children's Books

WOLF THE
  MECHANICAL DOG
NOBODY LIKES ME

Short Story Collections

WATCHING ME,
  WATCHING YOU
POLARIS
MOON OVER MINNEAPOLIS
WICKED WOMEN
A HARD TIME TO BE A
  FATHER

Non-fiction

LETTERS TO ALICE
REBECCA WEST
SACRED COWS
GODLESS IN EDEN

Auto da Fay

FAY WELDON

Flamingo
An Imprint of HarperCollins*Publishers*

Flamingo
An Imprint of HarperCollins*Publishers*
77–85 Fulham Palace Road,
Hammersmith, London W6 8JB

Flamingo is a registered trademark of
HarperCollins*Publishers* Limited

www.fireandwater.com

Published by Flamingo 2002
9 8 7 6 5 4 3 2 1

First published in Great Britain by
Flamingo 2002

Copyright © Fay Weldon 2002

Fay Weldon asserts the moral right to
be identified as the author of this work

A catalogue record for this book is available
from the British Library
ISBN 0 00 710992 X

Set in Sabon by Rowland Phototypesetting Limited,
Bury St Edmunds, Suffolk

Printed and bound in Great Britain by
Clays Ltd, St Ives plc

Auto da Fay

Photographs

Myself in Coromandel, aged eight, reading Captain Henty   viii

The town of Napier, after the earthquake, 1931   3

My mother and Nona with baby Jane, Alassio, 1929   7

My Aunt Faith, as a child, 1911   10

My grandfather, Edgar Jepson   18

Myself, aged 3, in Amberley   35

My mother, Margaret   47

My father as a young hopeful. Frank Birkinshaw in 1915   52

Jane'nFay, modelling on the sand dunes in 1943   74

Coromandel, the Golden Age, 1940   76

In the garden of Christchurch, 1937   89

My father and Edna, on their wedding day, 1942   112

Jane in pensive mood   150

Dashing Uncle Selwyn, beloved by many women   162

Myself with baby Nicolas, 1954, in the yard at
    Saffron Walden, taking refuge from the ghosts   264

Mrs Bateman on her wedding day, 1957, rightly
    fearful of the future   283

Ron Weldon and myself, (extreme right) in the
    Primrose Hill of the early Sixties. The occasion was
    Roger Graef's wedding. Pick out Bernice Rubens and
    Jonathan Miller   348

Myself as ad-woman: with my second son, Daniel, aged 3   367

Pre-name

I long for a day of judgment when the plot lines of our lives will be neatly tied, and all puzzles explained, and the meaning of events made clear. We take to fiction, I suppose, because no such thing is going to happen, and at least on the printed page we can observe beginnings, middles and ends, and can find out where morality resides. Real life tends to fade out into entropy, all loose ends, and grief for what should have been, could have been, had things turned out just a little differently. Yet probably the life that was lived was the best that could be done: even, to the outsider, better than could have been expected.

This is an attempt to narrate a real life, my own, and to find the pattern within it. The pattern can't really be completed, of course, until death, when autobiography so rudely turns into biography, but so far as I can do it, I will.

There seems to be a general overall pattern in most lives, that nothing happens, and nothing happens, and then all of a sudden everything happens. You are swimming out to sea, you're rocking gently in the wake of a wave, all seems tranquil, but water is mounting beneath you, unstoppable, and suddenly you are the wave, breaking and crashing, sucking back into a maelstrom – and then all is tranquil again.

When I was three months in the womb, in a period no doubt of nothing happening and nothing happening except a general warm all-pervasive dullness, an earthquake in Napier, New Zealand, had my mother Margaret running from the house with my two-year-old sister Jane in her arms. The year was 1931. My mother was twenty-three. Our house stayed upright but the grammar school opposite and the hospital down the road, both made of brick and not New Zealand's usual wood, collapsed. Everything else seemed made of matchsticks. My mother, in search of my father, one of the town's few doctors, ran past the grammar school and saw arms and legs sticking out of the rubble. But with a small child in your arms, what can you do for others? Everyone else was running too, some one way, some another: the ground was still shaking and changing and whether you were running into more danger or less how could you be sure? But still she ran.

All the water swept out of Napier harbour that day and never came back: the town had to be entirely rebuilt, and became the Art Deco gem it is today.

Dr Frank Birkinshaw, my father, was too busy with the injured to take care of his young wife. He was a man of great charm, tall, well built, blue-eyed, adventurous and impetuous – at the time in his mid-thirties. Margaret was small, dark, fastidious and very, very pretty, with high cheekbones, big brown eyes and a gentle manner. The Birkinshaws were recent immigrants from England. He was from the North, had joined the army when he was sixteen, been invalided out of the trenches, and qualified as a doctor in the face of many obstacles. She was a bohemian from the softer South, an intellectual by birth, breeding, and temperament: her father a novelist, her mother a musician. She kept the company of

Evelyn Waugh and his gang of friends, she was at home in literary soirées and in fashionable nightclubs, not in this harsh pioneering land. But she was also clever, determined and tough and failing to find my father, she left word for him, and by nightfall she and Jane had taken refuge in the tented city that went up overnight on the hills above Napier. The town was uninhabitable.

The stars had never seemed so bright, my mother said, as if nature were showing off its beauty to make amends for the terrible thing it had just done. But the lice, she added, were very active. I have met others who mention these two things about the tented town, the brightness of the stars and the liveliness of the lice. And they smile and seem to prefer not to go into detail. Perhaps licentiousness reigned: it would not be surprising; the ordinary answer to death is to create new life, and the normal inhibitions of small town life had been suddenly and drastically removed.

My mother was rescued from her makeshift tent by a sheep farmer and his wife, grateful patients of my father. They took her and little Jane to their homestead, where there was, my mother said, mutton for breakfast, mutton for dinner and mutton for tea. She helped around the farm, and cooked and ate the mutton with gratitude. I inherit this gift from her, I daresay, in that I do what is under my nose to be done, without too much lamentation.

Although the ground shook and trembled for weeks after the initial quake, meals continued to be served in the cookhouse, which had a tall brick chimney. My mother lived in fear of it collapsing and killing everyone inside, but no one would listen to her. She was dismissed as an alarmist. She was right, of course. There was another bad shock. 'I felt the trembling begin beneath my feet. I snatched Jane from her cot on the veranda and ran for open space but I was flung to the ground by what seemed a wave of dry land. I saw the hedge flick first one way and then the other. And then I watched the chimney fall into the cookhouse and destroy it. I always knew it would. I had already seen it happen.' As it fell out, dinner had finished just minutes before, and no one was killed, though for a time meals had to be eaten in the open air.

I have not inherited my mother's gift for prophecy: true, as you grow older you may begin to know what is going to happen next, but this can be put down to experience, not second sight. It is not a happy gift to have: because of it, for one thing, my mother never learned to drive, seeing too many scenarios of disaster ahead for comfort, too conscious of what might be going on over the brow of the hill. My father was very different: he was over-confident: he saw to the pleasures of the here-and-now and let the future go hang. I was born more like him than her, in this respect. She prophesied that it would land us both in trouble, and she was right.

There was no word from Frank for three months. My mother became alarmed. He knew where she was. It was true that, post-earthquake, communications were near-impossible: civil structures had broken down, there was no working telephone system for a time and no post – but surely in three months he could have managed some kind of message? Perhaps in the second big shock the earth had swallowed him up? Perhaps he'd run off with another woman? Women were always after him. Perhaps he had amnesia, and didn't remember he was married? Or perhaps this was just the way men were? She had no friends of her own age to talk to. The Birkinshaws had not been long in Napier: she'd been too busy adjusting to pioneer manners to make friends: in London people left calling-cards in the front hall: not here, where luxuries like hall-stands were rare.

The truth was hard to avoid: that here she was alone, penniless, on the wrong side of the globe, with no past, no future, just the shaky earth beneath her feet and two children, one born, one yet unborn, and no one to look after them but herself. Pregnant, she must for the time being be dependent upon the comfort of strangers. But once I was born, somehow, she would get us back to London. There were advantages to having no husband – at least you could make your own decisions. In the meanwhile she had better make herself useful and help in the kitchens and try to hold her tongue when her hosts started rebuilding the cookhouse chimney just where it had been before. It did not do for 'homies' – immigrants – to put on airs or offer advice.

She made mutton stew for the farmhands. Trim and cut the meat, brown in beef dripping – better than mutton fat – add onions and carrots, stew till the meat is on the point of

5

disintegration, thicken with flour and serve. She learned to make the basic cake which accompanied my childhood. The weight of an egg in sugar, the same in butter, a cup of liquid, a cup of flour, and never close the oven with a bang or it sinks. This is the same sensible basic cake which she now has every evening for supper in her retirement home seventy years on. Sometimes, for variety, they put sultanas in it, sometimes not. She looks at it and shakes her head. How can they make something which ought to be so light, so solid?

She would write home, of course, though it hurt her pride. Margaret had married, at nineteen, in the face of a great deal of advice to the contrary. A letter could go no faster than the ship which carried it: five or six weeks to get to London – via Panama or Suez – and the same for a reply to come back, and supposing Frank turned up in the meantime? Her parents would send her money if they could, but supposing they couldn't, all she would succeed in doing was worry them. Because back home in London, needing no earthquake to achieve it, or only those of the emotional kind, the Jepson family too had collapsed in disarray.

Her father Edgar, at the age of sixty-nine, had made his mistress Lois pregnant. Her mother Frieda, unable to bear it any longer, had fled the marital home and gone to be with her own mother, Mary Francis Holmes, widowed and in San Francisco. Frieda, now in her early fifties, had no income of her own and lived by her mother's courtesy, and anything Edgar could afford. It was not much. Edgar was a prolific writer: he wrote seventy-three novels in all – light but popular: *Lady Noggs Assists*, *The Reluctant Footman*, *The Cuirass of Diamonds* and so on – but hard as he worked, his age was beginning to tell against him, public taste was changing, and

the financial depression of the times affected everyone. Now he must do the decent thing and marry Lois, and he would have another child to keep.

Nor could there be any support, either financial or moral, from my mother's elder sister Faith, whom Margaret had loved dearly and greatly depended upon during her childhood. Faith had gone 'mad', and was now locked up in the lunatic asylum where she was to live out the rest of her short days. Only their big brother Selwyn, then a fashionable young man about town, already making a good living selling articles and short stories, was prosperous enough to offer any help. But it seemed doubtful that he would. He had been very much against Margaret marrying Frank and it was his general principle that if people made their own beds, they should lie in them.

I have a photograph of Selwyn at this period. A wraith of cigarette smoke curls from an elegant ivory holder. He does not look the kind of young man to see earthquakes as an excuse for failure. In the Second World War he was to become a major in the SOE, in charge of recruitment, his task to find and send agents to a likely death in occupied France. I think he became kinder then: certainly he was to develop an air of benign consideration, and to be of great help to us, until my mother quarrelled with him over a matter of principle. But as it was, my mother chose to write to Edgar.

No sooner had she done so, of course, than through the post came a letter from Frank. He was apologetic: he had been looking for work and hadn't liked to write until he had something good to report. Now he had. This was the Thirties, the depression had hit New Zealand badly: there was massive unemployment, and the professions were not immune. But he had finally found a job as houseman in the hospital at Palmerston North, a township further inland. True, it was a live-in job, there were no married quarters, and he had had to pretend he was single, but he had found her and Jane lodgings in a nearby boarding-house.

My poor mother: out of the frying-pan into the fire. She had her husband back, at least when he could slip out unnoticed from the hospital, and all the energy and exhilaration that accompanied his presence, but it wasn't enough. She was lonely, traumatized, uncomfortable because I kicked a lot, unable to sleep at night because of the trains which in those days ran through the middle of the town, Jane's crying and the landlady's suspicions about her respectability. When a letter finally arrived from Edgar telling her to come back home, no matter what, and enclosing money for the fare, she took ship back to England.

She did not stay in London because now Lois was installed in the family home as Edgar's new wife, and Margaret saw it as an act of disloyalty to her mother to stay there. It would upset Frieda too much when she heard of it, which she would undoubtedly do. Instead my mother went to Frank's parents, Herbert and Isabel Birkinshaw, then living in Barnt Green, outside Birmingham. And that's how I happened to be born, on 22 September, 1931, in a nursing home in the village of Alvechurch, Worcestershire, and not in Napier, New Zealand, as everyone had expected.

Franklin Fay

Before I was so much as named Edgar had drawn up my horoscope. I was never to meet him, other than for a few weeks when I was newly born. He was a Balliol man, a classicist, a collector of Chinese antiquities, something of a dandy, neat, small of build and a favourite of the ladies, as the euphemism went. Like many of the literati of the time, he was greatly interested in the occult; a fashion, or habit, or curse, kick-started by Annie Besant and the Theosophists, side-winding into the Cabbala and diabolism and ending with Aleister Crowley, Number 666, the Beast, with whom the movement expired from its own excesses.

Edgar was a good friend of Arthur Machen, writer of 'stories of horror and evil' and a member, with W. B. Yeats and

Crowley, of the Order of the Golden Dawn, a secret society dedicated to cabalistic magic. I do not think Edgar was very serious about any of this. In his autobiography (*Memories of a Victorian*, written in 1933, and dedicated to 'his wife', by whom – poor Frieda! – he must mean Lois) he complains that 'in these degenerate and sinister days few are at pains to learn how they stand with the stars' but notes that he himself is pleased to be born under the sign of Libra – 'for they have fine hair, and a beard less bristly to have than the beards of any of the other children of the universe, and write a more lucid prose'.

I was born at 5.30 in the afternoon, when the sun was just moving out of Virgo into Libra, and it was hoped I too would have the gift for lucid prose, though according to Edgar the position of the stars made this marginal. I certainly have fine hair, which has proved very difficult and costly over the years.

It was Arthur Machen who introduced my grandfather to the practice of astrology. Edgar taught my mother, my mother taught Jane, and Jane declined to teach me. But my mother had *Teach Yourself Astrology* on her shelves, in a bright yellow jacket, next to *The Cloud of Unknowing* and *The Writings of St Teresa of Avila*, and I have a clear vision of myself, at the age of twelve, sitting on the lawn of the Christchurch Girls' High School on a sunny day, with an ephemeris of the planets' places and some blank horoscope forms, successfully drawing up the chart of a school-friend. I did a handful of these for my classmates and then no more. They seemed to offer a fair enough representation of the temperament of my subjects but what was the point, since they themselves were sitting next to me? And casting horoscopes – or even reading palms, another party trick – left me with a strangely unpleasant feeling of remoteness and passivity: as if (a contemporary simile) one had taken too many painkillers in order to get rid of toothache, and one's liver was affected. In other words I got to feel 'spooked' – a teenage word but the only one available – which is the normal punishment for dabbling in the occult, and a sure sign one should stop. I do not watch horror films on my own in the house. To acknowledge the devil is to bring him nearer; best to ignore him.

I read Machen's novel *The Hill of Dreams* around that time, and still carry in my mind its feeling-tone; and the description of the aura of evil which sweeps one evening over an English landscape which has a terrifying past of cruelty and massacre, centred on a Roman fort. That novel was published in 1907, a year later than Kipling's collection of stories and poems, *Puck of Pook's Hill*, very much on the same theme, but seeing evil and horror where Kipling saw good and the human capacity for renewal. I wish it had been the other way round: it is not right for evil to have the last word.

My sister Jane had a 'blessing' by Arthur Machen in a frame upon the wall until my mother took it down. She never liked it. The blessing, given to baby Jane on the occasion of her christening, consisted of a sheet of parchment, in the middle of which was a paragraph in tiny writing in a language and script no one recognized. I was probably fortunate I did not receive one too.

In my father's absence my mother named me Franklin. The registrar wrote 'boy' in the 'sex' column, and then had to cross it out and write 'girl'. I was to feel vaguely apologetic about this later; my parents had a girl already and would obviously want a boy and I had failed them. My mother – Mrs Bored of Barnt Green, no doubt – had been studying numerology, a way of divining the future through the relationship of names to numbers, while she waited for the birth. Franklin Birkinshaw, she discovered, 'came out the same' as William Shakespeare. My being born a girl had left her unprepared. But Franklin was a most auspicious name.

And was not 'lin' the female diminutive, and was not Frank my father? Franklin still made perfect sense to her, and she hoped to others.

Alas, it did not, no doubt least of all to my father when she first showed him the new baby. It was going to be, he reckoned, citing the registrar as evidence, too confusing for others. They took in time to calling me Fay, I hope not after Fay Wray, the screaming heroine of so many horror films, but you never know. If it was, I grew up to be a sunny enough child, if only in defiance, though there were to be King Kongs enough in my life. I was left with the name Franklin on official documents, while being Fay at school. But it was Franklin only at the Christchurch Public Library. They would not recognize Fay, though I pleaded. I had to sign my full name, Franklin Birkinshaw, every time I took out a book, while the Beryls and the Dulcies, the Meryls and the Aprils, looked on askance, and the librarians shook their heads and took pleasure in wondering aloud what kind of parents I must have. Thus I started out in a state of ambivalence. I took out library books as Franklin and read them as Fay.

Names are important. I was only to become a writer when I added Weldon to the Fay. Other names had intervened, leaving me stranded, if often entertained, and occasionally scared. But Weldon was the one which best suited. It lengthens with the years, of course. This morning I signed a document under the name Fay Franklin Weldon Fox. With every change of name comes a change in fortune. I never took to numerology, all the same. No change in fortune should be seen as magic, only as a function of altering views of the self. As babies, of course, we are helpless, dependent upon our mothers' expectations, and in my case these were perhaps too high.

13

Edgar and Selwyn, father and brother, did not want Margaret to go back to New Zealand. It was too far away: the ends of the earth: things had not gone well for her there. If she went back to Frank, who was to say how she would ever afford to get home again? It was not as if her husband was particularly good at keeping even a roof over her head. They were quite right, of course. In March, 1938, shortly before he died, Edgar wrote a brief note to Frieda in California. He has moved house to spare himself the stairs. He gives his new address. 'There is nothing else in the way of news,' he writes. 'Margaret seems stuck in New Zealand, and I wish she wasn't . . .' He hopes that Frieda's giddiness has stopped. 'Perhaps the spring will be helpful.' And then – 'I have sold some sword guards to a North American and I send you the cheque. You must buy a spring frock with it.' He finishes, 'With best love, E.' It is a poignant letter. He would do better for her if only he could, one reads between the lines, and perhaps even still loves her, only Lois and her pregnancy came between. His obituary in the *Telegraph*, found yellowed between the pages of his second volume of autobiography, *Memories of an Edwardian*, reads 'He was a distinctive craftsman of remarkable personality, whose many friends included practically all the literary men of any note during the past half-century.' My mother cried when a letter came to us in Christchurch to say he had died, and Jane and I cried to keep her company, though we did not know what we had lost.

But my mother, back in 1931, was not to be dissuaded by family advice. It was her duty to go back to her husband; she had promised to go back and besides, she loved him. 'You have no idea,' she said to me once, 'what fun your father was in the early days. What light he brought with him into a room.'

She had not given the new land a fair chance, she told Edgar and Selwyn. New Zealand was a better place to bring up children than foggy, smoky London. And besides, things had changed. Her father, old enough to be great-grandfather not father to a new baby, was with a woman not her mother. The good days were over. And as Margaret embarked on the liner which was to carry her back to her unchancy husband, with little Jane clutching her hand and myself at five weeks held against her, and appreciative porters buzzing around with her trunks and cases, she must have felt a certain relief. At least she would not have to stay around to witness the sorry state to which two generations of Free Love and the Life Force had brought her family. To see the shadow of itself which 120 Adelaide Road, once so full of wit, energy and creativity, music and laughter, had become.

The House That Once Was

Terrible things had happened at Adelaide Road in the past, of course they had. It was not in anyone's nature to play safe – neither in the Jepsons', nor the Holmeses'. Where there are angels there are devils as well, and sometimes they both take up residence in the one person. At one time Edgar had installed Lois in the house over the way, and Frieda had been summoned in the middle of the night to help her rival through a miscarriage. It would be a rare wife these days who would put up with such a thing, but wives were more helpless then, and besides, the doctrine of Free Love was offered by the bohemians of the time as an excuse for a great deal of hurtful activity.

15

It was in its name that my seventeen-year-old Aunt Faith was seduced by her mother's brother, to the destruction of her life but with no apparent difference to his. Men are great theorists and when in full pursuit of ends which to them seem noble but are simply not, it's an unwise woman who allows herself to be persuaded. Body blows can be dealt to family life, and a family seem to reel and recover, but not for long. The next soft tap can bring it tumbling down.

But while it stood how well it stood. Houses have heydays, just as people do, and that of 120 Adelaide Road ran for twenty years, from 1910 to 1930. In the good days Edgar would write in his study, Frieda play the piano, the nanny look after the three children, and the cook and maid who lived and worked in the basement in times of plenty, looked after everything else. There were literary parties to give and attend, nightclubs to go to, and the talk was of socialism, Free Love, eugenics, and Fabianism. The household income was erratic, and entirely dependent on the skill of Edgar's pen. The carpets might stop at the first landing, yesterday's cold rice pudding turn up in today's soup (a habit of Frieda's, my mother would complain) but there was comfort and conversation and good cheer. It was true that at one time Edgar tried to forbid talking at meals, following the example of Joseph Conard, but the attempt was doomed to failure. 'Joseph Conard was a very bad-tempered man,' said Frieda, 'and hated his children. He said it was they who had driven him mad. Edgar could be moody and difficult, but at least he liked his children, and when it came to it, liked to hear what they had to say.'

There were twelve bedrooms in the house and the children could take their pick of them. All were unheated, all contained a bed, a rug, a mirror and a wardrobe and that was all, so it made very little difference which one they chose. They moved on every night, trying not to hurt the feelings of particular rooms by leaving them out.

During the four years of World War I, from 1914 to 1918, Londoners went cold and hungry and were bombed by German Zeppelins and that was the end of the cook and the maid. They left to take up war-work, which was better paid than domestic service. 'I am not surprised,' my mother said. 'They lived in and had one afternoon a week off and were at our beck and call night or day.' Frieda took over the cleaning and cooking and Edgar's life continued easily enough. He was able to write of that time, in his *Memories of an Edwardian*, published in 1937, that 'the war was the chief thing in one's mind but it made little change in the routine life of a civilian past the age of active service. Bacon and eggs came to my breakfast: beef or mutton to my dinner with quiet punctuality; I did my day's writing; I went down to Central London to play bridge at the Omega, or poker at the Savage.' But presently he and his friend the poet Walter de la Mare were seconded to work for the Ministry of Food. Walter was put in charge of sugar rationing and Edgar produced *The Win the War Cookery Book* and a notable advertising poster, carrying a picture of a loaf of bread and the simple slogan, '*Eat less bread*'.

Many years later I tried to persuade the Smirnoff client to run the slogan, '*Vodka makes you drunker quicker*', but they wouldn't go with it. Too simple and to the point, though research had shown that people choose vodka rather than other spirits because it does indeed make them drunker quicker. Advertising must be seen to work, but not at the

17

expense of the dignity of the client. Effectiveness and profit come a long way down a client's list of requirements.

In his *Memories* Edgar speaks of Frieda thus. 'I fell desperately in love with a lady in London . . . she had a greater natural charm and a better figure than any other woman I ever met. When we met she had just finished her training for the concert stage and had given one concert in Paris . . . Her father was Henry Holmes, the only English violist who ever enjoyed a European reputation, and her mother was a daughter of William Gale, a Royal Academician so old he must have been a contemporary of Benjamin West. As a child she had been used to go to tea at Holman Hunt's.' In fact Frieda and her sister Sylvia had as young girls sat as models for the painter, having the strong, rather noble features and the plentiful hair the Pre-Raphaelites so admired.

I was not to meet my grandmother Frieda until 1941, when after her mother's death at the age of ninety-nine, she travelled from California to New Zealand, to join Margaret and 'help with the children'. At her own request she was known to us all as Nona, that being Italian for grandmother. And this is what I shall call her from now on, because this is how I think of her.

She too suffered many changes of name: born Frieda Holmes, she became Frieda Jepson on marriage: Susan Jepson at her children's request (Frieda being too Northern and too bleak for her, according to Edgar), and then she became Nona, because she couldn't bear – as many women can't – to be addressed as 'Granny' by her descendants. I think she was happiest as Frieda Holmes. My mother was Margaret Jepson, and then Birkinshaw, and that was that. She had a clearer personality than Nona or myself.

The run-up from Holmes to Jepson, for my poor grand-mother, and no doubt for my great-grandmother, Mary Francis Holmes, was troubled, indeed traumatic. Edgar puts it like this in his *Memories of an Edwardian*. 'We had been engaged but a little while when her father grew tired of Eng-land. It irked him to be at loggerheads, owing to his advanced views, which were almost those of Shelley, but rather more erotically practical, with the Council of the Royal College of Music, in those days a very stuffy and hypocritical band. It was said of them that they pooled the female students. He betook himself therefore to the city of Berkeley in California, and became its Musical Dictator, and when he died the inhabitants set up his statue in one of their public places.'

Which was all very well for Henry Holmes. Men have one name and stick to it. They go their own way, not having to

19

absorb others on the way. Henry Holmes and Havelock Ellis, the sexologist, had seen fit to circulate a pamphlet extolling the virtues of Free Love and the dangers of standing in the way of the Life Force, and had included the Archbishop of Canterbury in their circulation list. Unfortunately, the Archbishop actually read it. The ensuing scandal was such that Henry had lost his post at the Royal College, and was obliged to flee to California, dragging poor Mary Francis and her teenage twins, Herriot and Hjalmar, with him. Nona, at the time a young concert pianist in Paris, a pupil of Clara Schumann and with one concert already under her belt, smeared by the scandal, was offered no more work. She married Edgar instead. He had to persuade her. 'She had a theory that we were happier as we were,' he writes, 'but I did persuade her.' I fear she was easily persuaded. She no longer had a home and what alternative was there? So from the age of six to the age of ninety-six she played the piano for between six and eight hours every day, but seldom to an audience.

This was the first of the three great blows that the Life Force, that male conceit, was to deal Nona during the course of her life. The second was when her daughter Faith was discovered in love and in bed with her Uncle Hjalmar. Free Love was for the paterfamilias, on the whole, not for the rest of the family. The ensuing mayhem was to drive Faith into a mental home, where she died some fifteen years later. Edgar visited her weekly, but Nona went into a denial so profound that she blotted Faith, poor Faith, out of her consciousness entirely. When she was in her eighties, and I showed her a photograph of her three extraordinarily beautiful children, taken in about 1912, she could still see only two of them. And the third blow from the Life Force was when Edgar made Lois pregnant, and Nona was back to where she began, living with her mother.

It was hard for the family to see what Edgar saw in Lois. She was conventional and without any noticeable grace or talent, at least compared to Nona. She was a great complainer, about everything from her marriage, to the weather, to the state of her electric blanket. But perhaps her very difference from Nona was a relief to Edgar. She could look after herself. She made demands. 'We never quarrelled,' wrote Edgar of Nona, in 1937, by which time he was married to Lois, and their daughter Jennifer was six, 'I do not believe that she could quarrel . . . When we were young we were always hard up, and she had but a poor time of it. She never complained, not once. Sometimes she would look wistfully at a frock or a hat in a shop window, or at a hansom when she was tired, and that wistfulness I do not forget.' Perhaps that passage was written as a subtle reproach to Lois, as a suggestion that she mend her ways, and do as well in this respect as his first wife. Writers are not above sending coded messages to their spouses in their books.

In my teenage I went to the same school as Jennifer, but she was my aunt and the same age as me, though in a junior year, so it seemed prudent for us to ignore each other's presence, and no one ever knew we were related. We both still live within a mile of Adelaide Road, and these days enjoy a cordial relationship.

Nona's home collapsed when she was eighteen, thanks to her father Henry's behaviour, and so, homeless, she married Edgar. Her daughter Margaret's home collapsed when she was eighteen, thanks to her father Edgar's behaviour, and so, homeless, she married Frank. My mother collapsed her own house the month I turned eighteen, and left me homeless, and had there been a suitor around I'm sure I would have married

21

him, but there wasn't. I just hung around for a couple of years, rendered myself pregnant and thereby drew my mother back to me, and Jane did the same.

I made a real effort to break the run of compulsive behaviour – doing unto others as you have been done – and desist from rendering my own children homeless just at the wrong moment, but did not altogether succeed. Jane did it to hers by dying. The Life Force, once it's set going, runs through families for generations, and causes terrible havoc. 'I blame Arthur Machen,' said Nona to me one day. 'He cast too many spells.' But I daresay Freud could have produced a more rational answer, and Arthur Machen frightened himself by his own necromancy, my mother said, and though he never lost his allegiance to the Old Gods of his native Wales, concluded that they had lost their powers in the new world, and there was no point in dabbling.

My mother was not sent to school. That is to say when she was five they tried to take her and she refused. Her father came downstairs from his study wearing his silk dressing-gown and smoking a cigarette in an ivory holder, and said, 'What can be the matter with little Margaret. She's making such a noise!'
'She won't go to school,' Nona said.
'Do you not want to go to school?' Edgar asked his daughter.
'No,' she replied.
'Then don't send her,' he said and turned and went up the stairs again. And that was the end of my mother's formal education, apart from a couple of terms at the Slade School of Art when she was fifteen. She told me she knew at the time it was a major life decision and she had chosen wrongly. Her failure to go to school made her over-respectful of auth-

ority, I think, and she never felt permitted to lie when she filled in a form, though brave enough in other respects, and she never learned to deal with what she didn't like: all the important things one learns at school. They tried her again at the age of nine, but after a week of lessons she refused to go any more. She already knew everything they were trying to teach her.

Edgar's account of it runs thus: 'My daughter Margaret at the age of nine refused to go to school because it bored her, and it proved to be the wise course. Neither Susan or I [alas, for the poor forgotten Frieda, now subsumed into wife and mother 'Susan'] could conceive of any reason why she should go to school, and we raised no objection to her staying away from it. I do not know whether she regrets it ... but she writes better if gloomier novels than Selwyn or I, both of whom suffered seven years' schooling apiece, and if you doubt my judgement, read her *Via Panama*.'

In the three weeks after my birth, after Margaret had succumbed and gone to stay at Adelaide Road with her father and her new stepmother, and before she took the ship back to my father, Edgar and she managed to write a book between them, *Miss Amagee in Africa*. 'I shouldn't have gone to stay with them,' my mother said later. 'It hurt Nona very much.' But her own attitude to her mother was ambiguous. Her sister Faith had been betrayed by Nona, she sometimes hinted that Nona had been too fond of Frank: the clamour for emotional justice and the need to love battled it out.

Miss Amagee in Africa, of course, shows no sign of emotional stress: it is a stirring adventure tale about a brave American woman outfacing lions in Africa, written on the hoof, as it were, with wonderful descriptions of a landscape which neither writer had ever seen. I can only imagine that Lois was left to look after Jane and myself, and Jennifer too, while Edgar and Margaret worked. If so much was to get written in so short a time, someone had to look after the children.

And then it was time for Margaret to go home, though no one wanted her to go – except, I daresay, Lois. Frank was waiting impatiently for his wife and children to return. He had found a practice in the South Island, inland from Christchurch, at a township called Amberley, in the heart of the flat wheatlands of the Canterbury Plain. It was going to be all right, he assured her in his letter. He was starting a radio station. And he was standing for parliament as the socialist candidate.

Fay Franklin

Of Amberley, I remember the hot wind blowing off the mountains, day after day, and a bare flat landscape, and a lot of sheep there was no escaping. I remember being dressed up as Little Miss Bo Peep for a fancy-dress party. I remember the creaking of the windmill which pumped our water, and the hot dust beneath the macrocarpa hedge which you had to wriggle through to get to play with the children next door. I remember the milk being warm when it came from the cow, and wishing it wasn't. I remember the day I learned to read – I was three – and the way the letters suddenly made sense, and the excitement of that. I remember thinking now I could catch up with Jane but of course I never could. I remember my father coming home with a big new gold car, and how proud he was of it. It was a Voisin, imported from France; it had a starting handle and running boards on which we were allowed to stand. It was a magic car: I was sure it could fly, one day it would take off into the sky. But my father had a trick which I hated: he would stop the car in the middle of a dry river bed and tell us how we had to beware them, how people would camp the night in them, and be swept away in the darkness as the flood swept down from the melting mountain snows.

I was frightened, he knew I was frightened, why did he want to make it worse? Even today I still get panicky when driven through even the shallowest ford in the soft English country-side. 'Can't we go the long way round?' I plead, but we never can. My experience of men in cars has always been that if you don't want them to do something, they will. It is when they are behind a wheel that they most fear the control of women and children.

I remember my mother turning cartwheels on the lawn, white legs flashing, short skirt whirling, and being overwhelmed with admiration. None of my friends' mothers turned cart-wheels. They wore pinnies and made apple pies. We were different. I became aware that we were homies. We came from a far-off place called England, and didn't really belong here. This made you both better and worse, before you even began. Sometimes people didn't even understand what you said. Then you felt stupid. You wanted to speak like your friends, but your mother wanted you to speak as she did and was quite cross when you didn't. You wanted to say 'yiss' but she wanted you to say 'yes'. So you learned to speak two different languages, one for home, and the other for your friends. The picture books came from England, though, and showed children and their parents who were more like you than the other families around. You could read the stories to your friends and they liked that. People were like the pages of books. There were more and more of them, a page behind every page, and everyone with something new to say, and you never wanted it to stop.

In retrospect it is clear that my father took to life in the outback with enthusiasm, my mother decidedly less so. She had escaped the emotional stress of her family circumstances but at some cost, though at least there weren't any earthquakes down here in the South. The earth stayed steady beneath her feet and my father and she did indeed have a radio station to play with, or at least several hours' a week broadcasting time. My mother wrote radio plays, and even in these benighted parts found people enough to perform them, and an appreciative audience, and made friends: my father lectured on socialism and lost quite a few. New Zealand was an advanced country in social terms – first in the world with votes for women, first with an embryo national health service – and always, like my father, hungry for improvement, but actual socialism was viewed askance, particularly in rural areas.

My father was tireless and energetic: he wrote a detective serial for the local newspaper which went on for more than a hundred episodes. He wanted to stop but he couldn't because he didn't know who had done the murder. He was like a hotel guest who wants to leave but can't because he has no money to pay the bill. The longer he stays the worse things get. In the end my father offered a five-pound prize for anyone who could solve the puzzle, and someone turned up who did. There is always a reader out there who knows better than the writer, and just as well.

In my father's footsteps, I wrote a serial for a woman's magazine in the Eighties: *The Hearts and Lives of Men*. It was meant to go on for twelve episodes but ran for forty-nine before the editor called enough, other writers wanted their space on the page back. I was happy to finish: I had already had to divorce and remarry my hero and heroine once so that the eventual ending would stay feasible. To do it again would be absurd. The serial was about a lost child, little Nell, who must in the end be reunited with her parents and bring them to their senses.

This endeavour went on for nearly a year. A courier would call at the door at one o'clock every Thursday to collect the latest instalment, which I had most likely written on the train that morning. In those days I lived in Somerset but had an office in London. I marvelled at how trusting the editor was: had there been a train strike, had I been ill, he would not have been able to collect his instalment. I think he had a vague idea that the story was already written and all I was doing was cutting it up into bits and handing it to him section by section, out of meanness. Even editors don't seem to understand the make-it-up-as-you-go-along school of writing which I inhabit. But I am responsible in my own way: I couldn't be ill or have a holiday for forty-nine weeks, and I wasn't and didn't. The episodes, restructured, were eventually published in novel form, and when it was I was quite pleased with it, though I missed the 'story so far' sections, which I had loved writing. As you move through a story it is interesting to see how your own view of it changes, and how you see fit to describe those who inhabit it. But the central premise of the story held, that like calls to like and most of us are given second chances, and that virtue is more often rewarded than we think.

Second Chances

New Zealand, for my father, was a second chance, and perhaps that was why he took to the new land with such joyful ease. Its very air suited him. He had contracted rheumatic fever in the trenches of World War I and nearly died from it. The smogs and fogs of London were no good for him. He had run away from home in 1914 to join the army, in response to Lord Kitchener's pointing finger and '*Your country needs you!*' He was sixteen but pretended to be eighteen. In those days it was possible to lie about your age: now we are all so closely monitored and registered it is near-impossible. Life is much duller as a consequence. One's instinct is to hide from the state. I was always taken aback by the way schools asked to see my children's birth certificates – supposing there was something there that I wanted them not to know? What business of theirs was my offspring's parentage? Bad enough that school was compulsory – one could overlook that, because the children evidently so badly wanted to go – but what did they hope to find out? And where was I meant to find these bits of paper anyway, four or five years after the birth? As it happened I managed on all four occasions to fail to provide the required documentation, and no one ever followed up the initial request, but just assumed the children had the names and ages they said they had.

My father came from yeoman stock: his mother Isabel was a Garbutt, from a family who had farmed sheep in Northumbria for generations. His father Herbert was a Henderson on his mother's side: the family had been 'in wool' for as long as anyone could remember, but had diversified into carpets, and were 'in trade' which was not quite the thing. The Garbutts, who now included bishops among their ranks, saw Isabel as a cut above Herbert. He was spoken of as a bully, and Isabel as a saint for putting up with him. And she was indeed the sweetest, gentlest thing. My half-sister Barbara takes after her, and her daughter Naomi, though sweetness seems to have by-passed the rest of us, become too diluted in the genes. On the one occasion I met Herbert, in 1946, he seemed perfectly pleasant and gave me half-a-crown so I will not add to the slurs.

But he did seem to be anxious that his four children would not succeed, and almost to spite him, they all did. He took Frank away from St Edward's Grammar School in Birmingham and apprenticed him to an engineer, when that was what he specifically didn't want to be. Sheona, the oldest, was given away in infancy to be brought up by an aunt, and grew up to marry her cousin, an eye surgeon, and to became a poet. For fifty years, until her death in her late Nineties, a poem by Sheona Lodge, delicate and lyrical, appeared regularly in the American Fly Fisher's Journal. The second daughter, Mary, was active in politics, married Michael Stewart, later to be Foreign Secretary in Harold Wilson's government, and both ended up on the Labour benches in the House of Lords. Bill became a much respected dentist in the Midlands: once mysteriously married to someone who 'ran off', and whose name he would not have mentioned in the house. That was not so unusual a response at the time; the world was full of things too painful to be mentioned, because there was nothing to be done about them. Infidelity, illegitimate children, insanity, cancer – it seemed impolite to God to mention them, pointing the finger because he had failed to make a perfect universe. As cures became available, of course, one by one, they could be talked about, and now are, almost to exhaustion, as if we are making up for lost time.

So my father ran away from his apprenticeship and my not very pleasant grandfather, and was sent to the front line in France, but within the year was invalided out of the mud and slime of the trenches. Next he was posted to Arabia, where the air was all too dry. But he became T. E. Lawrence's driver: he had a Rolls-Royce to play with, adapted to desert use and armed with a machine gun, which he coaxed up and down impossible sand hills. I think he enjoyed himself very much. He once showed me a battered leather-bound copy of Shakespeare's *Romeo and Juliet*, inscribed to him by Lawrence himself. He told me he was captured by Bedouin but saved himself by offering them jam labels, which he told them was money and they believed him. It just so happened that he collected jam labels, there being lots to collect in a desert filled with soldiery who had to eat. They blew about the sand hills.

This part of The War he talked about: he would never speak about the trenches. Perhaps the time spent there was too traumatic: too full of exploding bodies for words to encompass. It made him neurotic. Those who have been soldiers often are: from time to time they behave compulsively. Those who are damaged feel the need to pass it on: those who are hardened try to harden others. Soldiers who emerge from wars are often cheery enough: they have learned the art of living in the present: they're good at that – today's friend can be tomorrow's corpse. Just sometimes they shake and shiver and are cruel to others, and want them to suffer too. Ron Weldon, my second husband, was an ex-soldier, like so many of the generation after my father's. He had spent time clearing bloated bodies from streams in Burma: he didn't mention this for a good twenty-five years into the marriage, when he started getting nightmares and handing them on.

After the Armistice Frank went to London and with the aid of demob money and contributions from his maiden aunts in Newcastle, studied medicine at University College Hospital. In 1922 he visited a nightclub and there met and charmed Edgar and Susan Jepson, who took him under their wing. Before long he was sleeping on their sofa, and had begun his assiduous courtship of their daughter Margaret, then a girl of sixteen.

Doors opened to my father. It was a life he had not known before. Those who have a natural and spontaneous response to books, paintings, music and the life of the mind are lucky: the gift of their enthusiasm strikes through class barriers: they find mentors. 'He was rather rough at the time,' my mother said of him. 'He'd been a soldier for years: he'd had no education. He swore dreadfully. He had no money: he slept on other people's floors and ended up on ours. His aunts came down to visit him and threw up their hands in horror at what they found.'

Perhaps the gift for standing in front of the right door runs in families? When Edgar gravitated to Nona, back in the 1890s, a new world opened up for him, and it suited him down to the ground. Here was the gossipy bohemia of the day: forget the waspish writers and intellectuals, here were painters and musicians, and another kind of delinquency. 'Through Frieda,' he wrote in his *Memories*, 'I came into the Bloomsbury Group of the day.' He picked up the ball and ran with it.

Thirty years later Frank was to find himself in the same situation. All he had to date was the copy of *Romeo and Juliet* from T. E. Lawrence; now Edgar and Nona offered him the culture he was starved of, and he realized he had finally come home. When that home collapsed, he carried the daughter off as a trophy. Another generation on and history repeats itself. My mother's world, by the virtue of war, divorce, poverty and circumstance had shrunk to subsistence level, and my world with it. Forget the arts and the life of the mind, what about the rent? But go to a party one night, just as Frank had been to a nightclub, and all of a sudden, there you are, back in your natural place: in my case Primrose Hill in the Sixties, the abode of the writers and painters. Go down to the launderette and run into the kind of people who hung out in these parts. Ted Hughes and Sylvia Plath, Patrick Caulfield, Kingsley Amis and Elizabeth Jane Howard, Adrian Mitchell, R. D. Laing and the George Mellys, Tom Maschler the publisher, Mel Calman and Michael Ffolkes, cartoonists, Alan Sharp and Lukas Heller, screenwriters, ANC activists by the handful, Bernice Rubens and David Mercer, and down in Gloucester Crescent Alan Bennett and Jonathan Miller, and as many names as you care to drop, rising young artists and writers all. And the parties we gave were many and wild, and not so different from those at Adelaide Road, except the beer was made in the bath, and the bath was lidded and in the kitchen, and I don't think Nona would have stood for that. With a permanent place in the lover's bed, comes a permanent place in their circle. Actual marriage cements it.

Patterns

I am very conscious of the patterns our lives make: of interconnecting cogs and wheels, of coincidence which is no coincidence but fate, of the quiet sources of our energy. All things connect. The lost wedding ring turns up on the day of the divorce; the person you happen to sit next to on the Tube happens to be your new boss. Destiny intervenes. We assume we are playing the lead, but turn out to be bit-part players in someone else's drama. Nothing is without result.

Even the maiden aunts, Madge and Augusta, who helped Frank become a doctor, were major players in his story, for all the quiet seclusion of their lives. They lived in Newcastle, in a house in which almost nothing had changed since the beginning of the century. Antimacassars protected the armchairs: oil lamps provided the only lighting.

In my student days, when I would hitchhike down from St Andrews in Scotland to St Ives in Cornwall, their house made a useful stopping-off point. The Aunts, who by then were in their nineties, provided a fine refuge from the hunger and tribulations of the open road, especially in winter time. Their ancient maid May lived with them. Most social inequalities had been evened out by the passage of the years, but not all. They would share the warmth of the fire but if more coal were needed it would be May who went to fetch it, and she was the one who got up to make the tea, though she was even more doddery than they. There would be a candle to light you to the unheated spare room, where the bed was so high you had to climb up into it. A flowered china

33

chamber pot was placed beneath it. Springs would creak if you moved: the mattress sagged. The sheets were linen and cold, and the pillow was stiff, but the weight of the many blankets was reassuring. After you had been a little while in the bed it would begin to steam with damp, which was oddly pleasant. In the morning ice crystals would have formed on the inside of the windows. You would put bare feet out onto cold lino, dress as fast as you could and make for the kitchen, where a purple-knuckled May would be making breakfast. The tea would be hot and sweet.

The aunts would give you some money to help you on your way, and wave goodbye from the door as you set out on the road, and you would worry that this was the last time you would ever see them. It seemed a miracle that they existed at all: this was the stuff of fairy-stories, as if they came into existence only to facilitate your journey. When you ceased to see them, they would cease to be.

Missing Mothers

It was when we left Amberley and moved to Christchurch that things fell apart. It could not have been expected. Christchurch was, and still is, a quiet, orderly town, the most English of all the New Zealand cities, the respectable face of the original New Zealand Company, which sold off land it did not own to the pioneers. The streets are laid out in rectangles around a central cathedral square, and rather grudging allowances made for the unreasonable curve of the green-banked River Avon. The flat Canterbury plains stretch off to the west

to meet the white peaks of the Southern Alps: and to the north, neatly separated off by a soft ridge of hills, is the port of Lyttelton, in what was once a volcanic crater. But all that natural violence and upheaval was long, long ago.

In Amberley we were part of the old original land: the ground was soft beneath bare feet: in Christchurch people wore hats and gloves to go shopping. The sky felt too huge, arched over a city which did not take up enough room. The sense that we were perched at the end of the world, that real life went on somewhere else was very great. Even I felt it, and I was only four, nearly five. My father was to set up his practice in a good part of town. We had a house which was not a bungalow. It had a staircase, and you could look out onto the trams in the front of the house, and a garden with walnut trees and a washing-line at the back. I had a theory that I could fly like an angel and had to be stopped from jumping from the top windows. And I don't know why it happened, or what exactly the move to the town precipitated, but I began to be conscious of a kind of trouble that ran through the house. I would wake in the night to sounds of discord. Jane frowned a lot. One day my mother put on her hat and gloves to go shopping and came back crying, with an empty basket. We owed money and it was my father's fault. She'd had no idea.

The King (that was my father) *was in his counting house,*
Counting out his money. (But there wasn't enough of it)
The Queen (that was my mother) *was in the parlour*
Eating bread and honey. (If she was lucky)
The maid was in the garden,
Hanging out the clothes,
Along came a blackbird and pecked off her nose.

The words haunted me. It seemed all too possible. Jane and I had a nursemaid who hung out the clothes and I beseeched her to be careful. Sudden and disagreeable things could happen. I knew that by now. Had we not moved from Amberley to Christchurch? And were there not blackbirds in the walnut tree? I had seen them. I met her fifty years on when I was visiting New Zealand, and I was glad to see she still had her nose. She remembered me more clearly than I remembered her. She said I'd say the oddest things. She'd offered to tell me a story and I said, 'How can you? You haven't got a book.' She said she'd make the story up in her head, and I'd replied, 'Then your head must be made of paper.'

The sudden and disagreeable things might have had something to do with Ina. Ina was the daughter of my mother's friend Winifred. Winifred had come to New Zealand as an immigrant foundling at the age of sixteen and been apprenticed to a milliner. She'd met and married a man forty years older than herself, on the understanding that she would nurse him through his terminal illness. This she had done, conceiving Ina on the way. Now she was free, with her husband's money in the bank. She was plain, practical and very kind. Her daughter Ina was always a trouble to her: beautiful, nervy, arty and spendthrift, running up debts her mother had to pay. She had a long neck and often wore a turban, and when my father read Aristophanes to us, and in one of the plays there was a bird called a Hoopoe, I thought he was probably describing Ina. She would turn up quite a lot at the house and when she did my mother would look baleful.

But nobody, surely, could compete with my beautiful mother? She was so special. She wrote a masque: I was not sure how that could be done, but whatever it was everyone dressed up in flowing robes and did what she told them to do. She spoke from the balcony of the Bishop's Palace, which looked over green lawns and the River Avon, and everyone clapped. Then there was strawberries for tea. I was very proud of her. But I was proud of my father too. He took Jane and me to Hagley Park, to watch a man with a parachute drift out of the sky. The world was full of marvels. But the marvels and the nightmares had begun to run side by side, racing to see which would win.

There was a night of bangings and crashings, shrieks and slamming doors, during the course of which I was told to go back to bed. In the morning my mother was not there to get me up. My father did it instead and said she'd gone home, for a time. That was strange. Surely where someone lived was their home? On further enquiry home turned out to be another country, up at the top to the right on a page of the atlas. Home was England. We came from England which was why we were called homies.

But if the world was round like an orange, as people tried to tell me, why was it flat on the map? The orange theory did not make sense. Half the people in the world would be going round upside-down if it were true. I did not much like being tucked away at the bottom of the flat page, so far from any-where else, tiny little lengths of red, set in a pale blue sea, so far from my mother on her way to the top of the page, but it was better than being on some huge orange. And at least now I had my father to myself.

But why had she gone and when would she be back? I couldn't get much sense out of Jane: all anyone said, including her, was that I was too young to understand. Without my mother in it, the house seemed curiously light and free, as if we could all now just have a good time. But within days, my father, Jane and I had moved out of the house, said goodbye to our nursemaid, and were living in a private hotel near Cranmer Square.

Cranmer Square

Cranmer Square was not actually a square but an oblong, its grass intersected by paths in the pattern of the Union Jack. In this city of boxy bungalows set in neat gardens it seemed to me a significant place, if sloppily named. Nearly all the buildings which lined it had stairs: that is to say they were more than one storey high. There was the Girls' High School at the north end, and St Margaret's to the west and the Nor-mal School to the south. In between were boarding-houses and hotels. On wet days, when heavy rain drummed on the ground and made the corrugated-iron roofs rattle, slugs and snails would come out in enormous number to cover the stripes of the Union Jack, making walking hazardous. The crack of a snail beneath the shoe or the sight of a squashed worm strikes horror into the little-girl heart. There were few wet days, of course: winter in Christchurch was an eight-week affair and then it was over. The nor'wester was a worse affliction; wake up to see the arch of cloud in a heavy sky, and know that within hours the hard, hot, strong wind would get up and blow for days, making everyone cross and tired.

Our winter was England's summer: that was strange. In the conservatory of the private hotel which was now our home the apples and the oranges would come out as my father and his friends tried to prove to me that the earth was round, not flat, and circled the sun, like this, and the moon went round the earth, like that, and why night happened and so on. It still did not seem convincing. As well claim we were all living in the fruit bowl.

Jane and I shared a high damp steamy bed in the front ground-floor room. The bedspread was made of bright green artificial silk which was chilly and slippery to the touch. I cried a little on the first night we slept in it, and was proud of Jane, who didn't cry at all. There wasn't a pot under the bed and we didn't know where the lavatory was, so that night Jane wee-ed on the round Chinese carpet. She said it was their fault, not hers, and I wondered as I have often wondered all my life, who 'they' were. I didn't like to witness her desperation, but marvelled at her pride and determination.

We ate our meals in the dining room with the other guests. I could see there were advantages to this situation. There was no one to fuss about washing your hands or combing your hair or worrying what you were doing. If there was anything you didn't know Jane probably would, and at least in an emergency she could be relied upon to tell you. My father took much more notice of us now my mother was out of the way, and I resolved to look after him properly, and make him happier than she had. I would never go off and leave him the way she did: I could see I was too small to take her place but I would do my best.

But my father had other ideas. I was not allowed into his bed, for one thing. Ina came in and out, wearing her absurd silk turbans and heavy strings of wooden beads, hooting and chirping away. Rita Angus the painter would drift palely in, look sad and drift out again. Then there was Jean Stephenson and Helen Shaw. Jean was thin and clever and edited the New Zealand *Listener*. How on earth did you edit a person and what was he listening for, I wondered. It sounded very important, like being Prime Minister. Helen was rounded and creamy skinned: I thought she was like Helen of Troy, in the Walter de la Mare poem my mother used to murmur.

> *Helen of Troy was beautiful,*
> *As all the flowers of May:*
> *Her loveliness from the walls looked down,*
> *Over the towers of Troy town,*
> *Hundreds of miles away.*

But my mother was beginning to feel very far away, and wherever she was, had taken herself there without much reference to me. Why should I care? Jane and I were both going to St Margaret's school now. We wore green uniforms and panama hats. I liked school, but could wish for more from home. It wasn't the kind that other children had. Other children didn't live in hotels and had a mother to collect them:

we had a different lady friend to do it practically every day. They all seemed to want us to like them, mind you, and were forever giving us things. At Easter I was given so much chocolate I was sick. I asked for a car for my birthday and was given a toy one, not a real one, and then they wondered why I was crying: if I'd had a proper mother she could have explained. Why on earth would I want a toy car? I was a girl. I was Fay. No one ever called me Franklin now.

Rita Angus, or Rita Cook, as we knew her, one of my father's friends, took it into her head to paint a portrait of Jane and myself. Rita was to be reckoned as one of New Zealand's finest painters, but at the time was seen as a rather eccentric dabbler in the arts. The portrait now hangs in New Zealand's National Gallery. We were put in our matching check dresses and told to sit still. Jane managed this very well but I couldn't. I kept running off to get a drink of water. I somehow lost the belt of my green cardigan and Rita had to paint it out. She sat our dolls in a row above us but dressed them up first in a rather formal way which in my opinion didn't suit their personalities at all. She put in some of the hotel teacups, and painted them to give us a rest from sitting still. She was very nice, though we didn't think we looked at all the way she had painted us. We were more real and lasting on the canvas than we were in real life. But we were very polite. We knew instinctively from an early age that the artist's sensibilities are to be protected, lest they give up altogether and walk off into the night.

I got up one morning and my legs wouldn't work. I had poliomyelitis, or infantile paralysis. It could kill you or lame you: I knew about that. Everyone was terrified of it all over the map, or up and down the orange. I was a map person,

Jane was an orange person. I could see by now that she was right but I wasn't going to admit it. I was given a bed in the conservatory and Jane wasn't allowed to come near me. The waitress would put my food down and run away. My father cried, but I knew it was all right: he was the best doctor in the world and would see to it. And nothing bad could happen to me: fate was on my side. And so it was. Today, when I'm tired my right ankle tends to turn my foot in a little, but that's all. There was some talk at the time about callipers, which happily soon went away.

By now Jane and I were so close I hardly noticed any difference between her and me. We seemed one body. Even our names were bracketed together. We were called Jane'nFay. My father was standing for parliament: I watched to see if he stood up more than usual but no, he sat down just as much as ever. What were they all talking about?

One day at school, as I lay sleepless on my mat on the floor, a woman I didn't know bent over me. It was afternoon-nap time, a torment if ever there was one. You had to lie in rows on the floor for what seemed forever, when all you wanted to do was run about. This still quietness, this 'rest', seemed such a waste of life. The stranger wore a scarlet pillbox hat with a little black veil, so her face seemed covered with small black dots. She kissed me and said she was my mother and I was to get up now. That was a relief. Jane confirmed that she was who she said she was and she took us out of school for the day. I asked her what her name was and she said it was Margaret. I seemed to remember that.

We sat in Cranmer Square for a bit and I told her about the worms. She said that at home it had rained a lot. I asked her

42

whether the ship had had to climb up the sea to get to the equator, and she said no, and dropped a stone and explained the theory of gravity. Jane said she knew that already. Then my mother took us back to the private hotel but did not stay. Nor did my father ask her to. It was amazing how the lady friends seemed to melt away, and how quiet everything suddenly was.

Via Panama

In his *Memories* Edgar remarks that my mother was a better writer than either he or Selwyn, and that her novel *Via Panama* was proof of it. He complained that it was gloomy, and it is perhaps not surprising if it was. It was written on her journey back to Christchurch, whence she had fled so impetuously from Frank's infidelities and his embarrassing failure to keep out of debt. She had been trying to establish a life for herself in London, and had found a flat and, miraculously, a job on the *News Chronicle* as a journalist. This would pay just about enough to enable her to support herself and her two daughters. She would return to New Zealand to fetch us as soon as she had got the money together.

The first letter she received from Frank said that if she did not come back at once he would take Jane'nFay to South America and she would never see us again. Rightly, she did not believe him. She did not reply. But his second letter was brief and to the point. Fay had polio and Margaret must come home at once before it was 'too late'. Overwhelmed by anxiety and guilt, she took the next boat home, giving up both the flat and her job. Trapped on shipboard for six weeks, without news of her younger daughter, not knowing what she would find when she disembarked, she spent the time writing a novel.

Via Panama was about the shipboard voyage out; and contained a thinly disguised portrait of my father, whom she clearly still loved, and of her fellow-passengers, mostly New Zealanders, whom she affected to despise for their drunken and provincial ways. The novel was published both in England and the US to critical acclaim – and for a thirty-year-old young woman it was a triumph – but when it reached New Zealand there was uproar. She had insulted her hosts: she was an ingrate, the worst kind of homie. She put on airs: she thought herself too good for New Zealand. She was not Public Enemy Number One – that role was preserved for my father, who was standing for election as a socialist candidate – but she was Public Enemy Number Two. Frank lost the election because of *Via Panama* – or so he believed – and my mother was so shaken and upset by its reception that she resolved – as her father had once done before her – never to write a 'serious' book again. From henceforth she would write only to entertain. (Edgar's first novel, *The Passion for Romance*, written when he was at Oxford, had been 'serious', had taken him three years to write and earned him only £6.19s. It was on financial grounds that he came to the same decision. Or so he said. Forget art, forget literature, forget enlightening his readers as to the ways of the world, and the state of their souls, the rent must be paid.)

In my mother's footsteps, some forty years later, I was to write a television play about an English husband going home with his new second wife to the New Zealand outback –

affectionately known as the boondocks – to an uneasy welcome which included Pavlova cake and separate beds. That got me into trouble, too. I was accused of stereotyping New Zealand women, portraying them as backward in their attitudes, cake bakers all. Useless to say but I'm not writing documentary, I am under no obligation to produce a fair and balanced view, this is a particular story about particular people – such arguments never convince those predisposed to take offence. But I was older than my mother was when she wrote *Via Panama*, and tougher, I daresay, and others came to my defence and I was soon forgiven. But for my poor mother, alone and far from home, the uproar was definitive. Had she been to school, I daresay, she would have been better able to cope.

For a time my mother was able to support us, just about, by her pen. Over the next few years, under the name Pearl Bellairs or Bentley Ridge, she was to write a run of romantic serials – *Velvet and Steel*, *The Cups of Alexander* – which were published in London by Herbert Jenkins, then Edgar's publisher. Her editor wrote in enthusiasm to say she had readers queuing up for them in the bookstores as they came out. She'd write by hand in bed, in tiny script, with a fountain pen; and then get up and type it all out on a clattery typewriter. My contribution was to pick out the ink which clogged up the keys. I used a pin. The o's and the e's, the most frequent of the letters in the alphabet closely followed by the t's, were always most in need of cleaning. I loved doing it. Typescripts, in the days of the typewriter, always had an individuality of their own. Microsoft produces a clean, uniform print, for which we should be grateful, but something's lost as something's gained.

My mother borrowed the name Pearl Bellairs from the vapid romantic novelist in Aldous Huxley's novel *Crome Yellow* – she was saying, I suppose, to anyone who might happen to make the connection: 'I can do better than this, I am worth more than this, it's just I have to make a living.'

She worried greatly about the morality of writing romance: she thought it was wrong to put false ideas into the heads of young women: better that they understood that marriage was not necessarily a happy end, and that poor helpless girl catches strong handsome rich man was simply not the way the world went. And she had a point: *Velvet and Steel* – with its overtones *of Pride and Prejudice* – the helpless shop girl wooed by her wealthy employer, bringing him to heel by virtue of charm, wit and personality, would today, alas, read as a sorry case of sexual harassment.

Then the war came, and forget principle, the sea-lanes became impassable. Ships were torpedoed, manuscripts went down with everything else: there was a shortage of paper, and none to be spared for frivolities like fiction: that was the end of that, for four or five years.

My mother took advantage of the impossibility of earning a living from these problematic works, and started what she called her *magnum opus*: a book of philosophy, which dealt with the relationship between morality and aesthetics. She did not type this out: it remained in handwriting: thousands of overwritten pages, which would get in a hopeless muddle on the kitchen table. I wished she would not; I knew even when small how important it was to keep papers collated and in moderate order. The eighty per cent behind you had to be more or less finished and complete, if it was not to

distract you and make you restless as you moved ahead into the unknown. What you were working on currently required chaos, what was behind must be orderly, or you would be overwhelmed by confusion.

After the war, my mother said to me, when she thought once again of aspiring to be a 'proper' writer, styles of writing had changed. Novels ceased to be discursive, writers could not hide behind their anonymity; politics and social comment began to enter in. The novel was becoming a confessional, and readers demanded that the writer speak the truth as he or she knew it, and my mother's truths were difficult enough to live through, she said, let alone writing about them as well.

Margaret, Jane'nFay

There were various to-ings and fro-ings between my parents and then it was Frank's turn to walk off into the mist. This was a literal mist, more than just the usual cloud of childhood unknowing. I was growing up. I was six. We stood upon a beach on a rainy day, my father, my mother, Jane and I, and my father walked off along the shore without us, saying, 'Don't ever leave the children with friends. Have them properly adopted.' And then the mist swallowed him up; the tall, dark, consoling figure faded away, without so much as a glance behind. My mother was crying, which is not surprising. He was divorcing her for infidelity. She had only thirty pounds in the world, we had nowhere to live, and my father had gone to catch a ship to England, 'home', which was due to leave within the hour. Once the gangplank was up he changed his mind but it was too late then.

Matters had come to a head between them. To demonstrate to him just how upsetting she found his persistent adultery she had spent a night with a passing stranger, and told him that she had. But instead of showing remorse for his own behaviour he had been outraged by hers, and had started divorce proceedings within the hour. It was different for a man than a woman, as common wisdom had it then. Even now women will do this kind of thing, believing tit for tat will somehow cure matters but of course it never does. I have never known a confession of infidelity work anything but harm. The couple who 'tell the truth to each other' after their first visit to the marriage-guidance counsellor seldom enjoy many more nights together.

My mother left us with friends, naturally, while she found us somewhere to live. This was to be two rooms in a boarding-house in Cranmer Square. Jane and I no longer went to St Margaret's across the way: it was a private school, there was no money to pay the fees. My mother, unlike my father, as she pointed out, would not spend money she didn't have. The green uniforms were sold. The rest of our clothes were brought round in a small suitcase from the luxury of the private hotel. We were to go to a state school, St Mary's Convent, to be taught by nuns. They would teach us manners, said my mother: we had been running wild. They would be very religious, but we were to take no notice of that.

The boarding-house was shabby and basic. There were no shiny green quilts upon the beds to hate, or round Chinese rugs to spoil. Now they were gone we missed them. The landlady was a harridan who wore curlers in her hair, did not like children, and had only taken us in out of pity. My mother was in disgrace, her name linked in the newspapers with a named co-respondent: guilty party in the divorce. She had not fought her corner: she did not have the money to do so, or the will. (My father was required to send us a meagre sum for our maintenance every month, but it was often late, if it came at all.)

The worst thing about the boarding-house was the magpie which guarded the backyard. It lived in a kennel like a dog, its wings were clipped, and it had a long rattling chain attached to its scrawny leg. When you opened the back gate it would run at you to peck your ankles, screeching 'Go on out, go on out!' in a flurry of black and white raised wings and gaping orange mouth. It was what the landlady would shriek as she swept the atrocious bird from her path with the garden broom, the flesh of her ankles falling in folds over her shoes: the bird had learned the phrase from her and now mimicked it to its own ends. I had no broom with which to defend myself: I would try to sneak in the front door in Cranmer Square, but this was forbidden to children, who must use the back yard and face the bird. My ankles were covered in peck marks and sometimes even bled, but I didn't complain: my mother had enough to be getting on with, so much was obvious, and would get us out of there as soon as she could.

I was so closely aligned to Jane that I had no vision of her as a separate being. She did not count as a sister, as a companion, rather she was an extension of me, and my mother soon became the same. We went round in a survival unit of three: Margaret, Jane'nFay.

My mother decided to paint wooden powder boxes for a living. Pretty women bought face-powder by the ounce, and transferred it to a decorated round box upon their dressing-table, and placed a powder puff on top of it, and a lid on top of that. It needed to look feminine. She would do the decorating. Alas, the pretty women did not want painted powder boxes in sufficient number for us to make any kind of a living: powder was for special occasions only. It lay on the top of the face in a floury film; Max Factor pancake foundation had not yet been invented. The limit of my mother's skin care was a pot of Pond's cold cream, to be applied at night.

I still have one of the powder boxes we failed to sell: pale glazed wood, with stylized flowers painted elegantly upon its lid. My mother's training at the Slade School of Art was paying off, though not perhaps in the way her tutors had envisaged. I love it and hate it, and as for using it, that's out of the question. Powder flies all over the room. I keep buttons in it, on the theory that one day or another I shall take up a needle and sew.

Letters came from my father. He made a book for us out of firm paper, and glued photographs and drawings to it, and scraps of poetry, and tales of things he had done and seen, and people he had met. He had taken a lot of time over it: I thought perhaps he missed us. I assumed he would be back soon and we would all live together again. (No one had mentioned the divorce.) He seemed to be quite rich: he sent a photograph of himself leaning against a KLM aircraft, in Amsterdam. He sent a book, *Ferdinand the Bull*. Ferdinand was stung by a bee and picked for the bullring because of it. When it came to the point he just sat down and smelled the flowers in the ladies' hats and lived happily ever after. A good pacifist book: even my mother admired it. My father was going back to school in London to get some more medical letters after his name. Yes, said my mother, your father always has money to do what he wants. But he's a very good doctor, never forget that.

I looked for Holland on the map. I could accept by now that the world was round. Europe took precedence in the scheme of things. They were on top, we were underneath. If anyone were to fall off it would be us.

I learned anxiety and fear. I was out playing sevens in Cranmer Square – you threw a tennis ball against a wall and caught it in a progressively difficult way – so many bounces,

51

overarm, underarm, a group of seven to be completed before you could move on to the next stage; as solitary and obsessive an occupation as any computer game today – when I was interrupted by a boy. I didn't know him. My concentration went: I dropped the ball and complained. He told me he had been in an earthquake, and how the earth yawned in front of you and if you weren't careful you fell down into the cracks, and even as you scrabbled to climb out the earth would close again, and squash you. It had happened to a friend of his. He told me about how erupting volcanoes could suddenly rise up out the ground, and how the boiling lava would frizzle you alive, and he hoped it would happen to me. If you felt the earth shake beneath your feet it meant earthquake or volcano was about to happen. Then he walked off. I was petrified. Every now and then I did feel the earth shake but I was never sure if it was in my head or outside. How would one know? You could look to see if the ceiling light was swaying, and sometimes it was, but your eyes must be deceiving you, because everyone said there were no earthquakes in the South Island, only in the North, and all the volcanoes were extinct.

I don't know whether Jane shared my fear: I assumed she did, but I may have been wrong. We were separate enough for her to love St Mary's Convent and me to hate it. The nuns liked her and were suspicious of me. Jane was good and quiet and looked holy: I was noisy and giggly and looked frivolous.

Convent Girl

The Convent was a tall building with gothic towers. Behind barred windows lived scores of women who wore black robes and white wimples. When they were angry, which they often were, they were like the magpie; they'd come screeching at you in a flurry of black and white, though rapping your knuckles or pinching you instead of pecking your ankles, and much more painfully. Fortunately most of them stayed in their cells in the towers: just a handful came out to teach in the school wing. Mother Teresa was nice and motherly, and would hug you and give you sticky sweets: all the others, from Sister Katherine to Sister Dorothy, ruled by sarcasm and violence. I liked their names, but that was about all.

The children, all Catholic except for a handful of heathen, which group included Jane and I, were on the whole cowed and snivelly. Their noses tended to run. I was a worse case of pious dereliction than Jane, who had at least been christened, albeit as a Protestant not a Catholic, but I had not even been that. My parents were freethinkers, rationalists, humanists – which was why I was spared Arthur Machen's blessing. Jane was allowed to stay in the classroom while the rest of the class said their prayers and told their rosaries – some six times a day – but I had to leave the room, and stand outside the door with my spelling book, and learn the hard words. I became very good at spelling. I did not mind the exclusion much: prayers were boring and rosaries were peculiar, but I could see it was more comfortable to belong. But belonging was already beginning to seem unlikely. I was a homie, I spoke with a fancy accent, lived in a boarding-house and not a bungalow, didn't get pocket money, and my mother put on airs. I was the youngest in my class by more than a year. I struggled to keep up.

The nuns decided that I had to be baptized. Otherwise, being unchristened, my fate was to go to limbo when I died. Limbo was the place, in their rather primitive theology, where all those born after Jesus's time but who weren't Catholics were doomed to go. It was a flat, featureless, grey landscape where nothing ever happened. The face of the Lord had been turned away. In retrospect it seems a fair description of a depression, and perhaps that's all depression is, limbo leaked over in life: but the prospect certainly terrified me. There was no getting out of it: limbo was everlasting, and my certain

54

fate, so I had better start learning my catechism and sign up for baptism now.

I asked my mother if I could be christened as a Catholic but she said certainly not. She did not seem to realize the full implications of what she had said or what she was letting me in for. I could see that the only way I would ever be able to save myself was if she were dead – but that would be bad for her because she would be going to purgatory, and I was ashamed of myself for wishing it. Purgatory was where she and Jane were going: they had been christened but didn't go to Mass, so they would be put into this kind of holding pen for heaven and tortured there until they were purified. If people prayed for you after you were dead you could some-times get out early. Then the gates of heaven would open and you would spend your time praising God.

I told them at school I wasn't allowed to be a Catholic and they were shocked at a mother who would condemn her own daughter to limbo. It was probably a mortal sin. If you committed a mortal sin you went to hell. I could see the only thing to do was to stay alive, and when my mother died of old age, I would be free to be a Catholic.

I sat next to an etching of St Anthony being tortured in hell by demons, and tried to concentrate on mental arithmetic, and pronouns. I could not get the knack of the latter, so in a test I copied the answers of the girl in front of me, taking care to change one so as not to be charged with the sin. That was the only one I got right. I realized the imprudence of copying. Better to rely on yourself than others. I had my knuckles rapped for doing so badly in the test. A nun seized your hand, turned it over and banged your knuckles sharply against the desk. For some reason the girl I had copied from did not get her knuckles rapped, but then she was a devout girl who even at the age of seven wanted to be a nun. Knuckle-rapping hurt: anything to get out of it, but I did not want to join the magpies in their high tower, or even promise to. How they lied and swore and cheated, all the little convent girls, to get out of trouble or make money. I had never known anything like it.

My friend Colleen borrowed twopence from the newsagent telling him her father had just died. Then she went into the butcher and borrowed threepence saying she had to take it back to her father or he'd beat her terribly. Then she went to the newsagent and spent the lot on colour balls which she shared with me. I thought I ought to refuse but the sweets changed colour as you rolled them round in your mouth and I couldn't resist. You had to keep taking them out of your mouth to see whether the pink had turned to violet, the magenta to mauve. It was a sticky process and the dye stayed round your mouth for days.

I was hungry most of the time. The boarding-house breakfast was meagre and my mother gave Jane and me sixpence between us to buy lunch every day. You could have a small hot meat pie or a cold apple pie or half a pound of broken biscuits from the biscuit factory down the road. The meat pie was nicest but it was also smallest. The biscuits were dry and dusty and hard to swallow. Drink came from the water tap.

There was a girl in my class called Beverley whom everyone hated. She had cross-eyes and spots, and was smelly. She crouched in a corner and whimpered, and the more they bullied the more bulliable she became. I thought it was outrageous. I played with her on principle: if I played with her the others would. I made her wash out her knickers. If her mother didn't she'd have to do it herself. She cheered up a bit. Presently the other children asked to join in: Colleen, Mary, Teresa, Marjorie, all the big wild popular girls.

The nuns were firm creationists: I was taught that the world began with the Garden of Eden and Adam and Eve. I was annoyed to discover that Eve was created out of Adam's rib as an afterthought, because God thought Adam needed company, and puzzled as to how Cain and Abel managed to have children without marrying their own sisters, which I knew was forbidden. My mother said that Genesis was not necessarily the only truth, but I knew her witness was not sound.

I took to reading the psalms in bed at night under the bedclothes. The nuns did not encourage us to read the Bible: on the contrary, they thought it should be mediated through a priest. It has always been my impulse to read what I am not meant to read and not to read what I am encouraged to. I fell in love with language, in what I can now see was in itself a kind of sub-erotic experience. I wrestled with the notion of the hills lifting themselves up and the valleys being exalted, and like Daniel wrestling with the lion, I won. If I could not understand, I osmosed. I do not think the *Good News Bible* could ever have done as well as this little, leather-bound, thin-papered Authorised Version we happened to have in the house. I wrestled with *Ecclesiastes* and the *Book of Job*, and came to the conclusion that the nuns were only telling half the story.

What the nuns gave us to read was *Little Lives of All the Saints*, a Victorian tract describing the tortures that young women of long ago endured preserving their virtue in the name of Jesus. Their breasts were chopped off, bits of them sliced up and fried, but they would not give up their virginity. They were beautiful and they were good, and pain was their reward. I was fascinated and horrified: I knew there was something wrong in my response but not quite what. Tremors, halfway between pain and pleasure, affected me as I read. Sex was a mystery to me, let alone the finer pleasures of masochism. I had no idea what virginity was, or what men did, or how babies were conceived. No one talked about these things at the convent for fear of knuckle-rapping or ear-tweaking: nuns slid about the corridors overhearing what was said, invisible until suddenly you saw them. All you knew about sex was that it was exciting and forbidden, and very secret.

On the way home from school one day a little boy with no clothes on ran out of his house. When I got home I asked my mother if there was something wrong with him, since he had this little bit hanging out in front. She said no but was too embarrassed to elaborate. I thought he was probably mal-formed.

Sin and Guilt

The main problem with the convent was that you never knew what would get you into trouble. It seemed to have so little to do with common sense. It shrieked at you out of a clear sky. If your mother made you meat sandwiches on a Friday there was terrible trouble, though it was not your fault. You would be lining up at playtime to go back into the classroom, jostling as ever, called into silence. 'You are touching one another. Never, never touch another person if you can possibly help it!' I stretched out my hand and touched the person in front of me, in defiance. I was seen. Deliberate disobedience! My punishment was the worst they could think of: I was not to be allowed to stand and clap and wave flags when the cardinal from Rome came to bless us, dressed in his scarlet robes with gold binding. I was to stay in and learn more spelling. I learned to spell 'theatre', I remember, though my mother had to explain to me what it was. I didn't mind at all not seeing the cardinal, which merely proved to the nuns how hardened in sin I was. But things were getting worse: I could not explain it: limbo was creeping round the outskirts, with occasional glimpses of hell showing through.

The nuns liked Jane and she liked them. She was quiet and clever and good at art and never got her ears tweaked. She embroidered exquisite flowers and made a little cloth book to contain them: it had a white vellum cover, on which she painted bluebells: it seemed something out of the past, from long ago. If I tried to do anything like that it got covered with ink and was tatty within minutes. Jane also painted an entire set of the Tarot pack: small, fine, perfect replicas of those sinister cards. I don't suppose she did this in the school art class, and where she got the originals or whose idea it was I do not know. My mother half admired them and half hated them. I thought they were very spooky, especially the one she did of the Tower, the edifice splitting apart beneath the black hammer blow of a bolt of lightning.

A nun slammed open a window in the gothic tower of the convent as I ran up and down shrieking and splashing in the mud and called out to the world that I was a wicked girl and a heathen and the ringleader, and she would let my form teacher know in the morning. I spent a night of terror so abject nothing has been as bad since, not even the night in the haunted house in Saffron Walden years later. Nameless horrors, scrabbling to get in, the worse for being un-named. In the morning nothing happened. There was no hammer blow. I did not tell my mother because her life was hard enough.

I got a bad sore throat and lay with my pecked ankles in bed and couldn't go to school and was tremendously happy. The doctor came and said I might have scarlet fever and if so I would have to go to an isolation hospital. I prayed to God that I could go, and to the Cardinal in his wonderful sweeping scarlet gown, all the way from Rome, the Holy City, to intercede for me with God. My prayers were answered, which was gratifying. I had begun to doubt the deity. I thought it said in the Bible that if you threw your bread upon the water it would be returned threefold: I'd throw some of the stale biscuits into the Avon but nothing ever came back, though rather more ducks than usual would come by. The ducks seemed so happy and free, though sometimes they too would turn on one of their number, a Beverley duck, as it were, and peck it to bits.

I loved the fever hospital. The nurses were kind and the other children were friendly. My ankles healed and fears of limbo receded. My confidence in the deity was restored. Invalid food, the like of which is not known in today's hospitals or sick-rooms, food to tempt the reluctant appetite, was cooked and served. A little pale and white, it's true – clear beef broth, steamed fish and mashed potatoes, and vanilla blancmange

– followed by hot sweet milk and white-iced biscuits – but every spoonful you got down you was applauded.

Anything parents brought in had to be sterilized in great steam cupboards, and if they visited us, which they were only allowed to do once a week, they had to sit the other side of a thick glass partition. I had a fit of neurosis which I remember to this day: a girl in the bed opposite had a bag of sweets: she threw me one and missed and it went under the bed, but I chose to believe she had not thrown it, and had treated me badly, and wept and wept until a nurse came to comfort me. I knew perfectly well it was an accident but preferred to be miserable, for the sheer drama of it. Later in life I would treat lovers and husbands in this way. Taking offence and suffering because of it, knowing in your heart they are not in the least to blame, you just want a drama, and your turn at being a victim.

One day unannounced, it was not my mother sitting the other side of the glass screen when I was led in for the family visit, but my father. At least that was what the nurse said he was, and I had no reason to mistrust the nurse. I didn't know what to say to him. He seemed tall and handsome and I was immensely flattered that he had come to see me, and to think that I was his daughter, which gave me some kind of right to him. He talked about his plans: they did not seem to include living in the same house as us. That was fair enough, I could see he would hate the magpie. He gave me two shillings, and then he disappeared again.

Convalescent

When I came out of hospital my mother said my father had gone to the North Island to look for a job. North! The island I had never seen. That was where the excitement and energy lay, I was convinced. It was the land which contained my father, where the weather got warmer with every mile you travelled, where I had never been. Further south and all was bleak and next stop the South Pole, where there was nothing but penguins. I was increasingly awed by the map. How vast the globe was, and how proud I was to be British: why, a whole third of the nations were coloured red, which meant we governed it. The disgrace of being a homie was balanced by the specialness of being English. But how far away we were from the rest of the world! I knew only too well, because of the time that lay between my parents' coming and going, what distance meant. You measured it in days and weeks, not miles.

School was on hold for me, while I recuperated. I managed to forget about it. One Sunday afternoon Jane and I were sent out to play in Cranmer Square. Frank had come south. He was to take us out for the afternoon; we were to drive to visit the black swans which lived on a lake outside the city. No, he was not coming into the house, the landlady would not like it, we were to wait for him outside. We had ribbons put in our hair. I had the check dress Jane had worn for the Rita Angus portrait, which fitted me by now. There was no choice. We were given no option as to what to wear. There wasn't much to choose from, anyway. School uniform and Sunday best and that was about all.

Jane'nFay went out to play. She skipped and I played sevens. We didn't speak much. We improved our skills while we waited. I could read what was in most people's heads but seldom these days what was in hers. I thought it might be something to do with the colour of her eyes. She had dark, dark brown eyes like my mother's, and mine were bright blue like my father's. I adored her and felt apologetic, the cuckoo chick in her nest, growing larger and larger, wearing her cast-offs, and resented for something I couldn't help, for being there. I daresay most younger siblings feel like this.

Time was getting on. No sign of a father. I wanted Jane to go back inside to ask what the time was, but she wouldn't. I went. It was three o'clock. I played more sevens but kept dropping the ball: Jane kept stepping on the rope. In the next hour hope and disappointment fought it out, and minute by minute disappointment gained ground until there was no hope left. The sun sank lower across Cranmer Square: I came to the understanding that I was not central to the universe, and that no amount of wishing and hoping would twist it to my convenience, and the sun would just go on sinking.

Around four-thirty my mother called us in and said, 'Well, he's not coming, is he?' in the tone of one who was disappointed but not surprised. I sat down to read *Ferdinand the Bull* yet again, practising insouciance. I did not like people being sorry for me. Just sit down and smell the flowers, like Ferdinand. I have, and I date it to that day, become expert at receiving bad news. I keep my face still, gain time to reassess my situation, to retreat or advance as required. Grit the teeth, face a changed world, go back afterwards to mop up the emotion. I was more like a New Zealander than a homie in this, and have stayed so. New Zealanders go into

63

danger gear at the drop of a hat: you don't see them emoting all over the place. That's why they run Aid Agencies and such like: they don't panic.

Later my mother said he'd had flu and hadn't been able to come. I didn't quite believe her. I thought it was probably something to do with Ina, or Jean, or Helen. Be that as it may, he had gone back to the North without stopping by.

We left the boarding-house. I was so pleased I tried to set the magpie free of its chain: my mother said it only attacked because it was unhappy. But it preferred its imprisonment: it wouldn't let me near it. I had rather hoped for a bungalow like other people had but my mother had found us rooms above a disused stable in an old mews on the road out to Papanui. Poverty is a stubborn thing: you seldom escape it with one bound. But the great thing was that I no longer had to go to the Convent. I was to go to a school called Elmwood instead.

Jane and Fay

There had been some upturn in the powder-box trade, and my mother had sold a novel to her publishers, and received a cheque for fifty pounds. She seemed to have changed her mind about the desirability of a convent education for me, though Jane was to stay at St Mary's for another year. Now I was at a school of my own our names began to separate out.

Elmwood was run on progressive lines: there were no turrets and towers, it was just a great space of green grass interrupted by low, airy custom-built classrooms. There was a swimming-pool. Nobody lied or stole or cringed. Teachers read us stories. Lessons were out of doors on the verandas. We sang English folksongs about nightingales and strawberry fairs: we English-country-danced. 'Home' was respected and I was a homie. We practised the Alexander Technique once a week, and learned how to stand properly, and no one did anything dreadful or sudden. It was observable that education was meant to prepare you for adult life, not terrify you into sub-mission.

The headmaster did for a time instead of a father. Mr Eggle-ton was a plain, kind, dull man with a face as long as his legs: I could see the advantage of dullness: it went along with reliability. If Mr Eggleton said he'd be at a certain place at a certain time he would be. He taught us calligraphy: joined-up writing was not enough: now you must make the words look graceful. We used his name to practise on because of all the above the line and below the line loops, and when my handwriting becomes indecipherable I will practise it the sooner to return to legibility. He would let me hold his hand. There were boys at this school, which was thrilling, but the girls didn't play with them.

My only social problem at Elmwood was the march into school when the bell rang for the end of playtime. It was 1937. Militarism was beginning to infiltrate even here on this grassy slope at the back of beyond. Ferdinand the Bull might prefer to sit and smell the flowers than fight, but he was increasingly on his own. We marched into school in pairs, heads held high, in step, swinging arms. I was the new girl, arrived mid-term. I had to walk on my own, unpartnered. I hated that.

I did not want to be despised, to find myself in the wrong place in the pecking order. I was beginning to read other people's thoughts: it was quite painful. It was not for many years that I realized other people tended not to be able to do this. They heard what people said, not what they meant. They did not interpret silences. No wonder they went round so confident and bullish. But soon the marching-in problem was solved, when a new girl turned up to walk in with me. She didn't have the gift of marching: she was too languid for that, but at least we were a pair. Her name was Aliz: she was a refugee, she said, a runaway from Germany. Like me, she didn't have a resident father. She slept in a feather bed and was always ill. I had to defend Aliz against accusations of being peculiar, of which being 'delicate' was evidence, as was coming from a country you had heard about in geography but certainly couldn't place on a map. Then she changed her name to Alicia which suggested to my other friends that she was getting worse, not better. She was affected. I tried to get her to desist but she said Alicia sounded less like a servant than Aliz.

I was always amazed how fancy people could be. She'd tell me stories of people walking along roads carrying suitcases and being machine-gunned by aircraft, but seemed to worry most about her name. I tried to find out why her family had had to run away. She didn't seem to know the answer either, other than that she was Jewish. When I asked what that meant she said she wasn't supposed to turn on the light on Saturdays, which seemed much the same as not eating meat on Fridays. The adult world baffled her as much as me: but she was inclined to shrug and comb her hair in the mirror, while I bounced up and down in indignation or curiosity.

In retrospect it is remarkable how little the adult world at that time confided in its children, even when it came to explaining why others were trying to kill them. Reticence and decorum seemed almost more valuable than personal survival.

I developed my playground skills. I became knucklebone champion of the playground – knucklebones is the same as five-stones: only we played it with scrubbed sheep's knuckles from the butcher, not metal crosses. You toss the bones in the air, catch all five on the flattened back of your hand, and then perform deft scooping and collecting tricks with your fingers. I was good at that, having a wide hand, and also at spelling, for which I was famous, thanks to the St Mary's passion for excluding me from prayer, and the spelling book. I could walk on my hands, do back-bends and touch the back of my head with my foot. Such are the accomplishments of young girl children.

At home things were looking up. My mother stopped painting powder boxes and we moved into a proper house at the end of the tramline. We had a garden with a stream running through it and a walnut tree which we could climb. Jane and I shared a room. We even had the luxury of a bedside table each: plywood apple boxes up-ended – the partition making a convenient shelf – and covered with a piece of curtain stretched on a wire: a bit splintery compared to Alicia's smooth maplewood, but bedside tables nonetheless. There was an outside loo, as was normal enough in a mild climate, before the advent of indoor plumbing. Sit out there at night and see the Southern Cross rising, that bold four-pointed constellation, somewhat skew-whiff, totem of the southern hemisphere.

Even my mother was obliged to admire the Southern Cross, though she sorely missed the northern skies of her youth. There seemed no way she could ever get back to England now. She was trapped. Some points of light in the heavens were shared, she explained to me. She taught me to distinguish Betelgeuse from Mars – the former trembles in its redness, the latter stays steady – to recognize the cool splendour of Venus, to find the North Star and its pointer the Plough.

A telegram came to say that Edgar had died, and I remember weeping to keep her company, but she was weeping for someone I had never met and a world I didn't know. I felt oddly out of sympathy with her, knowing that the more she regarded the old world, the less she regarded mine. I saw the big burnished Southern Cross as belonging to me and my vanished father: my mother could have the little point of the North Star, and all it stood for, as her part of the heavens.

I realized that my mother was a remarkably good person. She got off the tram home to rescue an injured dog, which she'd seen lying in a gutter. No one else took any notice of it, but just walked by. She taught us to love our enemies – or better still, avoid making any. She stayed in bed every morning and wrote her *magnum opus*, and I would rather she made our breakfast and got us to school but I held my tongue. I no longer wanted to be a Catholic but I still had ambitions of sainthood. I learned the art of reading while I walked. There wasn't much traffic, though I do remember being nearly run over by a van, and the outrage of its driver. I was allowed to read at meals: Alicia never was.

At the end of every month money from my father was expected in. Then my mother waited for the post. It seldom turned up, or if it did it wasn't for the right amount. I didn't like to ask where he was and when he was coming back, it seemed impolite. But I was sure he was doing the best he could.

The Doctor's Daughters

My father had a proper job. He was to be medical superinten-dent of the whole Coromandel Peninsula. Even my mother was impressed. We were to visit him: we were to stay for the summer, for a whole eight weeks. No, she wasn't coming, she didn't have the time. We were to go on our own. It seemed good news could come as well as bad, and as suddenly. Out came the map: Jane already knew where Coromandel was. She knew so much I didn't, though she seldom bothered to pass the knowledge on. The North Island stretched up into the Pacific as if groping for the rest of the world: it divided like a hand up near the top, we were to go onto the thumb.

My mother packed our clothes and everything we would need into one small thin brown leather suitcase which Jane was able to carry. She was nine, I was seven.

How neatly and carefully my mother folded and packed: even so, one of us always had to sit on the case to close it. That same suitcase did us for the six years during which summer-with-my-father became ritual. We were the first of the shuttle children. Who else's parents, in those days, lived in different places? (No one used the word divorce: like insanity and cancer, these tragedies were too irrevocable for words to lightly describe, and mercifully, were rarer then than now.)

The journey in itself was excitement enough. It would take two days. Overnight on the ferry from Lyttelton to Wellington: our mother came thus far. Seagulls, a tiny cabin with bunks and portholes – why do ships have round windows? – the smell of oil, the great brass-edged pumping machinery of the engine, pounding through the night, breakfast in company, the kind of food other people ate, not us. Bacon and eggs, and a fried slice. Then we'd spend the day in Wellington, the capital city, bigger and busier than Christchurch, whipped by wind and with ground that trembled, go to the zoo to see the lion and the kiwi, to the Botanical Gardens to look at rare ferns. Disloyal to be too happy and excited, too ready to leave my mother for the eternity of two months, to be the doctor's daughters.

In the evening she put us on the overnight train to Auckland and went back home on the ferry. Jane and I had a sleeper, a delight: seats which turned into bunks, hidden lights, little tables which pulled out, miniature shelves for fob-watches, a tiny basin and tap and cut-glass tooth mugs. I was in Jane's care. In those days children travelled alone: Jane was nine and I was seven, sixteen years between us, old enough added together to meet all eventualities.

The train hooted and whistled out of Wellington: the sky was red and orange against hills, night fell, the whole future spread out in front of us, secret black, shot by moonlight. The train took its time, edging its way up through the centre of the North Island, the crevices between hills opening out into farmland and closing back in again: at five in the morning it began to get light, mist wreathed the landscape as it declared itself, a rising sun replaced the moon and the bush turned slowly from black to green. Farmhouses built before the railway had their WCs at the end of the garden. They had been built without doors and so they stayed, though now they looked out on to passing trains. If you looked, you could see people sitting there, unabashed. We were hungry: we'd eaten our breakfast sandwiches the night before, of course we had, thinking hunger could get no worse. The guard bought us grown-up tea and biscuits.

But would our father be there to meet us? He hadn't managed Cranmer Square, would he manage Auckland Station? What would we do if he didn't? But he was there, large and dark among pale, streaming passengers and friends, cigarette sticking to his bottom lip: we were too stiff and self-conscious to hug – people touched so much less, once upon a time, even in families – though he sniffed a bit and I thought he was crying. He took the suitcase and admired the way we travelled light. He was taller than I remembered. I was instantly in love with him. He strode off through milling crowds and we ran after. He assumed, in his lordly way, that we would and so we did.

The journey was not finished yet: now there was a six-hour drive to Coromandel, out of the quiet limbo of Christchurch, through the eventful purgatory of places in between, to arrive at the unknown. My father owned a Ford V8 imported from America, solid and black, and the newest thing in engines. People stared after it as we passed. Cars till then had been square and upright: this one was curved; 'streamlined', my father described it. This made it go faster, apparently: the shape offered no resistance to the air, which would stream away on either side as we went. I loved the importance of it. With my father, going north, we were on the top of everything, looking down. Not, as with my mother, peering cautiously upwards, fearing the descent of the untoward.

The road was flat and straight at the base of the thumb of land and we travelled fast: too fast for my liking – I am easily frightened in cars – but after the mangrove swamps outside the little town of Thames the hills began and progress was slow. As we went further north the landscape changed: now we were in sub-tropical bush, and soon the only way forward was along the winding, unmade-up road which skirted the coast. Red pohutukawa trees leaned down from the cliffs to meet the rocky sea-line, where cormorants shrieked and dived, past rough shacks where Maoris, brown, beautiful, glistening, lived and fished, and on to Coromandel bay, and the ghost town of Coromandel itself. And even then as a child I knew how privileged I was, to be in that place, at that time, in the Golden Age.

The real gold had gone, the seams exhausted, but the memory of it remained. The Coromandel Peninsula saw a gold rush at the beginning of the century – there were rumours that you could pick up nuggets on the hill tracks, or just sitting there on the stream beds – but the seams were soon exhausted and a population which had suddenly swelled to hundreds of thousands, as suddenly dwindled again to be reckoned in thousands. The goldminers were long gone – other than a few reddish hairy old men who stumbled out of the hills from time to time to consult my father, like survivors of some forgotten war. But they had left behind not anger, disappointment and despair, which you might have expected, but a benign ambience of hopeful exhilaration. The High Street was like something out of the Wild West: wide enough for a gunfight or so and the Wells Fargo coach to rattle through, lined by wooden shops: the general store, the outfitter, the bank, the lawyer, the chandler, drinking-houses by the dozen and a couple of wooden churches, and a little further on, on the dirt road out of town, was the wooden hospital and opposite it the doctor's house. All are still there, largely unchanged. The hippies have moved in, and marihuana floats through the air, the tourists come and go, but the coast road is much as it was and keeps the bus parties away.

My father was medical superintendent to the whole sparsely populated peninsula. He was not just a GP, but his own specialist surgeon, physician, obstetrician and consultant. He had to be, since there was no one else to do it. He held his morning surgery in the cottage hospital across the road. The hospital was grand and pillared, with a wide sweep of lawn and drive in front, and had been originally built by a mine-owner for his own use: the doctor's house had housed his chief of staff. There were seldom more than a handful of patients and a ward sister and some four or five live-in nurses to help. There was an operating theatre, and I pleased my father by being able to spell the word without trouble.

Every summer for the next five years Jane and I were to go to Coromandel. One year when my mother was ill we stayed on and went to the village school. I loved it: it was such a casual affair. You could go barefoot, and sit in a class with others younger and older than you. They gave the cane – the thwack of a stick on the hand for misdemeanours – but it was seldom used: the only time I can remember is when one of the big boys held the headmaster's head under the school

cold-water tap and kept it there. And after the caning he got expelled as well. It would not happen to us: we were children of status now, we were the doctor's daughters, no longer Margaret, Jane'nFay, on the wrong side of things. I made friends, Dulcie Strongman in particular: she was the shipwright's daughter. We ran wild. We'd go up into the bush where we weren't meant to go, because it was pocked with mine shafts, and slid down the hills on the great green bucket leaves of palm trees. We looked in the streams for little frogs which were said to date back to dinosaur times, and for gold nuggets which might still be lurking there. Deep in the bush everything was quiet and you didn't like to shriek or make a noise. It was dark, dark green, except for a scatter of white clematis hanging from the kauri trees, which stood like the masts of ships, piercing up through the forest roof to get to the light of the sky. These secret parts of the forest were the temples of unknown Maori Gods; we went quietly through them, following streams, not wanting to stir up things we didn't understand.

It was unusual for a man to be in charge of children, and not a mother in sight. The nurses took us under their wing. For food we relied mostly upon morning and afternoon tea served up at the hospital. Morning tea was meat or fish-paste sandwiches and scones and strawberry jam. Afternoon tea was the same but with potato scones, Afghans, brandy snaps, sponge cake filled with jam and cream, and lamingtons – pink or yellow sponge squares rolled in desiccated coconut – added. Those were the great days of New Zealand bakery, a cold-climate, carbohydrate-rich habit of cooking brought to the antipodes by Scottish pioneers, refined and developed in days of warmth and plenty into something inspiring, if fattening.

But mostly we were out of sight and out of mind. We played in the orchard behind the house; it had an orange tree and lemon tree and a banana grove: cherries, apples, plums, figs and apricots. We carved out rooms in the bamboo grove and lived in those for a time; we moved our beds out into the veranda and slept there. On Wednesdays we'd drive over the peninsula with my father to the cottage hospital at Mercury Bay – where Captain Cook first observed the transit of

A merry Christmas from the Birkinshaws.

COROMANDEL
1940

Mercury, as everyone kept telling us – and if there was an emergency there and he had to stay over we'd go to the village school there, and show off our mental arithmetic and our pronouns, but subtly – *noblesse oblige*. We were the doctor's daughters, and wherever we went we were welcomed. Out of term it was the beach, the surf and paradise.

We looked after animals on first principles. They had to eat, to drink, to sleep like you did, and you combed out the fleas to do them a favour. We had a pen for the livestock the grateful patients who couldn't pay would leave in lieu. Usually hens or ducks but sometimes a sheep and once a pig. Sometimes the old men from the hills would pay with gold nuggets. They sat in a row along the mantelpiece, greyish, disappointing lumps of stone. They needed polishing, my father said.

On wet days we learned poetry. My father paid sixpence for every Shakespeare sonnet. Jane learned all the *Ancient*

Mariner but that was at a lower rate and I gave up after the first two pages. Soon I could recite all *The Lady of Shalott*, and poetry extending into prose, could deliver the first page of John Stuart Mill's essay *On Liberty*. That was my party-piece.

We were the cow in the Christmas pantomime which my father put on. Jane was the front legs, I was the back. We sold programmes for Ibsen's *Peer Gynt*, which he directed and the whole town out of loyalty turned up to see in the tiny Town Hall. They were baffled – what had Norway's mountain trolls to do with them? – but they were receptive. He loved them as they loved him. He is still remembered. They wear his appendix scars to this day, some with pride and some with alarm. I think he was quite innovative when it came to operations. His clock is in the tiny town museum along with what I'll swear is the laundry wringer we never used. These Coromandelians were not people turned out by the button-maker, they were sharply individualistic.

If my father were called out in the night he'd take us with him. We'd take our pillows and blankets to the car and settle in and go back to sleep. I woke once in the early dawn and found my father gone and the car parked on a hillside. Along the ridge of the hill above us was a row of horsemen, looking down at us. They were very haughty, Maoris in ceremonial dress. We were intruders. I woke Jane. She was as frightened as I was. They galloped down the hill towards us: horses milled around the car in a flurry of cloaks and feathers. An angry tattooed face hung upside-down to stare in at us. Then the mouth broke into a smile the wrong way up, and someone whooped something, and they galloped off to where, as the sun rose, I could see the carved roof of a Maori meeting-house. Presently my father came back. 'It was a boy,' he said. 'It was difficult but it's okay now,' and we drove back home.

The second year we left to go back south to Christchurch on the morning of 4 September 1939. We were up at five to be at the Thames airstrip by eight. We went up to the hospital for breakfast and found everyone in a state of alarm. War with Germany had been declared.

Wartime

Germany was a long way away and it was hard to understand what the quarrel was about. But Hitler had 'walked into Poland' with tanks and guns and couldn't be allowed to get away with it. We were shown maps. All the young men were to leave New Zealand to fight for 'home'. This they would do with bayonets, guns and in hand-to-hand combat. They were to be put in the way of the Germans and meant to kill any they came across, unless the German said 'I surrender', in which case the German was put in a prison camp to stop him cheating and continuing to fight, until the end of the war. The end came when one side said 'pax'. In the meantime it was permitted to kill German women and children by dropping bombs on them otherwise the German men would drop bombs on you. The rules of engagement seemed strange, and rather like a lot of playground games except people got killed.

We children were set to knitting balaclavas in khaki wool. We sang as we knitted.

Knitting, knitting, knitting, with a prayer in every row,
That the ones we love,
By God above,
Shall be guarded as they go.

It was exciting to wonder about the young man who would actually wear this strange garment, and stare out of the holes we had left for the eyes. He would never know us, but we would know him. It was quite an erotic feeling, though we didn't know the word or what it meant. I think we rather wondered, as we looked at the knubbly, crooked, khaki piles we had created, whether anyone would actually ever wear them, or what good it would do them if they did. Jane knitted perfect balaclavas, and was even allowed loose on the socks, but the rest of us weren't.

We were sent out into the wheat fields at harvest time to look for ergot, a black fungus which would cause madness if you ate it, but which also made a blood-clotting substance useful on the battlefront. We were told not to lick our fingers if we found any. I found some, forgot and licked my fingers, but I stayed sane.

We marched about a lot in parades, waving little Union Jacks on sticks. I wished I was a boy, and not doomed to knit and wave flags: I longed to march off with the men. I was proud to be English: it was as if everyone was coming to my defence. It turned out to be true that if you didn't bomb them they would bomb you – there were photographs in the newspapers of London burning. I felt with my mother then that it was my true home, and I wanted to be there if only for the excitement.

But death was real, not a playground game. I went into a corner shop to buy colour balls and the woman who ran it came out of her door crying. She had a telegram to say her son had been killed in action. I cried as well and held her hand and went home without the sweets. I felt the earth shake beneath my feet and knew that this time it was in my head: I could see that earthquakes and volcanoes were just an outer and visible sign of an inner state, what happened to you as you lived your life. Omens and presages, geological convulsions and emotional shiftings, sudden eruptions; everything inside and outside made the same patterns.

There was a shortage of tender young Canterbury lamb; New Zealanders were left with tough old mutton scrag. All the best cuts were shipped off to Britain. There was not a banana to be seen for five years. Oranges were a rarity. My mother's copies of the *New Statesman and Nation*, which used to come in clusters of six, every six weeks, now came in clusters of thirty-six. Ships still braved the torpedoes and got through, but cargo space was booked for essentials.

In 1941 the Japanese entered the war and things took a turn for the worse. Singapore fell. Darwin was bombed. Japanese submarines were seen in Sydney Harbour. There seemed no stopping them. It was believed that they would swoop down and take New Zealand and use it as a base to capture Australia. New Zealand was defenceless: a nation of women, children and old men. The warrior caste was away fighting other people's wars. The Japanese looted, raped, tortured, killed, everyone knew. Friends told my mother she must be prepared to kill her daughters to save us from a fate worse than death at the hands of the enemy. Instead she taught us to smile courteously and if spoken to by a

Japanese man to reply – what was it, '*konichiwa*'? – I think so. What those troops could possibly want of us girls remained a mystery. There were air-raid shelters in the school playground.

Then suddenly US troops were everywhere. Their ships were in the harbour, handsome men in swanky green uniforms strolled up and down the streets. They had got to New Zealand with a week to spare. The Japanese called the invasion off. We were saved. But now we had to stay indoors after dark, for fear of marauding GIs, of whom everyone seemed to be unreasonably frightened. If you spoke to them they gave you chewing gum, which you were not allowed to have at home. It was one of the vulgar things from which good girls were protected: chewing gum, comics, jazz music on the radio, the company of rough soldiery. We might be poor, the enemy might be at the door, but we were cultured and would not give in to populism.

Elmwood acquired two new men teachers, Mr Stuart and Mr Reid. They were communists, conscientious objectors, and had chosen teaching as an alternative to prison. Mr Eggleton seemed not noticeably grateful for their arrival. Mr Stuart was flamboyant, large and hairy, and Mr Reid was small, angry and hollow-eyed. They took it in turns to give us blow-by-blow accounts of the siege of Stalingrad: for five months the city fought off the German invader, prepared to starve rather than surrender. How innocent the times were: later it emerged that the citizens were forcibly kept inside the city by their own army, to score a propaganda point.

I quite fell in love with Mr Stuart, his descriptions were so vivid and his ideas so strange and complicated. But teachers were always far more impressed by Jane than they ever were with me. Indeed, Mr Reid mortified me by complaining about my untidiness, and asking me why I couldn't be more like my sister Jane, who was always so neat. I felt as bad as did Helen Burns in *Jane Eyre*, wearing the nameboard, with 'slattern' written upon it for all to see. But Mr Stuart did look me up and down once and observe that I was quite a clever little girl for my age. I have a feeling that Mr Stuart was a Trotskyist and Mr Reid a Leninist.

We sent food parcels to my grandmother Isobel in England and she sent us clothes parcels in return. Jane and I viewed these with trepidation. She'd send combinations, cast-offs from nameless cousins, scratchy all-in-one flannel undergarments with flaps for personal functions, which fastened with little rubber buttons. If my mother decided the day was cold, we were obliged to wear them.

The ship on which my mother sent her latest manuscript was torpedoed. Her publisher's offices in London were bombed. There was no spare newsprint for fiction anyway. That was the end of another dream. Now how were we to make our living? But the men were at war: women were able to take the jobs. They ran the farms and the industries: Mary Glover, wife of poet Dennis Glover, who ran the Caxton Press in peacetime but killed men in time of war, delivered our daily milk from an electrified float. My mother, who had been working as a typist in the Albion Wright advertising agency, took over when her boss was called up. She wore a little grey business suit, functioned perfectly if anxiously, kept the agency in profit, earned seven pounds a week – and once actually spent four pounds on a new suit.

In 1944 we had a special assembly in the Girls' High School to celebrate the end of the war in Europe, VE Day. Some 400 of us were crammed into the assembly hall on the first floor. The building began to tremble and the floor to tilt. Earthquakes were not meant to happen in Christchurch but this quite definitely was one, and a bad one too. We continued with Henry Vaughan's hymn to peace:

> *My soul, there is a country,*
> *Far beyond the stars,*
> *Where stands a wingèd sentry,*
> *All skilful in the wars . . .*

But we sang shakily, an inch away from panic . . . The earthquake calmed, the building steadied. We were lucky. People trusted far more to luck then than they do today.

Still the young men did not come back from the wars: they were moved on to the Japanese front. The Japanese were not playing the same game as we were, or else the goalposts had moved. The enemy just would not say 'pax'.

One day that same year my mother came home from work white faced. The Allies had dropped an atom bomb on Japan. It had destroyed a whole city, women, children, everyone. It didn't seem the kind of thing our side did, but we'd done it. No one knew much about the effects of radiation: it was just a very big bomb. Simple loss of civilian life was enough to horrify. But at least very soon after that the Japanese said they were giving in, war stopped, and we celebrated VJ Day in school assembly, concluding with hymnody in proper spirit of vigour and triumph. 'And her ways are ways of gentleness, and all her paths are peace . . .'

The great day came and the men came back from the war. Albion Wright took over the reins of the advertising agency: my mother was demoted to typing and making the coffee once again, and her wages were cut by half. Indignant at her treatment she handed in her notice, and took a job in the biscuit factory whose broken products I had eaten while at the convent. This earned her a couple of shillings more than had she stayed at the agency. She would come home from work with blistered fingers: her job was to lift hot biscuits from the oiled conveyer belt and place them on wire racks to cool. I was sorry that hostilities had ended.

And that was the course of the war for Margaret, Jane and Fay. After that flags went out of fashion, and we no longer marched in from school playgrounds but simply took our places at our desks when the bell went.

Playground Narrative

When Jane and I returned from Coromandel in the autumn of 1938 we found that our mother had moved house again. Turn your back for a moment and she was off. Mostly we lived in furnished houses, so moving was not a big deal. She has always believed there is somewhere better round the corner, and by and large she was right. This little house was surrounded by green trees and was dark and damp, but I could walk to school and I liked that.

We were not there long because my mother became ill with jaundice, and Jane and I were sent to stay with friends in

Sumner, a seaside town a few miles out of Christchurch. It was thought we would enjoy being on the beach but we had been spoiled by Coromandel and were not grateful. It was a flat dull beach, its only feature a large rock with a tunnel cut through its middle for the fun of it, but it always smelt of pee. So did the school we were now sent to: Jane hated it, I didn't mind it, but I was shaky on past participles and you got the strap if your homework had too many mistakes in it. The trouble with moving schools was that some things you knew too well and other things you didn't know well enough: but at least your past had no time to catch up with you. The strap was a leather thong: it did your hand less damage than the cane, but the hurt went on for days, or so they said. At least it was not the paddy, which was a flattish long-handled wooden spoon with a hole in the shallow bowl, to raise a blister in the palm of the hand. Only the boys got that: girls were spared. There were some advantages, I could see, to being female.

Once my mother was better Jane and I became ill. We caught whooping cough, quite badly, and were taken to recuperate on a farm at a little place called Kowai Bush.

We collected pails full of warm milk from the cows and warm eggs from the hens. By day I read and by night I coughed. I read all the Hans Andersen stories and as many of Andrew Lang's *Fairy Books* as I could. I began on E. Nesbit and Rider Haggard. The cough kept coming back at night, and was frightening, because sometimes I felt I would never breathe again, and die, like the Little Mermaid. When we were ill my mother was really attentive. She would get up in the night and bring us honey and lemon drinks. Jane and I became adept at presenting her with short intensive illnesses. I try to do as much for my children, but after three days' nursing I begin to lose patience, and the flow of tender loving care becomes erratic, and they by some miracle, or instinct for self-preservation, get better at once.

Jean Stephenson and Helen Shaw came to visit us, forgiven by my mother for any sins they might or might not have committed. They seemed to want to please. Jean took pride in knitting us Fair-Isle jumpers, made in lengths of different coloured wool to a traditional Scottish pattern. They were scratchy and ugly. If you chose the right place, snipped a single strand with the scissors or with your teeth, and pulled, the garment would fall in half. This seemed to me immeasurably funny and I took pleasure in doing it. Jean would patiently knit the pieces together again, I would snip, she would knit, until she finally gave up. This is the only piece of gratuitous naughtiness I can remember having committed through my entire childhood. Life was too precarious: we lived on a knife-edge, financially and socially: we knew better than to rock the boat. We were two very good, very polite and docile little girls. I was discovered weeping over *The Snow Queen*. It was the sliver of ice in Kay's heart that frightened me, which stopped him loving Gerda. I foresaw a life full of Ice Queens swooping down with the wind and freezing my beloved's heart towards me. I was not far wrong.

In the summer of 1940 Jane and I found our father's Coromandel bed filled by a tall, elegant, rather brusque woman called Dr Edna Mackenzie. She was the school doctor in Hamilton, a hundred miles or so down country. I had nothing against her personally: indeed, she was an extremely kind and helpful person who laid the table and sat us down to proper cooked meals, instead of the sandwiches my father favoured. I was not sure why she was in my father's bed at night: there was a perfectly good spare room: it was wives who shared beds with husbands and by lying close together, I had worked out, they had babies. I got up early one morning and slammed and slammed the kitchen door to get them out of their bed and my father called out in annoyance and I cried. I stood on the tap of the rainwater tank. But it was rusty and broke and all the water ran out and away, and I cried and cried. My father was irritated but Edna said, 'She misses her mother, poor little thing,' and I cried some more, full of self-pity. That was the first year of the war, my mother was ill again and we stayed on in Coromandel and went to school there.

When we got back to Christchurch six months later there were nits in our hair. My mother said, pulling and tugging with the nit comb, 'Fine school doctor she turns out to be!' and I decided that you didn't speak about the South Island when in the North, or about the North Island when in the South, there was too much antagonism around. I had tropical sores on my shins, too, which came, or so my mother said, from walking barefoot to school. I was quite proud of them. They ate deeply into the flesh, right down to the bone. I have the scars to this day.

On our ritual journey up to Coromandel the following year, when we were walking in the Wellington Botanical Gardens looking for rare ferns, my mother told us that Edna and Frank were married. The sky darkened and the ground seemed to open up. The weather had been dry and the lawns were sparse and networked by myriad little cracks where the earth showed through. Now these seemed to deepen and widen, and I had to stand very still for fear of being swallowed up by nothingness. I was not sure whether this was a real earthquake or one of the ones in my head. I kept my face still and said that was bigamy, since he was married to my mother. She said that she and Frank were divorced and had been for two years. She explained what divorce was. It was the first I had heard of such a thing. And why would anyone want Edna, when he could have had my mother?

What a strange family we were, and unhappy, judging from the look on my mother's face, and things had so nearly gone well. And how stupid I was not to have realized. I could tell that nothing was ever going to be right again. The pattern of my life was establishing itself, and it was not good, and there was never to be any curing it. Jane said nothing and stared at her shoes. They were well polished. Mine were scruffy. We were too embarrassed to look at one another, or indeed at my mother. The ground reverted to normal though it was some time before I felt safe enough to move.

I did not discuss the matter with Jane. We both kept our own counsel. Nor did I speak freely or easily to my father thereafter: I thought he must take me for such a fool. I was taken to the Botanical Gardens in Wellington a couple of years back, while on a book tour. It seemed rather a pleasant place and the lawns were well watered: nor did the earth yawn. But I still had the feeling that it was a place where the devil had once flown by, and we'd got caught up in the dark wind of his wings, because we just happened to be standing there, the three of us, Margaret, Jane'nFay, in his path.

It was shortly after that Jane got bored with my tagging along. She'd tell me to go away and stop following her: she turned and looked at me once with an expression so dangerous and manic that I was frightened: I never trusted her with a confidence again, or my mother, let alone my father. Life,

I could see, had to be borne on one's own. I smiled and skipped about as expected but I had learned to be wary. Being sociable, I put my trust in friends and learned to turn my family life into playground narrative, the better to entertain them. I knew it was a kind of disloyalty, even then. I have never stopped. I put it on paper now, elaborating further and further away from the original tale, with a succession of *what ifs, what ifs*, but the source, the riverhead, is the playground narrative.

A Burning Bush in Hagley Park

My mother was losing interest in worldly matters. She had seen angels in Hagley Park: where once I had held my father's hand and seen a parachutist floating down from a clear sky, now she saw, floating down, pillars of light: the light spoke to her, reassured her; she was in despair at the time, she said, as to what her life had come to, and ill, and anxious as to how to keep us, but they told her all would be well in the end. She was special to them.

I read a description in C. S. Lewis's *Perelandra* of just such pillars of light: he too described them as angels. They too appeared at a time of crisis. Such visions are both transfiguring and dangerous: the Church is suspicious of them (Joan of Arc ended burned at the stake) and psychiatrists spend a lot of time and energy trying to explain them away, as they do point-of-death-experience. Some neural disturbance, some hormonal imbalance, they claim. But I don't think so, I think she did see angels: and after that nothing that happened, nothing she did or saw, seemed quite real to her again, as if she was living in shadow, waiting for the sun to return.

Visions came to her from time to time, as if the sun came briefly out from behind the clouds. She described a vase of flowers to me, once, as it suffered a sea change into its proper self, floating with an intensity of being and beauty, before returning to its everyday self. She had glimpsed what Plato would describe as the perfect form, of which all mundane things are the shadow: it was the heaven even the nuns had spoken of, when it is enough just to gaze and adore in the Light of the Lord.

For all my bouncy practicality I was the one she talked to about these things. Others were embarrassed. Angels! Mystical experiences! In Hagley Park of all places! Floating vases of flowers? You're joking! Jane would walk out of the room if my mother tried to talk about it: her friends thought she

90

was a little touched; the local vicar didn't want to know. I was perfectly prepared to believe in them: I was well aware by now there was more to our existence than meets the eye. My mother wrote to Gerald Heard, a religious leader who lived in a community in California, where later Aldous Huxley was to take mescalin and write *The Doors of Perception*. Letters of reassurance and understanding came back to her. She read St Theresa and Evelyn Underhill's *Mysticism* and felt better. I understood but I was not totally in sympathy. If you were in the here-and-now that was all you had to work with, and you should get on with it and enjoy as much of it as you could. She should be concentrating on earning a living, not covering sheets of paper with tiny writing on the relationship of the aesthetic to the moral.

But I envied her. She had seen with her own eyes, clear and bold, what I only sometimes had just an intimation of, when landscape would turn silent and purposeful, or sunlight glitter on water – a flash of some glory only just vanished, caught out of the corner of the eye. It is not so fortunate a vision to have, of course: as my mother found. It sucks the vitality out of ordinary experience and nothing ever seems quite real again: it isolates you from others: it is anathema to most churchmen, who have no patience with it, and friends have no idea what you are talking about.

So much was said to me in a letter written in response to some passing remark I made on television about mystical experience. It was badly spelt and in an untutored hand. The writer wrote in distress. He described how the room he was in had suddenly become more real than he knew things could be: how a vase of flowers had blazed with a significance as if blessed by the presence of God. And after that nothing had made any sense, the blessing had been given and then cruelly removed, and he had walked in shadows ever since. He was a builder: he hadn't been a religious man. He had been to priests who didn't know what he was talking about: friends thought he was mad: psychiatrists tried to treat him with anti-depressants. All I could say to him was that at least he wasn't alone, and that you shouldn't expect to emerge unscathed from too close a brush with the Almighty, He who creates earthquakes and volcanoes.

Granddaughter

In 1942 I became a granddaughter. My grandmother came over from San Francisco to join us. Her mother, old Mrs Henry Holmes, had died in her late nineties and Nona, as we were to call her, was left alone in America. There was no point in her going to London – and there were so many U-boats in the Atlantic the passage was dangerous – the life she'd known there was long since gone: her son Selwyn had vanished into SOE to do secret war work: her unacknowledged daughter Faith had died, and so had the husband who had driven her to distraction and divorce, but who had written her affectionate letters to the end.

There was only Margaret left, and Margaret was stranded in New Zealand and in desperate straits, and needed somebody to help look after the children while she was out working. So Nona came. And indeed, she had little choice in the matter. With her mother's death she was left without means: she had a small annuity left to her by a friend, and that was all. She was now dependent upon Margaret and anything that Selwyn would or could send her. There was no way she could have stayed in California. In those days the State did not help those who could not help themselves: it was left to relatives to do it, and sometimes they did, and sometimes they didn't.

It was a dangerous journey. Since Pearl Harbor the Pacific had been alive with Japanese submarines, and though in theory civilian liners were not torpedoed, who was to say when the rules of engagement might not change for the worse?

She came with trunks full of beautiful things: embroidered fabrics and beaded bags, delicate gloves and exquisite belts – a tall, elegant, gentle woman with a strong chin, beautiful eyes, upswept grey hair and a flirtatious manner which New Zealand soon knocked out of her. This was a nation of practical, competent women in wartime. They didn't mind her playing the piano, but they didn't listen. She smoked, which was a male habit, and through a dainty little ivory holder. She made jokes which they didn't think were funny, and asides, which they didn't understand. She wore little strappy sandals instead of sensible shoes, which was absurd, and behaved in her sixties as if she were still attractive to men, which was even more absurd. And she didn't bake. Her new compatriots were perfectly polite but they left her alone.

I think Nona was too stunned to be unhappy. She had not expected a country still raw with newness, bedside tables made of plywood apple boxes, a house which hardly had a mirror in it, or two granddaughters who spoke with New Zealand accents, and hardly a man in sight. She had not seen her daughter for ten years, and her daughter no longer did as she was told. There was a brief power struggle between them, which Margaret won easily, being by far the more powerful personality, and Nona settled down to being comfortable and making the best of things. Again, she had no choice. This was what her life had brought her to and this is what she must accept.

She was meant to be looking after us, but mostly she played the piano and read detective stories. This suited Jane and myself very well. She tried to teach me the piano but her attempts filled me with insensate and irrational rage.

I have had great sympathy ever since with the reluctance of children to accept instruction from family members. It can drive you mad. Let strangers do it. Being taught by close relatives aggravates the child's sense of inadequacy and incompetence: I just could not bear the comparison between the way Nona's fingers tumbled over the keys and my own pathetic efforts: we both acknowledged it and gave up. Jane of course didn't, and became quite a competent pianist, but the true gift was to miss generations before surfacing in my son Nicolas, who only had to look at a piano to be able to play it, and now does so for a living.

Nona was a great reader. We became complicit in this. She would read a detective story a day if she could. She trusted me to borrow them from the public library for her, and since it was assumed they were for my grandmother, not for me, I was allowed to take out adult books. I read them after she had finished with them. I read Raymond Chandler and Agatha Christie, and every green-coded paperback Penguin books had to offer. I veered off into science fiction myself and read Jules Verne and Olaf Stapledon and then discovered H. G. Wells and *The Time Machine*, but Nona did not share my excitement over Wells. She said it was because she knew him too well, and nobody you knew well could you take seriously.

It was a small library but a good one. I fought an ongoing battle with the librarians for years. I would take out three books a day from the children's library and come back for more on the same day, and they would refuse to believe that I had actually read them and would test me on the contents. It was an absurd ritual. They never caught me out. Now, on the back of Nona's requirements for every detective story available in the country, and having read nearly every book in the children's library with the exception of Enid Blyton, whom I could never get on with, and Arthur Ransom, whose books I found painfully patronizing, I had an entrée into the adult library. They soon succumbed, gave me my own library ticket, and I was free to borrow what I wanted.

But mostly Nona played the piano. As soon as my mother left for work in the morning she would begin. She played Beethoven and Mozart, Haydn and Scarlatti for sometimes seven or eight hours a day, and when we came home from school she would still be at it. Today I daresay she would be playing computer games. The house was made beautiful by sound, and we took it for granted. I knew my mother would rather she didn't play so much, but only in the same way I would rather my mother didn't write her *magnum opus*. I resented what took her attention away from me.

Mind you, as a child-minder, Nona wasn't much good when it came to a crisis. Show her a mouse and she would jump on to a chair and scream in fear and anger, and had there been a man about would have required him to stamp it to death and remove it from her sight. Show my mother a mouse and she would address it, console it, and remove it for its own good to some distant place where it would live somewhere else comfortably and well. Nona was a social creature, not a maternal one, and if Jane and I presented her with any kind of emotional problem she would look vague and wander off and play some Chopin, a composer whom she found particularly soothing. But then she was the same woman who rather than face the tragedy of her daughter Faith's life, and her own involvement with it, chose to blot out the very existence of that life. And of course she was born in 1877. Successive generations have increased in empathy ever since. Indeed, we are now so weighed down by it that even a cockroach must not be harmed in the making of a Hollywood film, and the wretchedness of the criminal is as worrying to us as the distress of the victim. But to be in your sixties in the nineteen-forties meant, frankly, you had very little knowledge of human or social sub-text nor much desire to know.

She went off to play Chopin when I came to her in terror because blood was coming from between my legs and I thought I was wounded and dying. I was eleven. Jane, at thirteen, was as worried as I was. I wanted to go to the doctor but Nona just said I must wait until my mother came home and she would explain it to me. That was two hours away. I lay on the bed with pains in my stomach and waited, bleeding on to the sheets, and listened to Chopin. I have disliked Chopin ever since. When my mother got home she seemed shocked rather than alarmed. 'It's this country,' she said. 'Everything grows too fast, like the cabbages.' She always complained about New Zealand vegetables – all size and no flavour.

She then took our oldest, thinnest sheet, and tore it into sections, and used the scissors to cut the strong hemmed sections to make lengths of tape, which she knotted into a harness to go round my waist, with a strip hanging down front and back. 'This is a sanitary belt,' she said. She found two safety pins and told me not to lose them, and used them to fasten the pad she made by folding a section of sheet into a layered oblong. 'This is a sanitary towel,' she said. 'Change it morning and evening and wash the used one out and hang it to dry somewhere where nobody will see it, especially not a man.'

I was dumbfounded. This was normal? How long did the bleeding go on for? I could see it was the end of skipping about. Every four weeks for five days until I was fifty or so? Two thousand days of my life? Bleeding? Monstrous! 'It stops while you're pregnant,' she said. 'It's the body's way of getting rid of the waste which would otherwise go to the making of a baby.' So men didn't get it? It was just for women? Unfair, unfair! And the pain? The pain was only bad for the first couple of days: you took a warm bath or lay down. It was because of the pain it was called the curse: its proper name was a menstrual period but you didn't talk about it if you could help it. You just had to carry on as if it wasn't happening. I didn't see why Nona couldn't have told me all this, it would have saved me two hours' fear.

When I got used to it I didn't mind the bleeding too much. It even seemed reassuring: the monthly confirmation that the body just goes on functioning, in hopeful expectation, beat after beat after beat, in spite of the alarms and excursions of the outside world. It took no notice of what you did, or what you felt, or not much, though it would go on strike if you worried about it too much – if you were scared you were pregnant, for example – just to spite you for thinking that your basic function as a woman was anything other than to have babies.

By the end of the Forties the re-usable cotton rags – the worn-thin sheet of your own which your mother gave you to welcome you into womanhood – had given way for all who could afford them to bulky sanitary towels which you could buy discreetly at the chemist. At first they were not popular – they were made of some kind of paper filling which shredded as you walked, tending to leave a little trail of bloody bits behind. Over the years the quality improved until we have the slim, tactful wonders of today, and sanitary towels on our TV screens, though the graceful drops of blood must be shown as blue, not red, so we are not quite free from reticence yet. They say the Soviet empire fell because the grim men who ran it would not turn their attention to the shortage of lipstick and sanitary towels, and I would not be surprised.

It is not a fatal flaw in a grandmother to want to avoid discomfiture when faced by too much reality: Nona made an excellent minced meat roll on Tuesdays (roast on Sundays, cold on Mondays, mince on Tuesdays – we were sufficiently acclimatized for this) and on Saturday mornings we would do the washing. Washing day was meant to be on Mondays but we changed it to Saturdays so we children could help, while Nona regaled us with tales of the past as she bent over the steaming tub, or such portions of the past as she could bear to parcel out. The rest we had to piece together.

We had by now moved to a house in Jackson's Road in Fendleton, and here we were to stay for a full three years. We had time and space to accumulate a few possessions, and my mother had no excuse for not hanging Rita Angus's portrait of Jane and myself on the walls. She did not want to hurt Rita's feelings. But she hated the picture: it was everything she been trained to disapprove of at the Slade: it was almost caricature, the flatness of the paint, the lack of perspective, the crude colours, the hard edges – she hung it behind a door in the dark hall in the hope that no one would see it.

The Jackson's Road house had a back garden with a beautiful magnolia tree, an inside loo, a veranda, a pumphouse and a washhouse, for the sole purpose of home laundry. It contained a copper boiler, and three, not the normal two, rinsing sinks, and at the end of the row, built-in, and not the usual flimsy freestanding one, was a splendid wringer with rubber rollers, which you worked by turning a great iron handle, to squeeze out the water. It was, in fact, a fitted washhouse.

On Saturday mornings early Jane and I would bucket cold water into the copper, and add shaved Sunlight soap and washing soda. Nona would light the kindling for the coal fire beneath, and while we waited for the water to boil we would have breakfast. Then we would set to. Sheets were left on the boil for half an hour or so, and then, wet and steamy, would be heaved into the first sink with the washing dolly – a tough wooden stick strong enough to provide sufficient leverage without snapping. It was heavy work. While the next batch of washing boiled we moved the wet bedding and clothes from sink to sink, with three changes of water each, then through the wringer – I'd turn, though I had to stand on my toes to do it – and the long strings of wet compressed fabric would coil into wicker baskets – too early for plastic – to be pegged out on the line. We had two cold-water taps to accomplish all this. It was an exercise in logistics. We loved it.

While we toiled at the washing tubs Nona would regale us with tales of Adelaide Road. When my mother talked about the past I was uneasy; I suspected she was trying to remind me of my cultural roots, maintain my Englishness, stop me turning into a New Zealander, or as they now so quaintly say, this noble people diminishing themselves to flightless-bird level – a Kiwi. This was where I belonged; this was where my loyalties lay. My father stood for New Zealand, my mother stood for England, and I would not betray him. But Nona just wanted to talk, without sub-text, and the past came to life. I learned not to take the great and good seriously, for ever after.

Home Truths and Great Writers

Nona and Edgar married in 1899. She was twenty-two. He was thirty-seven. She gave up the piano to be his wife and mother to his children, and he gave up precious little at all. He had mouths to feed, true, but he went to his club, the Savage, as before, as was the manner of the times. Of his *Memories of a Victorian*, *The Times* had to say: 'Mr Jepson, though he would disdain the poses sometimes assumed by literary men is definitely a literary man. He is also a classical scholar, a product of the public school system and of Jowett's Balliol, a familiar inmate and keen domestic critic of the house of letters.' This rather chilly, intellectual but tremendously social man had married a generous-hearted, very young, very talented girl from the freethinking bohemian classes.

Marriages did last, in those days, because there was no alternative and divorce was a rarity, and if husband and wife found they were ill-assorted, they put up with it. This one was to last thirty-four years and in spite of expectations, a lot of it was good. And they gave parties to which everyone who was anyone in the literary world came, so there must have been at least the appearance of warmth and hospitality: people do not come easily to unhappy households.

The Jepsons held open house on Wednesday and Friday evenings. People came to eat, drink, quarrel, make statements and cut dashes. Nona had less time for the writers than did Edgar: she was a musician and the daughter of musicians and found writers pretentious. Edgar, one-time editor of *Vanity Fair* in Frank Harris's absence, overlooked their pretensions, but tended to dismiss musicians as of no account. Unless they were composers, musicians were interpretive artists, who depended upon craft and emotion to succeed but brought nothing new into the world. Nona simply could not take Edgar's writer friends seriously, neither when she talked of them over the washing tub in Jackson's Road, nor later, when I would pump her more assiduously for details. I had many years to do this – she died a week before her hundredth birthday, lucid and sharp as ever, saying how glad she was that she would not have to go through the embarrassment of receiving a telegram from the Queen.

She always had a good word to say about H. G. Wells – he was always fun and loved playing games, though she found his wife Jane very dull. But then she had a great deal to put up with, and anyone less dull might not have done so. 'All we young women,' said Nona, 'wanted a baby by H. G. His brains and our beauty! And of course poor dear Rebecca went and did it.' Nona was always pleased to be able to describe Rebecca West, who was Wells' mistress for a time, and actually did have his baby, as 'poor dear'. Rebecca apparently put on airs and thought herself very grand and clever. 'She didn't even start out with that name, she borrowed it from a character in some gloomy play by that Scandinavian fellow Ibsen. As if changing her name was going to make any difference, she was heavy and plain enough as it was.' And then, as she heaved the washing out of the boiler into the first sink, and we all leapt back to save ourselves from the splashes, 'The poor thing really thought H. G. would leave Jane and join her but it was never even on the cards.' And after that it got worse. 'The baby had both their looks and not much brain. It was born on the day war broke out, and never amounted to much, after all that.'

Nor was Nona fond of Jean Rhys, who was Ford Madox Ford's lover in Paris, before he moved in with Violet Hunt in Camden Hill Road. 'Such a *louche* young woman,' she dismissed her. 'Always after other people's husbands.' She didn't see how Jean could possibly have written anything of interest, and was incredulous, later, at the continuing popularity of Ford's *The Good Soldier*. 'You mean people are actually interested in that poor man's work? Whatever for? None of us thought anything of it at the time.' A dull, awkward person, she said, who made everyone in the room feel gloomy, and actually a German who'd had to change his name from Hueffer to Ford during the war.

She and Edgar would visit Ford and Violet Hunt, who had similar soirees in Kensington. Her liking for Violet was muted. 'She saw herself as very grand and artistic: but my dear, all those eccentric people!' Gaudier stole the stone he worked with: Sophie Brzeska was completely mad, Wyndham Lewis never washed. Ford Madox Ford edited the *English*

102

Review, and it was in his columns that the Futurists, the Cubists and the Vorticists fought it out. Also of course on the streets: Gaudier made ornamental knuckledusters which he and his Futurist friends would use to beat up roaming parties of Vorticists, until they came to some arrangement about the nature of art. I think Nona felt safer at Adelaide Road, where the antagonisms were less literal.

George Bernard Shaw never slept with his wife. Nona put that down to his being a vegetarian. Ezra Pound would come round when he was drunk and play her piano with his nose. She took it personally, as an insult to music. Arnold Bennett drew guarded respect: too clever and self-seeking for his own good, and he didn't know how to behave, but so attractive! 'He had to keep women off him with a stick.' Joseph Conrad was very bad-tempered, said it was his children who had driven him mad, had a persecution mania, and wouldn't allow talking at meals. I was amazed to discover that Edith Nesbit, the one in the gold writing on the red books I held so dear, was a real person, and not only that, was a chainsmoker who rolled her own cigarettes. She was very excitable and if you went to stay with her at her house in Dymchurch by the sea, you didn't get a wink of sleep. She'd run round the corridors at night screaming. Not that Nona was surprised: poor Edith was married to Hubert Bland, who ran the Fabian Society, and insisted that she bring up his and his mistress's children as her own. She too had a lot to put up with.

The early socialists were not afraid of hypocrisy. Hubert Bland and his fellow-Fabians had H. G. Wells expelled from the society for sleeping with too many of the members' daughters. They put great trust in 'the Life Force' as an explanation of the universe, by which, by and large, they meant sex. Fine

103

for men to be instruments of the Life Force, but their wives and children must desist, and take any extra children into the family.

But then there was Walter de la Mare, the poet, a much quieter kind of person. Along with Arthur Machen he was Edgar's best friend. 'A very spooky person,' Nona complained. She once found me reading 'The Listeners', that favourite of school anthologies: '*"Is there anybody there?"* *said the Traveller, /Knocking on the moonlit door*', and said, 'Of course no one answered the door. If it was Walter standing there, who would?' My mother described him as having a face like a pale almond. 'A very paranormal kind of person,' said Margaret. 'His wife kept seeing him floating past the window when she knew he was in working in his study.'

Arthur Machen was even worse when it came to spookiness. He believed in the power of the Old Gods, found traces of them everywhere, and would worship them whenever and wherever he could. It was he who invented the famous Angel of Mons, the apparition which floated over Mons Cathedral one Christmas Day during a lull in the fighting in World War I. He was battle correspondent for the *Evening News* at the time, his editor was harassing him for a report, there was nothing for him to say, so he invented the Angel and wired the story back. Or so he told Nona. Thus it passed into history or at any rate legend.

Family Scandal

When my great-grandfather Henry Holmes set off for California in 1899, leaving Nona with very little choice but to marry Edgar, he took with him his wife Mary Francis and his two sons, Herriot and Hjalmar, identical twins. He was for a time the musical director of the city of Berkeley, but scandal followed after him, reached the ears of William Randolph Hearst's mother Phoebe, and he was obliged to resign. It was thought, rightly or wrongly, that young girl musicians were not safe in his care, and he would not keep quiet about his theories as to the value of Free Love, the Wheel of Life, and the Life Force. He was not, at least, a hypocrite.

His father had been a Lincolnshire shoemaker, who had taught his two young sons the violin, and then toured with them as infant prodigies, Paganinis, through the courts and concert halls of Europe. He has a column in Grove's Dictionary of Music and the city of Berkeley, according to my grandfather's memoirs, put up a statue to him, and there is every reason to believe that Mary Francis, herself a sculptor, loved him deeply – though her own mother, Mary Francis Chubb, was not so forgiving and left her husband, the lock maker, and settled in Hove, where she was to write poems bewailing the lot of women and the bad behaviour of men. The tendency to marry faithless men comes running down the female side of the family, the tendency to faithlessness runs in the male.

Henry Holmes wrote a violin concerto which was never performed: the score was destroyed in the San Francisco fire in 1906, and was last seen as a kind of charred brick at the bottom of a labelled box. Where the box now is no one in the family knows, but the science of spectroscopy is now advanced: if they can decipher the words on the charcoal that is all that is left of the philosophical scrolls of Herculaneum, they could re-call my great-grandfather's symphony, and perhaps one day it will turn up.

The twins were to return to Europe in the Twenties to wreak havoc, both political and personal. Hjalmar and Herriot were stocky, bright-eyed, red-haired men whose lives were to mirror each other's. Both married women who had a child by a previous relationship and neither had children of their own. They were cowboys in Arizona for a time, and Herriot said the life was fine until the vigilantes came along, and took cattle rustling seriously and saw it as criminal – it had been a game rather than a profit-making exercise until then. The twins returned to Europe politicized by the Wobblies, the Industrial Workers of the World, and became active in the early pan-European communist movement.

Would that they had remained in the States. Hjalmar would stay with his sister Nona in Adelaide Road when passing through London. Hjalmar and Faith, he the uncle, she the niece, fell in love: and were discovered *in flagrante*. Nona was accused of encouraging it. Hjalmar was banned from the house, and Faith was tipped into what would now be called a violent psychotic episode, from which she never recovered. She was locked away, for her own protection and that of others. Edgar visited her weekly in the asylum until her death in 1935. Nona would not, could not, so much as go with him. She wiped her daughter from her memory: she went, as they would say now, into denial. It was the shock waves from this tragedy which echoed through the generations to disastrous affect. My mother lost her sister, ally and friend, the cohesion of the family was gone: the centre could not hold. Free Love, the creed by which the redheaded uncles also lived, is fine in principle but can be tragic in its consequences. The 'Life Force', invented as a concept by Shaw, taken up by Wells and all the other freethinkers of the day, the better to justify their often-ignoble sexual adventures, was a force indeed.

As for the mother so for the daughter: at the same age Margaret married Frank because he was there, she no longer had a home, and what alternative had she? I stuck it out for another few years, and I was twenty-five before I married a man because he was there, I had to have a roof over my head and what alternative was there? But it is only now, as I write this, that I see the pattern. As you're done by, so you do. All the mothers betrayed the daughters, looking after their own skin first. It is easier for me, I have no daughters, only sons.

I never met my wicked great-uncle Hjalmar Holmes: my father sent an edict out from New Zealand that I was not to, but I did meet his twin Herriot once in 1948: a romantic elderly figure, his once-red hair now sparse and dull, but still bright-eyed and talkative. He told me about Rosa Luxemburg, the revolutionary, and how he'd joined the Spartacist's, and how she'd been kidnapped and murdered by right-wing extremists. He spoke of the political magazine he and Hjalmar had edited in Paris through the Twenties. He advised me to be an anarchist when I grew up. He had no children and wanted little to do with his family and died alone, at ninety-nine. I went to his funeral in the early Eighties, and I was the only person there, other than a nurse from the old people's home where he'd been living.

The older you get the less likely you are to have friends to attend your funeral: the fewer children you have, ditto. The nurse had traced me only because Herriot had seen my picture in the paper and told her I was a relative. But of course the number of people you can expect at your funeral should not dictate the manner of your living. It can scarcely matter. Nevertheless it seemed to me to be profoundly sad: the same loud trumpets that attend the birth should always sound for the departure, and if possible louder.

The Inheritors

All that was in the past, in whatever measure it had contributed to the present, and here I was in New Zealand and it was okay by me. I was eleven, I had a bicycle, I loved the world of marvels that books contained, I loved the navy night skies and for some reason felt part and parcel of the Southern Cross. Sometimes, in the dawn of a bright day – I would always get up with the sun if I was allowed – I would be conscious of the exhilaration that infused the natural world, sometimes so acutely that it would stop me in my tracks, to hold my breath as the Creator brushed by. I knew what the psalmist meant about the hills rejoicing and the valleys being exalted: I knew what Wordsworth was going on about; I knew what my mother meant by the intensity of her floating vase of flowers.

But I was rooted in the carnal and instinctive world: my mother in the ascetic. If we had been male priests I would have been one of the fat jovial kind who drink too much communion wine and sleep with their housekeepers: she would have been of the lean, celibate, refined tendency. Both get to heaven in the end, I daresay.

When I grew up I saw sex both as sacrament and enlightenment, I saw the coming together of two people, male and female, in whatever circumstance, in mutual pleasure, as the best possible way of being part of creation, indeed of honouring the Creator. What else were we on this earth for? Perhaps, come to think of it, a belief in Free Love and the Life Force is inheritable? It comes down from Henry to Edgar, skipping my mother, to me? It was to get me into considerable trouble, anyway, as it did them. I stay full of sympathy with those bands of noisy bad girls they show us on TV, who go out to the pubs and clubs, wild and dissolute, looking for sex. Of course they do: what else is beautiful in their lives, but the dark ecstasy of being part of another person. Brief it may be, but never squalid, only what's around, intimations of immortality.

My mother had pleasures I did not share. Just as people now jog, then they walked. Everywhere the left-leaning classes took to wearing shorts and striding over the hills whilst discussing pacifism and whither and whence socialism. New Zealand was not immune, nor was my mother. We would go walking on the scrubby desolation of the Port Hills, the volcanic range which separates Christchurch from its harbour, our goal the Kiwi Teahouse where the old bridle path reached the summit. This was the route the early immigrants took, on foot, leading their horses from Lyttelton, over the hills to the fertile plain below. I don't think we ever found the teahouse open, but like them we travelled in hope. It was boring. Victoria Park, on the way, where the scrub gave way to a planted fern or two, was not an oasis but simply spooky: it was where two schoolgirls – their tragic and grisly story told in the film *Heavenly Creatures* – were later to batter one of their mothers to death, and even then seemed heavy with horrid foreboding.

But my mother would recite poetry as we walked, and this I loved to hear. The years she spent not at school not doing English literature had been put to good use. I loved to hear it. Tennyson, Byron, Keats, the mystical poets. Sometimes we'd gather tufts of wool from the barbed-wire fences, where the sheep had brushed by, and lichens from the trunks of gnarled old bushes. When we got home we would spin the wool, with either a spindle (me) or a spinning wheel (Jane), and boil it up with the lichen – its cobbled dull green sponge producing a bright unnatural orange in the pan. She would then weave the spun wool into cloth, or if we were unlucky, knit dresses for Jane and myself, knubbly and scratchy. I have always preferred silks and satins and crushed velvet, frankly, to anything that was too close to nature.

I won a scholarship, to my great surprise. I had seen myself as rather stupid. For one thing Jane could always do every-thing so much better than I could, and when my mother talked late at night with the Christchurch poets and I would get out of bed and eavesdrop on their conversations I could not understand a word of what they were saying. My school-friend Molly Banks was obviously the clever one. She was a plump bright girl with a pretty face, who grew up to be a credit to her country, probably the most intelligent person in it, and head of the International Welfare Agency, so I was up against heavy competition but had no way of knowing it. She came top in everything and I was lucky to come second or third. I was the youngest in the class. I seemed to have somehow missed out a whole curriculum year in my movement from school to school. My knowledge was patchy, and was to stay so, though it's noticeable, if you write for film or TV, the amount of background knowledge you can pick up over the years.

But with Molly Banks and myself in competition for the Canterbury Farmers' scholarship of the year, which as I remember would get me to Rangiruru school – *Rangiruru, rotten rats, go to school in Panama hats – do they stink, yes they do, like the monkeys in the zoo* – I was the one to win. I had beaten Molly Banks! It then transpired that since I wasn't a farmer's daughter I was not eligible for the prize, and neither was Molly, so that was that. We went to the Christchurch Girls' Grammar School along with everyone else halfway competent.

Stepdaughter

A letter had come from my father saying he and Edna had left Coromandel and gone to live in Auckland. I did not understand how they could do such a thing. I had friends in Coromandel – they were one of life's better permanencies – and I had not even been able to say goodbye. The house in Auckland, when summer came, turned out to be large, new, grand and dull, in Lucerne Road, Remuera, a long suburban road which ran round the rim of the hills which formed the harbour. The view was spectacular, and every evening at around five the flying-boat from Sydney would land down below in a flurry of white foam, but it was not enough.

111

There was nothing to do but play cards. Edna was pregnant and my father seemed remote, and so I played Patience. I was in considerable sympathy with playing cards. They, like me, were so much in the hands of fate. What could they do in the face of a shuffle? I began to suspect they could do something. Cards had some kind of relationship with your mood. Runs of good luck came when you *wanted* but not too desperately, runs of bad luck happened if you insulted your maker by wanting too badly. I remember one day shuffling and shuffling the cards and shutting my eyes and willing myself to pick out the four aces and succeeding. I told Jane, I showed her the four aces sitting there on the green carpet, but she didn't believe me. 'Then do it again,' she said. But of course I couldn't, not a single ace. I think every carpet I have bought since has been green, come to think of it.

My father took *Esquire* – it came all the way from America and was dangerously racy. It had fabulous drawings of fabulous girls, and the contents were very different from my mother's *New Statesman and Nation*. Jane and I could read and understand the *New Statesman* though it was deathly dull, and I was always thrilled at the god-like by-lines – Kingsley Martin, Bernard Shaw, Professor Joad – who seemed to know so much and understand everything, but the culture of *Esquire* baffled us. We studied the women carefully and we'd lie on our beds in our bedroom when it was too hot to do anything else and measure ourselves against what *Esquire* told us were the perfect proportions for a woman: 36–23– 36. Jane was doing better than me. Her legs were longer, for one thing, and she had a waist and an elegance denied me. She glided, I bounced.

Sometimes Jane was ordinary and friendly, and we took each other for granted, but there was a sadness and coldness growing inside her, which seemed to develop along with her breasts, and made her different from me. She could be contemptuous of my ignorance, she dismissed me as frivolous, a nuisance that she'd rather be without. I wanted company and she wanted to be solitary. The two and a half years older than me, which I had always reckoned on, began to feel nearer three than two. Even in our adult life, if I crossed a road with her, I would leave her to do the thinking, while she, assuming my greater worldly competence to deal with stupid and irrelevant things like traffic, would leave it to me. I am surprised we survived.

When my half-brother Alan was born there was at least something to do other than play cards. He could be dandled, fed and chirruped at. I lost him for about thirty years: then in the 1970s he surfaced in London, directing films with lurid titles which were in fact so cheerful and un-lurid that quite recently a sex shop selling *Confessions of a Sex Maniac* from under the counter as hardcore porn was prosecuted by the Trading Standards Office on behalf of indignant customers who felt cheated. Alan asked me to do a dialogue job on another of his films, *Killer's Moon*, handing me the script just as I was getting on a flight to New York. It was about a busload of psychopathic criminals stranded on a Yorkshire moor in a snowstorm, along with a busload of schoolgirls, and featured a savage three-legged dog. The dog belonged to Alan's next-door neighbour and was a perfectly amiable beast, but with a sound track fitted could be turned into a raving monster. Not even in the context of this chiller St Trinians could I honourably move from a scene in which a girl is raped, to the next, in which she seems to have forgotten all about it, without providing some covering dialogue. I have her say to her friend, who witnessed the attack, 'You pretend you didn't see it, I'll pretend it didn't happen, and we'll all grow up to be wives and mothers.'

The film, not surprisingly, because it was simply so odd, became something of a cult, if only because the dialogue sat so strangely with the plot, and is still about, albeit pirated, on the shelves of respectable video shops up and down the land. Alan and I have grown a great deal more serious since: these days we write worthy films together about Boadicea, or the SAS, or the Second Coming, which are always in the process of being nearly made but not quite made, after the manner of films today.

Alan was a joyous baby. He had a nursemaid known as Nursie, who had a GI boyfriend, and who on this account grew sloppy, left fishbones in his puréed dinner, and had to go, or so it was presented to me by Edna, to whom I was by now devoted.

My father now had a smart surgery in Queen Street in central Auckland and a silly receptionist to go with it. One morning at breakfast my father referred to her as 'the willowy blonde', and I caught the sad anxiety on Edna's face, and hated him for causing it. It would be so easy for him to reassure her, but he wouldn't. Men had too much power, I thought for the first, and not for the last time, to make women suffer.

I liked Nursie, and was sorry to see her go. She'd take us to the cinema and leave us there while she met her GI friends in the milk bar (or so she said) and would be waiting in the lobby to take us home when we came out, though sometimes she'd be late. We mostly saw war films out of Hollywood, of the kind in which Errol Flynn wins a continent single-handed, and war is presented as all heroics, and nothing truly horrible ever happens, so as not to discourage recruitment. It seemed a good enough trade-off, those films against our secrecy, and if Nursie was dismissed it was certainly nothing to do with anything Jane or I said. All the same, from the requirement of secrecy, it was clear Nursie was a bad girl, though exactly what constituted badness I had no idea.

In the Sixties I was to go to a psychoanalyst who was astonished at what she saw as my wilful ignorance of sexual matters. Surely I could have worked the details out? But how? I had never seen a picture of a naked man, let alone a real one, and if you had said 'penis' to me I would have had no idea what you were talking about, let alone to what purpose it was used. Those were the days when parts were nameless: when the dark mysteries of procreation stayed exactly that. Something happened in bed which resulted in babies, that much I knew, but what?

It observably also happened out of wedlock, in spite of what they said. When I was twelve my mother took in and housed an eighteen-year-old unmarried mother, Christine, to the shocked surprise of many. Christine eventually turned into that Christine Cole Catley who is now a publisher and a leading figure in NZ literary life. She had a copy of *Married Love*, by Marie Stopes, on her shelves, and I would creep into her room to read it when everyone was out, in the hope of finding out what went on in the marital bed. I read in vain. Babies, according to Dr Stopes, should be 'conceived' out of doors for the sake of the health of the nation, and not in a squalid slum – but what did she mean by conceived? I knew that people conceived ideas, but babies? Perhaps you just had to think up a baby and you started growing one? People who wore spectacles should never conceive babies, said Marie Stopes, because they would be handing on birth defects. Did that mean short-sightedness was catching? It was all a puzzle, and one I preferred to defer.

My mother discovered me with the book and took it away saying it was not fit reading so I gave up and went back to Dickens, Rider Haggard, G. B. Shaw, H. G. Wells, Upton

Sinclair, Samuel Smiles, Bunyan and *Eric, or Little by Little*, without protest. But I did think it would be a wonderful and extraordinary thing to share a bed with that rare creature, a man, whatever it was that happened in the bed. It would be so warm and companionable, and you could presumably talk into the night as long as you liked: once you were grown up who would there be to stop you?

Schoolgirl

Christchurch Girls' High School was a deeply serious and miserable place. It was the wrong end of Cranmer Square, a tall brick building with staircases and corridors where you were not allowed to run, and which shook with every earth tremor. I went back to the school in 1990, on a rainy day, and watched a demolition ball swing into its walls, and great chunks of its brick structure collapse in dust which floated out over the Square, and discomforted the worms. I was pleased to see it happen. I believe it is an Arts Centre now and I hope that whatever happens there turns out well. Personally, I think it was haunted by the *Heavenly Creatures* murder that was yet to come. Building up to it, as it were.

They taught us well, out of the Scottish tradition – never argue, don't discuss, simply learn from your elders and betters and repeat what you have learned – but it was an uneasy place. Classrooms would darken for no reason: no one ever wanted to be alone in the locker room. We twenty girls in 3S (Form Three special: we were to take our Matric a year before the rest) would sit in silent terror waiting for a teacher

117

to turn up when there was no cause – or seldom – for terror at all. Parts of the playground would never be played in – but perhaps that was just because of the overshadowing trees. Sometimes everything was okay, but sometimes it felt we swarming girlchildren in our bright white shirts, navy gymslips and ankle socks were extras in some kind of horror film of which we would never be told the plot. But I could never quite put my finger on what was wrong.

I and my good friend Molly Banks went round together, laughing and joking and trying to lay the encroaching ghosts, but the panelled walls were redolent with doom and no matter how bright it was outside, the contrasting dark inside always seemed too dense. Or perhaps memory clouds the past. The headmistress was tall and elegant and had an abundance of grey hair swept up on top of her head. She never spoke to us, and never smiled. Few of the teachers smiled, come to think of it.

Girls' schools can be unhealthy places, and this one was. Crowd females together, in convent, hospital or school, and they fall into psychic step and menstruate together, in tune with the phases of the moon. It is a shocking thought. A tableful of women in a restaurant, on leave from their homes, is all laugh and noise. Give them no homes to go back to and a sad silence falls by the end of the third course. Men may annoy women but by and large they are very good for them, as women are for men.

So perhaps it was the undisclosed, misunderstood, unexpressed and guilty passions we Christchurch schoolgirls felt for one another which, festering, somehow got into the walls and blocked the good light of common sense from the windows. Like Queen Victoria before us we had not heard of lesbianism and wouldn't have believed it if anyone tried to tell us. Freud had pointed out years back that adolescent boys and girls turn their passions to their own sex while preparing for a mature sexuality, trying out love for size, as it were, but Freudian understanding had not yet trickled down to the antipodes. Later, of course, with the growth of the gay movement, such Freudian views became heretical anyway. Once gay, always gay. Gay now, born gay.

Be that as it may I was at the giggling stage anyway, easily embarrassed, as girls were then, innocent or ignorant, depending on how you see it. Molly Banks and I were in Whitcombe and Tombs one day and on the cover of *National Geographic Magazine* was a native woman with bare breasts. How we giggled! For weeks afterwards one of us only had to say 'In Whitcombe and Tombs' and it would set us off again. How annoying and silly we must have seemed to our elders. But we had never seen such a sight before. Parents took good care not to be seen unclothed by their children and clothing was intended to shroud, not to enhance. Spouses were accustomed to undressing in the dark, or putting on their nightclothes in the privacy of the bathroom, before getting into a shared bed. No one much worried about their figures. Why should they? Who was ever going to get to see them clearly? *National Geographic Magazine* enjoyed a large circulation for years, it being the only way anyone could get to see female breasts: 'native' women somehow didn't count.

I had it explained to me by my school-friends within my first week at the new school that it was the done thing to have a pash or crush on some older girl: head of netball was the preferred option, or the art teacher was quite a favourite.

119

When you had a crush, it seemed, you thought about the object of your interest a lot, especially before you went to sleep at night, wrote them little notes saying how much you admired them which you'd shove into their pockets before running away, and you'd stand round to watch them come out of class or getting on to the bus. This seemed very strange to me.

I did not want to be left out. I looked the sixth form over as we stood in assembly, and my eye fell on one Alison Grey. She did not play netball, she was not particularly pretty, or particularly anything at all, though she did wear slip-on shoes, not the heavy laced-up kind the rest of us wore. She was on the platform because she was in the choir and I was looking up at her. She had curvy lips, not the straight trapdoor ones so many had, and I could hear her voice above the others, pure and bell-like. The more I looked the more fascinated I became. I wanted to be like her, I wanted to be part of her; the idea of the gap that divided her from me became intolerable. Why couldn't we just merge with other people, be one instead of two? Within five minutes I was head over heels in love with her, and wanted to gaze at her for ever, and that was the end of giggling.

'*Did you not see my lady,*' my grandmother would sing, '*Go down the garden singing, Silencing all the song birds, Because she was twice as fair.*' And that was it. It was romantic love, of the courtly kind. The idea that my profound love for Alison Grey was open to physical fruition would have sent me reeling. I grew out of her, of course, and by the time I was wrenched away from her she no longer played such a large part in my life. And I daresay, just as you can suffer from free-floating anxiety, an acute anxiety which attaches itself

120

to any convenient and mildly plausible source – a child not back by midnight, a friend taken offence, a pain in the back perhaps presaging cancer, a cheque which might bounce – so you can suffer from free-floating love. Mine floated and attached itself to Alison.

In a different environment, in a different age, it would have attached itself to a pop star, a male teacher, or even a boy on a street corner – but there weren't any around. Tuesdays and Thursdays became my special days because these were choir-practice days, and I had joined the choir so I could gaze at Alison. I still wake on Tuesdays and Thursdays with a slight extra enthusiasm for the day. Simply setting eyes on my idol was enough to make me happy. Once or twice she said hello. Then I could scarcely endure the marvel of it, but blushed and stumbled simply to say hello back.

Molly Banks thought I was mad but was tolerant. She didn't have pashes. They were silly. I tried to explain about Alison Grey's shoes – pale brown leather, slip-on, with a seam down the front and the leather coming up to a peak over the instep, in a mildly oriental kind of way – so extraordinary. Molly Banks thought shoes like that were just stupid. Lace-ups gave more support for the feet. If I see such shoes today – they come and go with fashion – I still catch my breath. I see them in shop windows but wouldn't dream of buying them. They are hers and hers alone. I didn't know she had even noticed me but one day just before the Latin class Alison Grey actually came to my classroom and asked to speak to me. 'I think you'd better lay off a bit,' she said, 'people are beginning to notice,' but not as if she minded too much, but just wanted to get a closer look at me, talk to me. And she smiled at me with curvy lips, slowly.

So I laid off. I stopped going to choir, singing 'Nymphs and Shepherds', over and over, 'In that grove, in that grove, let's sport and play, let's sport and play', and Vaughan Williams' 'Will the ships go down, go down, go down, upon the windy sea'. Alison Grey had spoken to me. And I would make this sacrifice for her.

> My heart aches, and a drowsy numbness pains
> My sense, as though of hemlock I had drunk . . .
> . . . and Lethe-wards had sunk.

There was such a sleepy sensuous pleasure in it all. I cannot believe that today's teenagers, kissing, cuddling and more behind the bicycle sheds or down a dark alley, have it any better. They have to take their ecstasy in pill form. We created our own.

But we were a hysterical lot. There was an epidemic of fainting in school assembly. It went on for a week. It started slowly: a girl would crumple to the floor, then another, then another. The hymn or the prayer would be stopped, the victims would be revived, taken to sick-bay, doctors called. On the third day twenty girls collapsed. The health authorities were called in. Food poisoning was suspected. We were tested for disease, asked what we'd eaten. Parents were scared. The press came round. On the fourth day some forty girls toppled. I was one of them. Round and round the world went, the gorge rose, blackness fell and so did I. That afternoon a special assembly was called and we were told that anyone who fainted hereafter would get a detention. On the fifth day no one fainted, and that was the end of that. Hysteria – a favourite word of the time, not much used now – the customary treatment being a slap to the cheek, and a detention having much the same effect. Hysteria comes from the Greek word for the womb, and wombs are now seen as optional extras to the female, not the root of their being, as once they were. But such outbreaks still occur, nevertheless, in all-girl schools.

I had quite a stout bosom by this time, but not as stout as Molly Banks's. These bouncy growths of ours were nothing but a nuisance. We were all firmly encased in navy gymslips with pleats, and belts, which made us look like beanbags, and I would dutifully press the gymslip every Sunday night. The knife-edges became thin and shiny: I needed a new one but there was no money for such extravagances.

Molly had a string of merit bars: you got these for coming top in exams. Merit bars were strips of engraved bronze attached to a narrow corded ribbon hung from the school broach. Molly had so many that the ribbon with its precious cargo would hang swinging in thin air from the shelf of her bosom and look absurd. I never came first in anything, so I did not have to suffer likewise.

Not for we S stream girls subjects like Domestic Science and Religious Knowledge, these were the options of the dullards. We did Latin and French phonetics and two hours' homework every night. We read Ibsen's *A Doll's House* and the English teacher, Miss Birch, who had small bright button eyes, explained to us that women did not have to be married to be worth anything: better to be Nora, she said, than an unhappy wife. I had decided I was so plain no man would ever look at me anyway – it was not the fashion for mothers at that time to praise the looks of their daughters, this being likely to make them silly and vain, and develop too early, but from her silence I drew my own conclusions – and thought that chance would be a fine thing. But I was glad to know that at least in theory there would be no shame in spinsterhood. But Molly and I were not quite convinced by Miss Birch. She wasn't married herself and perhaps she was protesting too much.

There were no boys around to test our theories upon. 'Dating' had not been invented. Girls in school uniform were out of bounds for males of any age. Not until they left school could the processes of courtship begin. Girls, especially the clever ones, could stay at school until they were seventeen or eighteen. No wonder we fell in love with one another. We seldom went to one another's homes and if there were brothers around I for one certainly never got to meet any. Nice girls stayed at home and didn't hang around street corners. I'd see my father in the summers, of course, but now we were older the relationship had become awkward. I would long to see him but when I did I could never think of anything to say. I filled up the Auckland days playing Patience, waiting for something to happen which never did, dandling my little brother and buying hokey-pokey ice cream at the corner shop.

One way and another the world seemed pretty much female. Only girls at school, only women as teachers, only women at home, except for the visiting poets, and they didn't seem to count: they were good New Zealand blokes, who got drunk and beat their wives like anyone else, but saw themselves as having special dispensation so to do, by virtue of their own sensitivity and their wives' crassness. The muse is there to have the life sucked out of her, barefoot, pregnant and at the kitchen sink, up to her arms in soapsuds. Once upon a time they did it gladly. No longer. (No wonder there's no great art any more – living sacrificial victims are no longer available. The Ted Hughes–Sylvia Plath story continues to fascinate, becomes an industry, because that was the turning point. She was the last of the victims: she died for love, but was an equal artist: the struggle was who was to be whose muse, and he won, but only just.)

My mother did introduce a man lodger into the house in order to expose us to some male company, but beyond having an artistic nude photograph of a young girl on his bedside table, all interesting parts fading into blackness, he showed few signs of maleness: he was a Quaker and gentle in his manner but since he complained about the texture of the meat-loaf Nona made every Tuesday out of the remains of Sunday's roast, froze conversation at the dinner table and frowned about reading at meals, he didn't last long.

Life for my mother was becoming quite tolerable. She was working at Albion Wright's and earning a decent income. She wore a really smart tailored grey suit in which to go off to work, and had friends and gave parties. She kept company with poets and experimental writers, and those involved with the *Caxton Press*, one of those small magazines that did so well during the Thirties and Forties, with wood engravings on quality paper. The late Allen Curnow, grand old man and poet laureate of New Zealand, said to me that my mother was the most beautiful woman in New Zealand. All she said when I reported this was, 'My dear, if you knew what New Zealand women were like at that time, you'd know that wasn't saying much. I wheeled little Wystan Curnow, now a literary agent in Sydney, about in his pram for pocket money.' The Curnows were an advanced family. It was even said the parents went around the house wearing no clothes.

When Rita Angus painted a portrait of Jean Curnow with what my mother considered to be a disagreeable expression on her face she was moved to ask Rita why. Rita said she didn't approve of the way Jean brought up Wystan and thought the portrait should reflect her subject's inner soul, not what was visible on the face. She could be very self-righteous, as only the childless can be. I don't know what became of Jean's portrait. Jane's and mine, in our check dresses, was to become quite famous. My mother, as I have said, despised it – it broke every rule in the Slade's book, with its hint of caricature and its hard edges – and not content with hanging it in the darkest corner of the house, tried to leave it behind when we left for London. However, a friend ran to the docks with it, just as the gangway was rising, crying 'You left this, you left this!' My mother said she nearly dropped it overboard, but good manners intervened and instead she told the friend to give it back to Rita. The next time she set eyes on the painting was forty years later, as a postcard from the New Zealand national art gallery. Some artwork, my mother remarked, appalled, is simply indestructible. Van Goghs turn up in attics, Mozart scores emerge out of vaults, when by rights they should have withered away and vanished. Lately my mother has admitted she can see some merit in the painting, but I think that's only because all the representations of me she has seen since have in her opinion served me worse.

I turned into a teenage reader. Not that the word teenager was in use. We were expected to turn from children to young adults without any intervening phase. Young people had no purchasing power. We were not yet a market, other than for colour balls and aniseed drops from the local shop. Advertising was confined to the occasional poster, about which there were always complaints – vulgarization, Americanization, same thing, consider *Esquire* – and small ads in the local papers. 'There's a war on, remember' – the normal response to any complaint – paper was in short supply and not to be wasted selling things nobody really needed. I read all Georgette Heyer, superior bodice rippers, set in Georgian times, about virtuous virgins, seduction, kidnappings, and lustful rich and powerful men subdued by true love. Somewhere between *Little Lives of all the Saints*, *Pride and Prejudice* and my own mother's *Velvet and Steel* I thrilled.

A very hairy Professor Binswanger, a refugee from Berlin, would visit us in Jackson's Road from time to time. He seemed like someone out of *Emil and the Detectives*, other than that he would grab me and hug me and smell rather beery as he kissed me with slobber lips, and that was not the kind of thing that happened in *Emil*. I did rather wish he would not, but with the dark embraces came a sense of impending future, of an excitement I did not understand, but wished I did. Oh the hairy, tobacco-smelling, sense-muffling tweediness of it all.

I was gratified that for once it was me he chose for his attentions, and not Jane, who in everyone's view was the interesting and exciting sister. I was Martha to Jane's Mary: doomed to be the practical one and do all the work while Mary sat at Jesus's feet and got all the attention and praise. Unfair, unfair. No doubt she felt the same of me. It has always been my experience, since an initial spat with Molly Banks, when she partnered me in a cooking lesson when I was eleven, and I complained she left me to do the dull and boring and messy work, and she took all the fun and all the credit, and I told her so, and discovered she felt exactly the same about me,

127

that one tends to suspect others of what one is guilty of oneself. The unfaithful wife is quick to suspect the husband of infidelity.

The Professor's wife Ottie was not Jewish but had fled with her husband Paul, who was, to New Zealand. There is a certain kind of professor, often in the sciences, who seems to keep a wife only to insult her. It's a notch up from the artist, whose ambition it is to destroy the spouse. If Ottie had a remark to make, her husband would dismiss it with 'That is not important, that is not important,' said twice with an angry, rising inflection.

My mother reports that the professor would do the same to her, even while he claimed to be infatuated with her. It has nothing to do with lack of love – which can be very confusing to the wife in question – and indeed such men often tend to marry the most poetic and imaginative of women – but with the necessity of keeping all things in a square box, a snapshot of a universe which follows a decided set of rules, and allowing nothing extraneous in, lest doubt creep in the edges.

I generalize, of course I do, when did I ever not, but 'that is not important' said often enough to a wife either breaks her or makes her, as she struggles for personal survival. I have two such female friends, one who has grown rich, renowned and competent in the arts through the very difficulty of her marriage: and one, renowned when she began, came to be defeated and curl up and die, in the face of too many literal and metaphorical 'that is not important's. The phenomenon has little to do with gender, more with the scientific view of the universe, which must be so rigidly preserved in the face of what is seen as creative whimsy: I daresay a female Professor of Physics, married to a poet, would be equally dismissive. How would Ted Hughes have survived, married to Marie Curie?

Ottie was a good friend. She made us do exercises: we were not allowed to neglect the face, which must remain as limber as the rest of us. The jaw muscles must be strengthened. We had to say U-X, U-X over and over, very carefully, moving the mouth to its limit. We must practise self-improvement: we must say into our mirror every morning, 'Every day in every way I'm getting better and better.' She was the forerunner of so many today who live in the hope that if only you can believe enough, so it will be. That to be vegan is to be moral, that pear juice will cure cancer, that there is an inner self to be found. I could see why her husband, the rational man, could get irritated. But on the other hand she was nice and he was not.

Later, when Ottie moved to London, my mother would take the bus to her house in Platts Lane, Hampstead, and together they'd coil flax ropes to make laundry baskets to sell in the craft section of Liberty's. It was hard, finger-blistering work, very badly paid. Making tasteful, natural craft objects in the home is never an effective way of making money, though my mother never quite lost the belief that it could be done. There is always someone else round the corner doing it better, charging less, and cornering the market. (One would like to think this law did not apply to writing too, but I'm afraid it does.) Paul and Ottie eventually received reparation money from Germany and went to live in Florence, where Paul became an honoured professor and Ottie an honoured sculptor. 'And then he died,' says my mother, 'and then she died, but otherwise it was a happy ending.'

But for our family the search for a dignified and not too terrible a way of making money continued to be a necessity. At one time we made pomanders at home – sticking cloves into dried mandarin oranges and dangling them from ribbon. Pomanders were great favourites at the time of the Great Plague, believed to keep infection at bay. These went to Liberty's too and went on sale but within weeks the oranges grew a white mould on their skin and shrivelled and had to be withdrawn from the shelves. Entropy can be very rapid in the organic world.

It was a lesson fate seemed determined to teach me. When I was a young copywriter working at Ogilvie and Mather for the Egg Marketing Board, it fell to me to compose a full-page ad for the various women's magazines so popular at the time. It was a recipe for a Christmas pudding containing more eggs than were strictly necessary. If ten million housewives could be persuaded to put an extra egg in their Christmas puddings, the reasoning went, they would buy an extra ten million eggs over the season. So they did. The ad appeared in October. Some ten million women made their puddings according to my instructions, and left them in their basins to mature until Christmas morning. Then they were to be boiled up, sight unseen, as it were, a two- to three-hour job. (Microwaves take seven minutes or so.) The turkey course done and cleared, the brandy warmed and waiting for the flame, ten million women decanted their Christmas puddings on to waiting, heated plates. All were coated with a green whiskery mould. I had left the sugar out of the recipe. Complaints and outrage came pouring in: no use my saying but it wasn't poisonous, just scrape it off and it was okay – too late: no use my offering the excuse that the mistakes of the parents are repeated by the children, as with the pomanders so with the puddings, no one was listening, they were too distraught. I felt really bad at the ruination of so many Christmases, but I was not fired, or even taken off the account; those were the days of the Sixties, of frivolity, of full employment, when others were slow to blame, and if people could laugh, they would. Years later, emotion recollected in tranquillity, as in Wordsworth's 'Daffodils', I wrote a short story called *The Year of the Green Pudding*, about a young woman who felt great remorse but always for the wrong thing.

Chicken-Licken

Forget earthquakes and volcanoes, now the sky fell in. I gave up turning cartwheels and walking on my hands upon the lawn – everything was upside-down enough as it was. At school the classrooms got darker, the locker room was icy cold, even on a hot day. We were in a horror film and I was not even one of the extras, but one of the principals. I got to school one Monday morning and found my desk had been moved. I was not allowed to sit next to Molly Banks any more. The relationship was too close, it was unhealthy. We were forbidden to go round together, or talk to one another. I was bewildered. What was their reasoning? We chattered a lot, true, but we worked hard and passed our exams; we had passed the giggling phase, and were seldom in trouble. We were a double act: we were popular: we saw it as our business to stir our friends up to fresh sensibilities; we were suave commentators on the scholastic and social scene. Molly's string of merit badges dangled from her bosom, tribute to her many talents. She had more than anyone else in the school.

She kept them well polished. (I took equal pride in them, for some reason. What was mine was hers, and vice versa.) We were, we had assumed, rather important and useful members of the community. Beyond 'too close', 'unhealthy', no further explanation was given. I went home and my mother was saying the same thing. I must spend more time at home, less time with Molly, in and out of school; I must find different friends, different interests. The infection had spread to home. Mysteriously, home and school had joined forces against me, talked about me behind my back, and in terms I failed to understand. I was betrayed.

I asked Nona to explain it to me but she just shook her head and looked sympathetic, played the piano harder, and sang her sad romantic songs to herself, gazing out of the window at trees she had not been born to, and a night sky she could never get used to.

> '*Did you not see my lady,*
> *Go down the garden singing,*
> *Silencing all the song birds,*
> *For she is twice as fair.*'

Poor Nona. Carefully folded in her jewellery box is a love-letter from a journalist on the *Economist*, Robert Crozier Long, posted in Berlin, dated 23 December, 1929. 'Write to me, my dearest, and tell me where you will be: Rome or Berlin? Tell me how it is with Edgar, and whether Miss Daughter (who turned up her nose at me) has married the doctor. I hope not. Has she stopped writing *Saturday E. Post* rubbish and done something better?' But now it was 1943 and all that had been fifteen years ago, and Edgar was dead and Miss Daughter had indeed married the doctor, in the face of the wisdom of friends, and had given up writing altogether on moral grounds, and Berlin? or Rome? was not the kind of question anyone asked any more, and here Nona was, altogether without power, in Christchurch, New Zealand, her time running out. I think life and its sadnesses was altogether beyond her: if she could never explain anything to me it was because she didn't understand herself. She would smile vaguely and kindly and take refuge in the piano, or find a soft cushion for her head – she never travelled without a down pillow – and wait for trouble to pass. And by so doing, as it happened, she lived to be ninety-nine.

So all was bad at school and all was bad at home. I don't know what was said to Molly Banks: she stayed away from school for weeks: she who was never ill was now ill. When she returned to school we stayed away from each other, not so much because we were forbidden to speak but because we were embarrassed. We were polite but ceased to share intimacies. The heart had gone out of us both. And I still hadn't *learned*, alas, if only because I didn't understand the lesson – and I then did something to compound this sorry state of affairs. When a sixth-form girl, Louise, who tended to hang round with us fourth-form girls, suggested that we wrote love letters to a prefect in another school whom she happened to know, and gave them to her to pass on, and the stranger would decide which one was best, I started writing.

I saw it as a literary brief: I asked for a description of the prefect's attributes and appearance, and on the basis of Robert Herrick's '*Whenas in silk my Julia goes, / Then, then, methinks, how sweetly flows, / That liquefaction of her clothes,*' worked hard and long at a prose poem, writing and rewriting until the sentences sounded right. I also borrowed, as I remember, from passages of the many Victorian novels I had read, full of swoony delight and offstage passions. New Zealand bookshelves were rich in literary tradition: all the novels anyone had ever loved and thought worth transporting across the world were there on the parlour shelf. I was pleased with the letter but saw no point in sending it.

I came home from school to learn that my mother had found it and read it. Now she confronted me. She was seized by a terrible anxiety which expressed itself in rage. She said she had always suspected it: now she knew: I was a lesbian. I didn't understand what she was talking about, or how I had suddenly become loathsome, but to be a lesbian was something perverse and horrible, not just something you did, but what you were as well, and you were despised and hated by everyone.

It was a lesson that was to repeat itself at intervals through life. You could be going along calmly and cheerfully, and suddenly the ground beneath you would erupt and a whole spew of nastiness and corruption would toss itself out like lava from a volcano, the horrid truth about how people saw you and thought about you, and like lava would solidify and be there for ever. You could get accustomed to it, but it would never go away, like scar tissue. It was a live volcano, pretending to be extinct, quiescent, lulling you into a sense of security, then erupting without warning, or only an initial sulphurous whiff or so which was easy to ignore. It was a wonder anyone could function at all. My Aunt Faith, faced by the volcano, unable to run, had failed to survive.

There seemed a line drawn in my life: a time before this had happened and a time after. I was left wandering in the grey desolation of limbo, stuck in its dead lava landscape. My mother insisted that I wrote a letter to the unknown girl 'breaking it off', and posted it herself. No point in saying that I hadn't sent one in the first place; it was a draft of a writing exercise. Who would believe me? Shame and absurdity would follow me all the days of my life.

The next day I sat on the No. 9 tram coming home from school and contemplated suicide and wondered how to set about it. I was in dread of reaching my stop. I went as far as the terminus and then, because there was nowhere else to go, had to walk home. Recently, because of the Molly Banks fiasco, it had been the other way round, and home had been preferable to school, but now both were equal in shame and embarrassment. I did not want to reach the end of any journey, whichever way down its tracks the tram was going.

One of the terrors of divorce is the knowledge that the safe place, home, has become the source of danger and betrayal: and there is nowhere, psychically or physically, to which to return. When you're adult there is usually somewhere to run *to*, if only these days by virtue of the American Express card in the wallet – but not if you're thirteen. I could not think of a decent way of killing myself. There were no cliffs around to throw myself off, no asps to hold to my bosom. I would be hard put to find a truck in Christchurch big enough or fast enough to throw myself in front of. I didn't know how to poison myself: Madame Bovary had been lucky: she had lived next door to a chemist and could steal arsenic. I had been to Guides for a time, but nobody taught you how to tie a hangman's noose, and I was bad at knots, in any case. What would Nona think if she came upon my hanging body? Had the tram been a train I daresay I would have thrown myself out, but trams do trundle along. Fortunately I had not read *Anna Karenina* or I might well have gone to the station and flung myself under the great iron wheels of the train to Lyttelton. The suicidal fantasies went on for some weeks: then the danger passed, but danger I think it was.

It soon became apparent that people forget, remarkably quickly. The incident was never referred to by my mother or myself, and other events obscured it. Little by little Molly Banks and I crept back into each other's company, and nobody seemed to notice – they had other things to think about, and today's newspaper is nothing but tomorrow's fish-and-chip wrapping – to use a pre-EU analogy – but it could not be the same. We were wary of each other: the adult world had infected us. As for my love for Alison Grey, whom I had never touched, let alone embraced, having discovered that my excitements were shameful, defiled and defiling, that diminished as my shame and self-consciousness increased. Though whenever I see pale brown leather shoes with a seam up the middle, coming to a point above the instep, I still think of her. From that time on I seldom trusted my mother with an emotional confidence, but kept my own counsel.

My mother took Jane out of school, for reasons I did not quite understand, other than that Jane now hated going there. She did a correspondence class from home. She was working for her matriculation. She was never to be upset. I was not allowed to quarrel with her. She was Mary-kind, I was Martha-like, she saved her pocket money, while I spent. I took after my father and my Uncle Selwyn, my mother said. My father was hopeless with money: Uncle Selwyn had borrowed money from Edgar and refused to give it back which was why Edgar had died: his heart attack had been triggered by anxiety. I hated the idea that I was the victim of my heredity: I was being traduced. It was as bad as being judged for what you were, which you couldn't help, rather than what you did, which you could. As bad as getting into trouble because there was meat in your sandwiches on a Friday, when it was something over which you had no control.

My poor mother: she wanted us to be perfect and we weren't. We were growing up and showing ourselves to be not prodigies, not the validation of everything she aspired to, but just more people. Jane was increasingly remote, nervy and unsociable, I was increasingly sociable, still defiantly spending too much time with my unhealthy friends and scarcely two minutes a night on my Latin homework, instead of the required fifteen. I never liked it to be seen that I was working. I would learn my Latin verbs while apparently brushing my teeth.

Later, when I began writing, in what I would call early kitchen-table period, perforce with pad and pencil, forbidden as I was to use a typewriter because of the antisocial clatter it made, I would write while pretending to read, or sit on the stairs and do it, so I would not be detected. It was childish and absurd, but one learns best, and writes best, in a state of defiance.

But all was not bad, not at all. I was fourteen and emerging from limbo: the future was re-establishing itself as more hope than despair. The flat featureless land was now rimmed by mountain ranges, snowy-peaked. Beyond them, over the rainbow, was the land where you could create your own past, in what you chose to remember, and sin and shame would be forgiven and forgotten. *Ding, dong the witch is dead!* sang the Munchkins in the Wizard of Oz. One day I would be grown up, make my own judgements, choose my own friends, re-start my past. True, I lived in an all-female household – mother, sister, grandmother, me – but on another island, if you travelled for a night and a day, my kind stepmother Edna lay in bed with a man, my father. It was not impossible.

I read Tolkien's *The Hobbit* and was awed: I waved it about and demanded that others read it and one or two of my friends obliged, but then looked at me in baffled incomprehension. What was I going on about? It was absurd. Stocky little creatures called hobbits, living in tunnels, hissing Gollums, rolling thunder in the east, the gathering of primeval forces. *One ring to rule them all!* What had all that got to do with them, with life in Christchurch, South Island, New Zealand, the Pacific, the World, the Universe? But there it all was, in my eyes, the great parable of good and evil, in this small, dense, unassuming children's book, prelude to the mightier, more flawed, more adult, more ambitious *The Lord of the Rings* to come. I despaired of them. It simply never occurred to me, when it came to books, that I could ever be wrong.

I had much the same feeling when later I read Salman Rushdie's *The Satanic Verses*, and was exhilarated, and insisted on recommending it to everyone, though the penalty for doing so suddenly turned from the baffledom of friends into death by fatwa. The death threat from Islam extended to anyone who spoke about the book in public, let alone translated it, published it, sold it, or gave sustenance or shelter to Rushdie, and is in theory still in force. My sense of the unreason of this has led to my categorization as an Islamophobe: I can only respond to this by thinking that my accusers are not only in error but Rushdiephobes.

But here I was at fourteen, rescued by the hobbits from evil forces, out of the depressed land and into the fertile alluvial plain of Canterbury. The magnolia tree in our garden was the most splendid in all Christchurch. We had a little sausage dog called Aggie who refused to go for walks. But carry her for half a mile under your arm and she'd run back home in terror of the unknown, as fast as her absurd little short legs would carry her. Round and long and smooth and hot – I knew she was indecent, though I'd have been at a loss to tell you why.

My mother had a suitor whom I liked, though he smelt rather of beer. Children's noses are far too keen for their mothers' comfort. He was an Irish journalist called Walter Brooks. They would sit together on the sofa and when I came home from school they would spring apart, my mother looking flushed and bashful. But she soon dismissed him. Suitors got short shrift. '*Who, me? Wash some man's socks?*' She was cheerful. Her book on the nature of reality was going well. She would not write fiction any more: she disapproved of it. It put ideas in people's heads and made them think reality was other than what it was.

As for me, I had a new bicycle. No more tram rides. I could cycle to school across Hagley Park, where my mother had seen angels, and which in spite of its ugly name was beautiful, and on a frosty morning seemed blessed, and in a kind of waiting repose, as if the angels might swoop down from heaven any moment and reveal themselves even to me. The crisp white rime crackled beneath my tyres. One winter night it snowed: Jane and I had never seen snow before. The world increased in marvels day by day. Latin began to make sense: we moved from Caesar's *Gallic Wars* to Virgil. I loved the sound, metre and wit of this language which no one spoke any more but existed on paper only, which paid such rigorous tribute to the exact order of event, the exact placing of words for maximum effect, maximum irony. The Southern Cross was romantic, seen at night from the outdoor loo: I paid it homage. I borrowed my mother's lipstick and tried it out on my lips, hard and whorish, and quickly wiped it off again. I read Sinclair Lewis's *Babbitt*. I read Shaw's *Prefaces*, and even got to the end of *Back to Methuselah*. I tried to read *Moby Dick*. I read Wells's short stories but gave up on *Ann Veronica*. I read Georgette Heyer though my mother disapproved. I could make sense of the *New Statesman and Nation*. I couldn't bear Hardy and fell in love with Bonnie Prince Charlie. I thought that was safe: he was dead and at least he was male. Paul Binswanger, my mother's hairy admirer, stared at me through his thick lenses, and if I had anything to say did not come back with 'That is not important'. But then I was not his wife.

My mother made beer in the bath. She'd store the bottles in the pumphouse for the artesian well in the garden. Sometimes the bottles would explode and a myriad glass shards embed themselves in the walls, and all she'd do was laugh and throw a party. She was much more cheerful. Anxiety no longer nagged and snapped at her heels, like the little gnawing fox it is.

Anthony West, unfavoured son of poor dear Rebecca West and H. G. Wells, once described it to me as we walked up Haverstock Hill together. 'I don't want to look behind me,' he said. 'It's there again, I can feel its breath. Depression is a dog, anxiety is a fox.' His mother wrote to her publishers once and said that if they were publishing one of Anthony's books – as she'd read they intended to do – she was going to leave them at once, he was such a bad writer. What a mother to have! At least his father was genial.

Nona had discovered Raymond Chandler and she and I read our way through all of his novels. Writers never wrote enough: discover one and there'd always come a time when you'd read the lot. There was no avoiding it. But we could lament the fact together, even while others deplored our low tastes. I have always had, if only out of loyalty to Nona, what others see as low tastes. I like blockbusters out of Hollywood, thrillers, gold taps, country music, Chinese takeaways, kidney dressing-tables and Coca-Cola. People wince. I don't think it is affectation on my part. Other people usually have a good reason for liking what they do: things can be good of their kind, at whatever level of sophistication. And it has been gratifying, through the decades, to watch Chandler move from among the most despised of writers, to his current degree of literary esteem, to my mind perhaps rather too high. I will not deny my likes or dislikes: it is a matter of honour.

Now that my father had Edna to remind him, our maintenance came in on time. I could go to the cinema every Saturday, and to a milk-bar afterwards, and sometimes even after school, and chatter along with the ordinarily un-anxious. I was happy. There were the summers to look forward to – though Coromandel the golden had receded into memory – and the long hot Auckland days, with my father, and Edna, and baby Alan.

I fell in love with Verlaine. I was made to learn one of his poems as punishment for running in the corridors. '*Les sanglots longs des violons . . .*' What a language, breathed through the nose! Would one live to see France? It seemed unlikely. How could one ever find the money? I wrote a story myself and fell in love with that too: it was only two pages but see what words on a page could bring to life! Lyttelton railway station at night, its vaulted steam-filled arches, the melancholy of the steam whistle, tired travellers, drawn faces, the pleasure and despair of other people's journeys, forget one's own, which I'd nailed and trapped in time. Write and then rewrite: it was like bringing a piece of sculpture out of dead stone: you could make things more real than real, make something where there was nothing before; you could have new people come to you out of the steam, make them do what you wanted, send them off again into the mists and they'd go on walking for ever.

I wrote the story in Mr Eggleton's classic script: I remember the look of it on the page to this day. I was both awed and spooked: it was the same feeling I had when I pulled the four aces out of the pack of cards without really trying. I had struck lucky. I got a perfectly ordinary B for the story and a complaint that it was too short: it was obvious from the beginning you'd have to rely on your own judgement when it came to writing. No one recognized anything if it came without fanfare. This was a world in which reading Verlaine was a punishment.

I didn't attempt the trick again: writing stories was altogether too like hard work and too powerful. You could set demons walking as well as angels. Others kept diaries: silly pink and green things with roses and hearts, using tiny little pencils, onto whose flimsy pages they'd pour out their hearts. But why bother? They read so foolishly and by this time next year I knew well enough they would be embarrassing. I still didn't have a merit bar to my name, to dangle on my increasingly thin and shiny navy serge gymslip, but I had realized that to beat Molly Banks and a couple of others in the S-stream whose merit bars already fell to their knees, you probably had to be among the cleverest girls in the country. Things were going okay.

It was June 1946. The war had come to an end. My mother was back in the biscuit factory, coming home with blistered fingers. My father wrote from Auckland to say he had developed a new treatment for septic throats – a spray containing some new stuff called penicillin, which you found in cobwebs – and his practice had become very popular as a result. His willowy blonde receptionist had left to get married. He said he was looking forward to July and our visit, and perhaps this year we could manage a whole eight weeks.

I came home from school to find my mother reading a letter from England. It was from my great-aunt Gertrude, Edgar's sister, a widow who lived in Barons Court, in London. Tucked into the envelope was a banker's draft for nine hundred pounds, a legacy for Margaret from an uncle she had barely seen or known. My mother sat down, overwhelmed. Nine hundred pounds! Our troubles were over. It was a fortune: it could buy you a house, or pay ten years' rent: you could eat leg of lamb and not scrag and for ever: now I could have a new gymslip and have three school blouses not two, like Molly Banks.

'I never have to go to that place again,' was the first thing my mother said, by which she meant the biscuit factory. Nona went to find some sherry. Even Jane looked happy. We examined the banker's draft to make sure it wasn't a joke or the noughts were a mistake, but they weren't. Nine hundred pounds!

'We have to celebrate,' my mother said, 'and not just sherry,' and she gave me half-a-crown and sent me off to the baker's shop down the road to buy some brandysnaps – thin crispy toffee tubes filled with whipped cream. Brandysnaps! We never normally had brandysnaps, they were too expensive and too frivolous. But as I skidded out the door I heard her say, 'Now we can all go back to England.'

I ran on but when I reached the shop I could scarcely say 'six brandysnaps' for trembling. She meant it. It was what she was going to do. She would take me away from my friends, my school, everything I knew, and wouldn't even ask me if I minded. The nine hundred pounds would just do it. Three adults (Jane was over fourteen) and one child, two hundred pounds the adult fare, one-way, and one hundred for a child. Extraneous costs would come to a hundred pounds or so. That gave her one hundred pounds to start a new life in London. It was insane, and I knew it. My mother didn't. She was sure it was more than enough. In London there would be jobs, money, friends, family, fun, novels to write and publish, theatres to go to: she wasn't yet forty. She could begin again.

I had seen enough of London on the newsreels. It was a war-torn, bleak and exhausted city: there were food short-ages, rationing: the people were thin, gaunt and tiny, ill-fed, women in curlers wearing pinnies, unsmiling men in cloth caps, squinny-eyed children. Slums. Piles of bomb rubble left uncleared. Did my mother realize what it was like? If she did, why were we going? She seldom went to the cinema, perhaps she hadn't seen the newsreels? How else to account for her unreason? A hundred pounds wouldn't last for ever, then what? How would we live? Even at fourteen I could see it was madness.

She was launching us off into the unknown, we were wilfully joining the refugees: we were becoming the Alicias of the world, and for what? She was fleeing an enemy, not the real and living danger of the Nazis, which the whole world had got together to defeat, but an enemy in her own head. There were ten million rootless and homeless, they said, now roaming Europe. Once we left there was no turning back: I would never get home again. I would never see my father again.

I managed a protest or two. What about my friends? What about my father? I was better off without those friends of mine, she said, they were the whole trouble, and as for your father – I had suspected my mother had never much reckoned fathers, or acknowledged that they had much input into family life, other than to leave one a few unfortunate genes; now I knew I was right. My father was too possessive: he loved us too much, he would never let us develop 'normally'. The more I protested the more implacable she became; the more sinister seemed the life I described, full of unhealthy emotions. It was because of me that we had to be uprooted. I had to be got out of there, saved from the sickly perversions of Christchurch Girls' High, and life thereafter as a Canterbury sheep farmer's wife in a flowered dress with permed hair and a shocking New Zealand accent.

Well, who is to say she was not right? Our names went down on the waiting list of the New Zealand Shipping Line for the next boat to England.

Jane and I were taken out of school for a week and sent up to Auckland to say goodbye to my father. I imagine he tried to talk my mother out of leaving, and that she was inflexible. She was going to get us out of there on the first civilian boat out of the country. The least he could do for her was let us go. I tried to pluck up the courage to ask if I could stay behind and live with him, not her, but I failed. It would have been too hurtful to my mother, too disloyal. And if my father had wanted me to, surely he would have suggested it. But so far as I know he didn't. He had Edna and baby Alan, and Edna was pregnant again, and what would he want with me? It was a dismal holiday, except that we all went to see *Holiday Inn* with Bing Crosby, and he said, 'Well, at least you'll have white Christmases in England.' Other than that the matter was not discussed.

I waved goodbye for ever to my father from the bow of the ferry out of Wellington, which would take us back to Christchurch. He'd never come with us so far south before. He was crying. I watched his figure on the dock grow smaller and smaller, and I knew quite well I would never see him again, and knew he knew it too. Then he went back to Edna and his new family.

There were compensations for the new, unhinged, temporary life, while we waited for our passage home. I ran in the corridors at school all I liked, and talked in classrooms and was thrown out of the art class, for too much hilarity. It didn't matter. It was like knowing you were going to die but without actually having to. I would be leaving the complications of Molly Banks behind, and all the disgrace of the past. I could start again. I would miss Alison Grey and her oriental shoes, but what was the point of caring?

And actually there were still glimmers of hope. The war was over but getting back to England was not proving so easy as my mother had believed. Great minds think alike, as Molly Banks and I had so often said to one another. All the stranded families in the world were trying to get back to where they belonged, before war had so crudely and rudely interrupted their lives. Ships were still requisitioned for army transport. Civilian travel was severely restricted. June, July, now August – and no available berths. My mother wrote to a politician she knew in Wellington and asked him to pull strings – she who never asked anyone for anything – and he arranged a passage for us, mid-August, on the *Rangitoto*, the first ship out of New Zealand for six years licensed to carry normal civilians.

We had a week to pack, and a single trunk to pack it in, marked 'not wanted on voyage'. I had very little to take, it was true. A few clothes, one doll to remind me of my past, the one in the painting, letters from my father, and that was all, and most of that fitted in our customary suitcase, the one now being marked 'wanted on board'. Jane was allowed to take the little white chamois leather book she had embroidered with flowers when at the convent. She had to leave the hand-drawn Tarot cards. I was glad of that. I never liked them, though well enough able to read them. Decades later I was asked to be the fortune-teller at the village fête in Pilton, in Somerset, and took on the role. But I removed all the nasty cards from the pack before I left the house – out went Death, the Hanged Man, the Devil, the Tower, the seven and nine.

See, the Ace of Hearts covers you (happiness and abundance), the Ten of Pentacles opposes you (too much contentment, if anything, a surfeit of wealth and joy). The Chariot (gravity) departs, the Lovers approach. Even the littlest of old ladies

147

could be made cheerful. It's the only possible way to tell fortunes.

Nona had a trunk all to herself. Her treasures went with her – the layers of silks, finery, engraved cigarette lighters, embroidered slippers, gifts from lovers, the little cushion for her head, all the silly worldly things my mother despised. In her battered jewel case, which sits on my office table today, and still carefully wrapped in brown paper, no jewellery but a miniature volume of the poems of Ovid, two tiny copies of *The Rubaiyat of Omar Khayyam*, and her love-letters.

Throw them out, throw them out, begged my mother, in her panic to be rid of the past, what is the point of lugging these things around the world? But Nona persisted and won, and by some miracle here is the box still today, retrieved from a top shelf in my mother's wardrobe, redolent of a century's worth of female emotion.

My mother bought me a new blue coat because it would be cold in winter in England, and a pair of plain court shoes with a little heel. I was the one who was now beginning to worry about money. If we spent it all now how would we survive in the new land? She was being spendthrift. There was room in the trunk for the pleated gymslip, so thin it hardly took up any room at all, ditto my two old white school blouses, and even the flannel combinations which had already crossed the oceans once, and were now to do so again. I wanted them to stay behind but they didn't.

Growing excitement mixed with spasms of desolation. I might as well have killed myself under the No. 9 tram. I was leaving myself behind and would never meet myself again. I felt it then and it turned out to be true. My mother ran from place to place organizing her family's destruction, which she saw as their salvation. She tied up loose ends, saying proper good-byes, leaving nothing undone and no reproaches to follow her home: she made sure she left the house swept and clean and empty. She exhausted herself. She gave everything she could away, and all she left in the dark corridor of the Jackson's Road house was the Rita Angus painting of ourselves when young and barely formed, and we caught the good ship *Rangitoto* by the skin of our teeth, the portrait following on our heels, as I have described.

As the ship left harbour my mother, finding herself on board surrounded by bags and boxes she had not had the time to sort and pack, but which we had insisted on bringing, and then left her to carry, simply dropped them over the rail and into the sea. The Monopoly money floated a while, tiny extra flecks in the waves, before sinking.

Refugee

The *Rangitoto* was a ship which had been plying between Wellington and London for decades and was old even in 1946. She normally carried some two hundred and fifty passengers in style but on this voyage was transporting some two thousand, having been used as a troop carrier and not yet having been converted to normal use. We were in a dormitory with ninety-six others, row upon row of bunk beds, bare metal and not a frill in sight, somewhere down in the bowels of the ship, near the engines. Nona paled as she came in

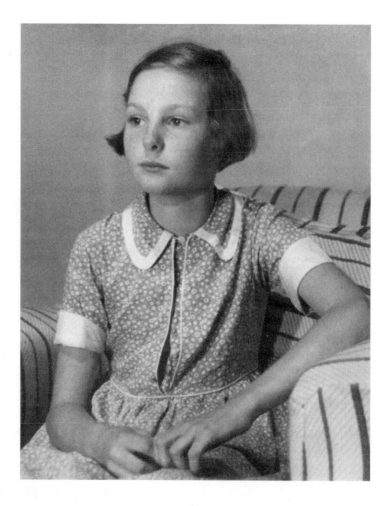

through the door. I had never seen anyone do that so dramatically. She had assumed there would be a piano in the lounge, but there was no lounge, forget the piano: there was sleeping and eating accommodation and the deck, and that was that.

My mother, exhausted, lay down on her allocated bottom bunk and went to sleep. Nona found her feather pillow and put her own head on that. She had a top bunk. So did Jane. I put on my coat and court shoes and went on deck and made a friend called Gail, my age, but who wore lipstick, and who came from Texas. She wasn't very nice and we quarrelled. She grabbed my belt when I tried to leave and stretched it and I said it was all very well for her but I was very poor and this was probably the only new coat I would ever have in all my life and I hated her. That is the only time (I think) I ever played the poverty card.

She let go and we made it up but she fell in love with the purser and spent her time in his cabin and even Nona said she wasn't a suitable friend. We were to be six weeks at sea, possibly longer because we were dropping off a party of GI brides on the way. For this reason we were to go via the Panama, not the Suez Canal. The GI brides were New Zealand's bad girls, the ones who'd got pregnant or made provable alliances with American servicemen, and the country couldn't wait to be rid of them. I thought perhaps Nursie might be among them but she wasn't. They were mostly peroxide blonde, cheerful and noisy, and somehow managed to find alcohol, and the more respectable of the families on board disapproved of them but I thought they were just fine.

We moved out of Wellington into black skies and tempestuous seas. No one was allowed on deck but I got out if only to breathe: inside smelt of hot oil and vomit. The ship was rolling from side to side. We were in a mist of spray, broadside to navy-blue waves the size of mountains. I was sure we ought not to be. Shouldn't we be head on into the seas? A sailor slammed me inside again before I was swept overboard. The engines were always breaking down, someone explained. It seemed clear to me that we were about to die, and what with this and that, and feeling fairly seasick myself, I didn't care one way or another. Seasickness is nature's way of making death by drowning seem attractive.

The engines were re-started, the boat eased round into the waves, the motion changed to the proper nose up in the air and flop down which was apparently preferable to the down on one side, then down on the other motion we had just been experiencing. I have never felt safe on a ship since. Even Aeroflot seems preferable to a sea cruise.

The ocean calmed, the sun came out, porpoises and swordfish followed the splendid *Rangitoto*. You can get to love a ship as you can a treacherous friend. Conjunctivitis and dysentery broke out: pus and shit dripped from two thousand orifices. Lice itched, swordfish leapt, porpoises played and there was phosphorescence in the ship's wake. Meanwhile my mother prepared us for our new life, walking us round and round the decks, practising proper modes of speech, getting rid of our colonial accents.

Oh my toe is frozen in the snow.
The rain in Spain stays mainly in the plain.
Mr Brown won renown, wore his britches upside-down.

Move the face, open the mouth, don't keep your chin in your chest, and speak up! Then off to bathe sore red yellow-crusted eyes with salt and water, which was the best the ship's doctor could offer. Were there weevils in the hard tack? Or do I imagine it?

Nona seldom got out of her bunk, not even for meals: she preferred to starve, but she had found the remnants of the ship's library and lots of detective stories she hadn't read, and relaxed with them into a stupor of denial. Afternoon tea was army style, from a giant metal teapot, one at either end of the ship. You queued up with your tin mug and if you were quick you could get a biscuit. I who had thought afternoon tea meant paste sandwiches, scones and jam, pikelets, chocolate fancies and sponge cake, found even this illusion gone.

After three weeks of nothing but sea one day dawn broke, and we were passing through the Panama canal. We struck land at a little port called Cristobal. Passengers were allowed on shore for six hours. It was good to have solid ground beneath the feet. I was astonished. The place was so pretty. Houses were painted as if they were fun, and not serious at all. People laughed and danced and ate food in the street. Men pinched my bottom and I squealed. Women wore bright colours and showed their figures and looked at me as if I might be some kind of rival. It hadn't been like that in New Zealand and nor was it to be again in London, when I was bundled back into the navy pleated gymslip.

My mother bought a handbag made of plaited white beads: it wasn't stiff as handbags were meant to be but flexible, as if even things like money and passports were not necessarily hard and fast. The bag yellowed with the years, and lost its beads, but my mother never threw the bag away long after everything else had gone. I think it contained her hope, and the memory of that exciting, liberating day between one world and another, with her new life opening up in front of her at last. I had to be glad for her.

An electrical storm blew up out of a clear sky and we fled back to the ship, while it howled and cracked around us. The

GI brides drifted back later on the arms of locals and made us all but late for the tide. Passengers leant over the side and booed the girls as they tumbled up the gangplank, dishevelled by more than weather, while lightning flashed and thunder echoed. The virtuous would have shaved their whorish heads if they could, and tarred and feathered them: their sins were many: they had turned their backs on their own country, they had failed to keep themselves for their own brave boys overseas, but gone instead for the fleshpots of the USA – and now this.

The brides were meant to be let off at Newport News, but a dock strike which spread north at the same pace as the *Rangitoto* meant that no sooner did the ship approach a port than it closed. We were carrying the curse of discontent with us – the brides, those female Jonahs, got the blame. We crept up the coast looking for harbourage, running shorter and shorter of food, to finally end up at Halifax, Nova Scotia, where it was grey and windy and very like Christchurch on a bad day, but colder. We walked about a bit in a dreary park. The Atlantic crossing thereafter was rough and further north than expected, but the passenger list was halved and by the time we got to Tilbury, on my fifteenth birthday, we were disease-free and even healthy. Not even a conjunctivitis virus could survive the icy sea wind.

Tilbury, England. I viewed it from the deck as dawn broke. Was this my mother's promised land? Where were the green fields, rippling brooks and church towers? Could this be the land of Strawberry Fair and sweet nightingales? Here was a grey harbour and a grey hillside, shrouded in a kind of murky, badly woven cloth, which as the day grew lighter proved to be a mass of tiny, dirty houses pressed up against one another, with holes gaping where bombs had fallen, as ragged as holes in the heels of lisle stockings. I could not believe that people actually chose to live like this.

'It's just Tilbury,' my mother said. 'It's always like this.'

Just Tilbury? The greyness was so vast, as far as the eye could reach.

But it was in the customs shed at Tilbury that terror struck. The scale of the building unnerved me: I did not know buildings could be so huge. I went into culture shock, as a visitor from the provinces might at the first sight of Imperial Rome. There were too many people: I could not make out what was going on. We could not find our two trunks among the hundreds. My mother's composure deserted her: she who never asked for help ran up and down uttering little cries of dependency, calling for porters who did not exist. Nona, for once moved to response, stood wringing her hands: or perhaps they were just stiff: it was seven weeks since she had played a piano. Jane stood apart from us, pale and remote, as if she'd disown us if she could: she was a burden, not a help. And not a man in sight specific to us: all the other milling family groups around had them in plenty, shouting, taking command, pointing, frowning, getting their own way – fathers, sons, brothers, cousins – but we were all female.

What had my mother done? Forsworn men and carted us across the world to this desolate, unknown, dangerous place? Why? 'War-torn Europe' was real, not a phrase: you only had to look at Tilbury to know it. We were as much refugees as any of the people we had seen on the newsreels, dragging their pathetic belongings behind them, only we had done it to ourselves. We were insane. It was one thing to survive on next to nothing in a land of plenty, but here?

It was my fifteenth birthday and nobody had mentioned it, nor were they likely to yet awhile. New rules would just have to apply. I was the youngest but the sanest, just too young to have any influence on the others. The England my mother had left was gone for ever – I could see the realization in her face as she struggled for a sighting of our worldly goods. The best I could do for her was not rock the boat, lest we all drown. I saw the trunks, and pointed them out. They were so close beneath our noses we had overlooked them. And then rescue came, in the form of Winifred, mother of the Ina who had once so entranced my father, brushing aside crowds as if they were flies, knowing what she was doing.

Immigrant

We spent that night in Winifred's house. It was in Bayswater, and the only building left standing in what had once been an elegant London square. Jane and I were to sleep on mattresses on the bare boards of the front bedroom up the first flight of stairs. There was a full moon. It was a clear night. I was too excited to sleep. I looked out of the window at piles of rubble and the craggy cathedral shapes of half-demolished buildings. Cats yowled at the moon. I thought, I will get the better of this town. I don't know how, but I will. This is the brave city from which the by-lines flow, and its future is mine. It's in a parlous state, an enemy has tried to destroy it, turned it with their bombs into a mouth full of missing teeth, but this is London and this is where I'm meant to be.

I still feel the same quiver of exultation: not always, just sometimes, as I cross the Thames at night over Waterloo Bridge, and see the Embankment lights dance, and the water sparkling below. St Paul's makes its patch of weighty dark beneath a glowing dome, the London Eye carves into the sky, and there are the familiar shapes of Westminster and Big Ben, and downriver the monster Canary Wharf with its warning Morse code blink, blink – then I remember the damaged quietness of what it once was, only the stray cats yowling, and I think again that I am part of this place and if the city can do it, so can I. And it did. Once I crossed the river to see my name running in lights over the National Theatre for some quite minor platform performance, and was taken by fresh surprise.

The bombsites stayed for decades. Nature quickly took them over, the split-apart houses, wild willowherb and buddleia creeping over ruined walls. Family rooms were imprinted on slabs of brickwork, ghost-like, floor upon floor. Different wallpapers, the faded patch where the cooker had been – once I saw a bookcase still with books in it – the plumbing for the loo, half a staircase. Stray cats abounded, the ones who ran away when the bombs fell and never saw home again or had no homes or owners to return to. Old ladies fed them their rations, and they bred and became plentiful, but weren't keen on stroking.

The world my mother knew had gone. 120 Adelaide Road was a boarding-house for refugees. The writers and artists had dispersed. Free Love seemed a luxury, so did a world in which ideas flourished. Ideas had produced fascism and communism, thank you very much, and communism was still very much alive. News of the camps was seeping out of

Germany. All the children in the country were shown footage of what had been found – piles of bodies, the living crawling over the dead – to show what man was capable of, to make sure it never happened here. We are used to these images now, we see them all the time, they are the stuff of Hollywood and entertainment. Then they were unimaginably obscene. If they were seldom spoken of it was for this reason.

Uncle Selwyn came to the rescue. He and his Russian wife Tania, an expert on rare books and manuscripts, lived in a little flat in Maddox Street, off Bond Street. They were ineffably smart. She was elegant and wore clothes of a kind I had never seen: Dior and Chanel. (Nona was thrilled when the New Look came along. The full skirts and tiny waists suited her figure and her imagination. My mother sniffed at the sheer wastefulness of it. So much fabric dedicated to nothing but vanity!)

Selwyn showed me a tiny radio, on which he could send and receive messages. He had been a major in the SOE – Special Operations Executive, the organization which helped downed airmen get back to England from Nazi-occupied France – and had spent years of the war as a restaurateur in Paris. He had always been a good cook.

Now Hitchcock had bought his novel *Man Running*, and was turning it into a film, *Stage Fright*, complete with a full complement of stars – Marlene Dietrich, Michael Wilding, Sybil Thorndike. Douglas Fairbanks was a friend. Selwyn was all confidence and kindness. I helped Tania 'do her Christmas presents', sitting on the floor surrounded by elegant and useless knick-knacks, wrapping and tying, any one of which passing gifts was worth the price of a week's rent for us.

Tania's secretary ticked the friends off from a list, and did the actual passing. I could see how pleasant life was among the rich.

Jane felt at home among so much busy elegance: she was admired for her sensitivity, her poetry and her looks. Increasingly, I felt I had little to offer: I was the fat, dull little sister, gauche and graceless, a poor relation, who blushed when spoken to and couldn't think of a word to say. I was my father's daughter, as Jane was my mother's. They were hostile to him, and though by now I had vowed to forget my father, since there was no point in remembering him, and anyway he had deserted me for his new family, I took offence.

When Selwyn remarked that he took care only ever to have friends who were rich and successful, since any other kind soon became a burden, I took further offence. Friends were sacred: you kept them for life and put up with them, for richer for poorer, for better for worse. Selwyn was a realist, a capitalist. I was a socialist.

My side was winning. Clement Attlee had won the election for the Labour Party, there was to be a free Health Service, National Assistance for unemployed men, and free university education for all if you could pass the exams to get in. About ten per cent of boys and five per cent of girls went to university, and though there was a female quota in many places, it was hoped the female proportion would increase. My mother thought I should work to get to university – presumably because she thought I was too plain, dull and lesbian ever to find anyone to marry me and keep me. As for Jane, she still wasn't going to be sent to school. I wanted to get back to lessons and my own generation, and quickly. I was good at

159

passing exams if not much else. The new school year had already started without me.

We were taken to see Aunt Mary, my father's sister, and Uncle Michael, he now a prominent member of Attlee's government. They were good socialists, but not Keir Hardie style, to my disappointment. They lived in South Kensington in a pretty little house. They were polite but not effusive in greeting us. Well, why should they be? My mother had blacked her copybook in being divorced by my father, and I daresay we looked like trouble. The left are ambitious too, and have to keep their noses clean, and poor relatives can cause endless trouble and scandal.

We visited Edgar's sisters, who lived in a dark little house in Barons Court in genteel parsimony and talked about Cousin Cecil the admiral. They seemed to me to come out of some other depressing age, and not to want to leave it. Tea was served on a mahogany tea-stand: tiers of round wooden shelves around a central shaft. The bread was cut very thin, being in short supply, and the rock cakes were bright yellow, being made of powdered egg, which now the US sent us on lend-lease, as a change from Liberty ships and guns, and all had to be paid for now the war was over. The US was not popular. Repaying the loans at the interest they demanded was making the nation's recovery hard.

I worried about train fares, bus fares, tram fares, and about the cost of cups of tea at Lyons Corner House. As my mother stopped worrying, at least temporarily, about money I felt obliged to take over. We had only some forty-five pounds left in all the world and no way I could see of making any more. The official school leaving age was fourteen and I could have started work but now I wanted to get to university.

In the meantime we were living in Uncle Selwyn's other house in Liss, Hampshire. The house was made of cedar wood: he had built it himself, staircase included, and the furniture as well. Everything was softly shiny, luxurious and smooth to the touch, very different from the splintery apple-box tables we were accustomed to. I did not like to complain that it gave me a headache: that we were living in effect in a scented cedar wood linen-chest. I had learned that this was not the kind of thing people wanted to hear. Aesthetics must come before comfort.

It was rumoured, such were Selwyn's talents, that he was not Edgar's son at all, but Ernest Gimson's, the furniture designer and craftsman, who was a friend of the Jepsons. It would not surprise me: Nona seemed sweet and placid, but she was unknowable. Her sister Sylvia had lived in a scandalous *ménage à trois*, with someone known to the family as 'poor Willie Beach the jam magnate' and a husband too. To have started life as models for Holman Hunt, as did the beautiful daughters of Henry Holmes, would not be a recipe for unswerving sexual propriety in the future.

On the other hand, if Selwyn inherited Gimson's talent for working wood he could not have inherited Edgar's talent for writing – and he was as good a writer as he was a carpenter. So who is to say? Now, ever ingenious, he was using papier-mâché to build up the wooded hillside around the Cedar House to make a lawn. The villagers would bring up their old newspapers, Selwyn would place them strategically on the slopes, soak them well with water, compact them and

161

sprinkle them with a coating of earth, and eventually grass seed. Grass grew green, luxuriant and weed-free. This early recycling went on for years until what had once been a steep unusable slope was flat and fit for croquet. Douglas Fairbanks lived along the road and Herbert Lom too.

The village of Liss looked exactly as villages did in wartime films out of Britain: the GIs had gone home but there were hollyhocks in country gardens, and ladies in cardigans riding high upright bicycles, and old men who doffed their caps to the gentry. I was alternately enchanted and bored and took to playing Patience again, but on the porch because inside gave me a headache. The autumn was beautiful, the country lanes lined with wild flowers and the blackberries ripened. We picked and picked.

I was given an Insurance number by the new Labour government – EEP something, as I remember, which was to be mine for life – and a ration book, which made me feel a proper citizen of my new country, and proud. At that time the butter ration was two ounces a week, and meat six ounces, bread was on points, as were the bright yellow powdered eggs from America, but vegetables were freely available, as was melon jam which came in tins from South Africa. The sweet ration was two ounces a week.

Frozen

My mother went back to London and looked for somewhere for us to live. Selwyn offered to buy us a house in Fitzroy Square – for a year or so after the war semi-derelict houses in London could be bought for almost nothing – but my mother didn't like to be indebted to anyone, let alone her brother, and refused. I tried to persuade her to say yes but she wouldn't. Instead she rented a single room, first-floor front, at 1 Belsize Lane, in northwest London, where the three of us were to live, cook, eat and sleep, and use a communal bathroom down the corridor. Here we were to live for the winter of 1946/7, the worst winter for decades, and on into the spring. Nona, lucky thing, stayed with Selwyn.

Winter was closing in, London was at its lowest, grimiest, hungriest ebb. So were we. We stayed in bed for days on end. There was no other way of keeping warm. Ice and snow closed the city down: there was erratic electric power, gas for cooking and heating came as a tiny flicker out of the jets and sometimes failed altogether. Water froze in pipes. There was whale meat in the shops and that was about all, off points, except a strange bright yellow powder called Cremola: you mixed it with milk powder, added boiling water and it thickened up into a highly scented dessert. There were posters for it everywhere. *'Cremola, tickles the world's palate.'* It always worried me. If you rhymed palate with mallet, as was the proper pronunciation, it didn't work as a strong statement: it you rhymed it wrongly as in relate, it did. Which was one meant to do? Pondering these things and reading in bed for days on end became intolerable. Jane and I would go and stand in the entrance of Belsize Park Underground, where blasts of warm body-scented air came belching out at two-minute intervals, with every passing Underground train, and unfroze us. There were quite a little group of us gathered there, and outside all the Underground stations in London, through that winter. The trains ran more regularly then than now. *'It's warmer underground,'* ran the ads. Oh yes, it was.

Belsize Park is on the Northern Line five stops up from King's Cross; next stop Hampstead for the Heath and Louis's Patisserie. It is halfway to everywhere; a step up from Chalk Farm, which is frankly depressing, a step down from Hampstead where people would live if they had the money, a quiet aspiring inner suburb chosen by young childless professionals: with a cinema to show art films and some useful shops, once family homes now given over to multi-occupancy, and with streets too narrow for grandeur and too wide to be companionable.

My mother spent the last of the inheritance on me, paying a term's fees at a private school run on progressive lines up the hill in Hampstead. It was called Burgess Hill School and modelled itself on Summerhill. It was co-educational, a rare thing in secondary schools at that time. My mother, I realized, hoped to undo the doom influence of Christchurch Girls' High and ensure that I kept the company of boys. I just knew I had exams to pass.

But pupils at Burgess Hill School, which was a large, messy, noisy house in a tree-lined street somewhere above Hampstead Station, next stop up the line from Belsize Park, studied only when they felt like it. They were expected to be self-regulated and self-motivated, but they were not: they were children. Treated as if they were normal adults, they behaved like psychopathic adults. They smoked, swore, put their clothes on and took them off when they felt like it, locked themselves into the lavatories in couples or threesomes and did goodness knew what. They were perfectly amiable, but had torn up most of the books in the library, and when I locked myself in a classroom with a Latin grammar they broke down the door to take it away. They did it, they said, for my sake. Learning by rote was bad for you and led to repression and war. Their teachers, who were a sensitive and idle lot, by and large agreed with this view. If the children managed to get themselves to a classroom on time the teacher seldom did.

The best of the teachers was Bernice Rubens, who became so good a novelist that she won the Booker Prize, and was later to turn up as an ex-girlfriend of my husband-to-be, and later still to be my friend. She taught English Literature from behind a veil of black tumultuous hair. She was seventeen, and very beautiful. She didn't think much of me because of my dissenting views on Keats's *Ode to a Nightingale*. I complained that it was mawkish, swoony, and full of self-pity.

'I' and 'my', I maintained, had no part in poetry. Bernice was very scathing, as she still can be. She has been known to throw guests out of dinner parties because she disagrees with what they say. In retrospect I was brave to maintain my opinion. She left to play Salome, unveiled, on the London stage, and I was left to continue my education unsupervised, at considerable expense.

I would laugh aloud on my way to Burgess Hill in the mornings, looking forward to the absurdity of it: it was warm, the school lunches were lavish. You didn't have to worry about the clothes you wore because everything was on points: girls wore their sisters' cast-offs and boys their brothers'. You would wear the same clothes for a week because how could you wash them if there was no means of heating the water? You didn't have to tell anyone you were living three to a room. I felt that God had me in his charge, giving me the life he did. I never got that feeling on the way to the Christchurch Girls' High. But everything was still alarmingly random: as random as the exam questions they chose to ask you when School Certificate came along, which would be in less than a year. You had to pass in all five subjects to get it.

The headmaster took me to one side and congratulated me on how well I had settled in, especially after the formality of my previous school. I was not so much settled, I said, as perched and having a rest, when actually I needed to work, and his school was too noisy and actively anti-academic to make that possible. He tried to persuade me that examinations weren't necessary for girls and most of the pupils went on to be something in the arts, but he didn't convince me. I was going through a self-righteous stage. I asked my mother if I could try South Hampstead School for Girls. My Aunt

Jennifer, Lois's daughter, went there and wore a proper uniform and did homework, which boded well for academic achievement. South Hampstead was, then as now, a fee-paying school but the new education legislation meant that if I could pass their entrance tests not only would my fees be paid by the State but I would get free lunches, and even a small grant to keep me in clothes and food.

The entrance test was a piece of cake. The convent and Christchurch Girls' High stood me in good stead. My spelling was just about perfect. I knew the Agricultural Revolution five times over, if the Industrial Revolution hardly at all. I had been terrorized and knuckle-rapped into a flawless knowledge of maths and grammar. Latin and French held no terrors. For the English paper I wrote a story which I remember to this day. It was about a lad in Pompeii who longed for the world to come to an end to save him from an embarrassment; his prayers were answered and as the sky fell in he was relieved to find himself dying. It was about a boy, not a girl, because that was the convention of the day. Nobody wrote about women: women's lives were too uninteresting.

I hadn't written a story for a long time and I was gratified by the power of the experience: I beckoned with my finger and all Pompeii slipped back into existence, and what was different then from now? If nature failed to make the sky fall in people would drop bombs on one another. I passed the entrance exams. I started mid-term. Spring was coming. With the clothing grant I was able to buy a new-style navy serge gymslip without pleats, that didn't have to be ironed every Sunday evening. There was even somewhere to hang it now, though there was a new danger, that of mould.

Servant Girl

My mother found a job as a live-in housekeeper at 21 Marlborough Street in St John's Wood. It was a good address, the house was white-painted and pretty. So long as I asked no one home to tea, no one would know we didn't live upstairs but in the damp dark basement, behind barred windows, where green mould attacked our clothes. We were the servants. There were four rooms, each one darker than the next. Not that I minded much; had not H. G. Wells' mother been a housekeeper? I was a socialist: I believed in the dignity of the working man, and woman.

My mother was under pressure from Selwyn and Tania to send Jane to a proper school. As it was, she stayed indoors in the boiler room which was her bedroom and studied for her Higher Certificate by correspondence course. No doubt Selwyn and Tania saw my mother as unreasonable. But my mother saw her sister Faith in Jane and could not, would not, tell them how much she worried that if Jane were thwarted she would follow in Faith's footsteps.

Insanity was the great dark fear of the age. It was undiscussed and untreatable – other than by locking the afflicted away and hoping it would pass – a matter of silence and shame within families. Freud had set up shop round the corner in Maresfield Gardens at Swiss Cottage, up the road from St John's Wood, across the way from Belsize Park, but to most decent people his ideas were anathema. 'Freud, Adler and Jung,' my mother would say. 'Fried, addled and hung.' She'd have no part of it, chanting:

'*It's no go the Yogi-Man,*
It's no go Blavatsky,
All we want is a bank balance and a bit of a skirt in a
  taxi.'

But she took us to Theosophist meetings, all the same, and for a time I was a Young Theosophist, but I found their languid handshakes clammy and soon left. I have never got on with the quietist movements: they lapse too easily into self-congratulation: *I have found the oneness, you have not.* I prefer to look outside myself if I possibly can, not inside. Meditation reminds me too forcibly of being made to lie on a mat at nursery school and take an hour's nap.

I did not hear from my father but then I did not write to him. What could I say? If I spoke well of this new land and our new life it would seem unfeeling of me: if I spoke badly of it I would be betraying my mother. But sometimes I got scared, and felt I needed rescuing from randomness, and wished he was there to do it. There was a rat in my bedroom which would come out from behind the water pipes and stare at me when I was undressing for bed. It had red eyes. It was the pecking magpie of Cranmer Square, back again, creature of ill omen. How long ago the golden age of Coromandel seemed.

We were in the world of Upstairs-Downstairs, and on the wrong side of the swinging green baize door that traditionally separated the haves from the precarious world of the have-nots. My mother was reluctant to mention the matter of the rat to Upstairs. She worried that if she did the couple for whom she worked, refined musicians both, would be horrified and insist on moving us out, calling in the ratman and laying down poison, and then where would we live? They thought my mother should be grateful for being allowed to have her two children live with her: they would not want any unpleasantness. Obscurely, we would be blamed for the rat's existence.

Years later, when I wrote the pilot for the TV show *Upstairs Downstairs* I wrote it with feeling, aware of the helplessness of Downstairs and the propensity of Upstairs to dehumanize its servants. Upstairs likes to pride itself that it's good to Downstairs, but is easily irritated by any show of ingratitude, and can't bear to be put to bother. The pilot went splendidly but after writing a couple more episodes of the show the curse of the red-eyed rat was upon me, and I was fired. The cast of both Upstairs and Downstairs very quickly began to vie in the lovability stakes. They had difficulty learning, let alone speaking, the lines I had written for them: they found them too sharp and horrid. Or this was the face-saving reason I was given by the producers. I thought it was just as likely to be my way of writing scripts at the time – give them a first draft, wait to be asked to make changes, do them, deliver them, and if you're asked for yet more changes deliver the first draft again: feeling somehow familiar, it is accepted at once. The producers alas had cottoned on: I had inadvertently disclosed to the press that this was how I went about writing scripts. I was seen as ungrateful and mocking. I wasn't: I just knew my first drafts were perfectly okay to begin with.

Back then in the barred basement – those same bars through which I had my weighty heroine Esther stare, in the first novel I wrote, *The Fat Woman's Joke* – I did my homework with my feet up on the bed for fear of the rat, and moved into Jane's room by night. She thought I should keep to my own room and brave the rat, but supposing it nibbled my eyes out while I slept? It looked as if that was what its ambition was, but was biding its time. I sat on a broken chair and punctured my hymen: I didn't know what it was, of course. It hurt, I bled out of turn, but it soon stopped. My mother scrubbed the kitchen floor for the musicians upstairs and took comfort at the thought of the statue to her grandfather in Berkeley, California, director of the city's music. What life could bring us to! And it was only just beginning.

Scholarship Girl

South Hampstead was not so different from Christchurch Girls' High. There was favouritism, emotional politics, pashes and hero-worship: there were cliques and Latin mistresses with favourites, and gym mistresses at whose touch you felt uneasy, and the same sense of brooding doom in the corridors, but more fitful, and I was older and less easily oppressed. The younger teachers liked me: the older ones thought I was too frivolous for my own good.

My name went up on the board every day for free school lunches, thus announcing my impoverished state to the world. I took some pride in this. It seemed to me I had earned the privilege of being here, and the others were here only by courtesy of their parents, give or take an entrance exam or two. And I was not aware of any discrimination on the part of the other girls. It was so soon after the war that even children were conscious of their good fortune in being alive, and in some kind of stable background. There was a large proportion of Jewish pupils, this being north London, and

171

many had lost relatives in Europe to the camps. There was no bullying, very little backbiting – the war had made outsiders of us all, and it was our instinct to support one another.

The headmistress was Miss Potter, serious sister of Stephen Potter the humorist; the history teacher Miss Stead was the daughter of Stead of the *Manchester Guardian*: most of the teachers came out of a long tradition of intellectual maiden ladies, descendants in spirit of Mary Wollstonecraft. We were one of the Girls' Public Day School Trust and we were taught, in the spirit of the male public schools, that we were the cream of a generation and must work for the benefit of the people: we were destined for public service. We would go to Oxford and Cambridge and then into the Civil Service or teaching, and only the dullards would have personal lives.

In those days careers and family didn't mix: women chose one or the other. We knew which we were meant to choose. We played hockey in our navy bloomers in Regent's Park and men stood on the sidelines and watched but no one so much as condescended to shoo them away. What harm could their lascivious fantasies do to us?

My half aunt Jennifer was in a class below me and neither of us wanted to have to explain to others the ramifications of this relationship, so we barely spoke. I fell in love with a girl of my age, Jean Francis. I thought she was amazingly beautiful, calm and still. If she saw something in a shop window that she liked she would just go in and buy it. I decided this was what gave her so glowing and smooth a complexion. If you could do what you wanted it improved the looks no end. She took no notice of me and I barely spoke to her. I just wanted to be her. She did not suffer from doubt.

On my first day at the new school I sat next to a pale, willowy girl called Flora Goodwin: she reminded me of Helen Burns in *Jane Eyre*, the schoolgirl who was to die speaking of a better world to come. As indeed was to happen, forty years on. I can feel Flora standing behind me as I write this, the Angel of the House whom Virginia Woolf speaks of, the one who's meant to whisper in the ear of women writers and tell them to be good, noble, positive, never destructive or unkind; but Flora is reproaching me for snivelling.

She is also suggesting that I hold my tongue, and I will, beyond saying that in the crises of our lives, from the minor disturbances of love and career, to the tragic descent into madness and death of my sister, and later, that of her middle son, we could make sense to each other, and of the layers of complexity and paradox which underlie even the most apparently obvious of tragedies: how you had better keep your head down or the Gods will notice and take their revenge. She was to die of brain cancer and though far from lucid at the end – how could one be – the sense of the separation of the spirit from the flesh was so great, the energy, determination and strength of both so stunning, even in the light of a fading intellect, that when all were finally gone the emptiness left behind was terrible. I could not go to her funeral, such were the exigencies of my own life at the time, and I will feel bad about that for ever.

The writing of this memoir causes pain as well as pleasure. It is not in the least therapeutic, on the contrary, but then I have never been a believer in the theory beloved by psychotherapists that recollection cures, or 'closes'. But then I daresay you get what you expect. To me, who believes that all re-living does is scrape off a scar tissue mercifully left by the passage of time, to reveal still bleeding wounds, this is all that happens. To those who have faith, no doubt recollection does indeed serve a healing function, or helps them understand better what they are, or how to change. But I have always felt like Mr Collins in *Pride and Prejudice*, who, when it was suggested to him that he might have to change, expressed surprise and could see no virtue in it. Or like the husband in the James Thurber cartoon, who says to the great troubled lump in his bed, 'But what do you want to understand yourself *for*, Martha?'

Flora, aged fifteen, with her large pale blue eyes and tumbling brown hair, smiled at me as I sat down next to her on my first day at South Hampstead School for Girls. Her name is engraved in gold on the school notice board: winner of an Exhibition to Oxford. Mine, needless to say, is not. I seldom win prizes, though I am often called upon to give them. (I like to think, when it comes to literature, that it is because of the shortness of my sentences, which makes the books appear to lack gravitas.) Though it's true I did once win four prizes in one evening at the Writers' Guild annual awards, back in the mid-Seventies. Best this and best that, mostly in radio. The prizes were given by the Duke of Edinburgh. 'We can't go on meeting like this,' he said, as I went up to the platform for the fourth time. 'I've run out of things to say. I'll say rhubarb rhubarb and you say the same.' So we did. I have been a royalist ever since, as those who brush up against royalty tend to be. They are more impressive than you could rationally conceive. I remember that occasion well because on our table was a skinny little woman from New York dressed in gold lamé and wearing a gold skullcap. She was astonishingly well turned out. She sighed as I sat down and said, 'And you don't even *care*, do you. What you look like,

I mean.' I was hurt, I had spent all afternoon at the hair-dresser's, and it didn't even show.

But that's another story: see how I wander off in a trice when faced with the memory of Flora? Grief and loss is never over, no matter how we are trained towards this thing called closure. Mourning comes in waves through the rest of our lives, and so I think it should.

It turned out within the space of the day that Flora's mother Louise had been a friend of Nona's in the days of free love and careless rapture. Nona described her as a plump, pink-cheeked laughing country girl, who, unmarried, had had nine children by the late Mr Goodwin, a writer of musical plays. Flora was the eighth. Goodwin had installed Louise in Old Conduit House, a gothic pile on the corner of Lyndhurst Gardens, next door to the house in which he kept his wife and legitimate brood. When he died Louise had inherited Old Conduit House. She had used the equity to buy up property through the war when nobody wanted it. At the time I met Flora her mother was converting houses all over Belsize Park and Hampstead to bed-sitting rooms, complete with sink, gas ring for cooking, gas fire for warmth, with use of communal bathrooms and penny-in-the-slot hot-water gas geyser. A penny a wash, twopence a bath. There is no record of what became of Mr Goodwin's original wife and children. Louise wore ankle socks and sandals and long skirts and decided I needed looking after. Old Conduit House became my second home.

I wrote about the house in a novel called *Splitting*: it is the place where identity vanishes and people and the woodwork become one thing, entangled and indistinguishable. It has arches and turrets and magnificent stained-glass windows and a fresco by Epstein under the window of one of the garden rooms. I fell in love with Flora's brother Laurie. He was lithe and slender. He kissed me once. That was astonishing. Wet, warm and powerful. But he didn't do it again. I thought I must be very unattractive. I wasn't accustomed to young men. Andrew, the eldest son, rather admired me and I think Louise wanted me to be his wife. He was as stiff and formal and ramrod as Laurie was lithe.

Flora and I would sit in the garden in the sun and discuss Shelley and dig chewing gum out of long lengths of carpet which Louise had bought up from bombed cinemas. 'Nothing wrong with this except the chewing gum!' But how the stuff stretched and stuck, how difficult it was to get rid of. Louise blamed the Americans, who had brought it over with them in the war, though she acknowledged that without it she would have had to have paid five times as much for stair-carpeting.

At school Flora was the teachers' favourite. She had the pallor and transparency of the natural academic. She was being groomed for an Oxford Scholarship, not just an Exhibition, and knew everything about the Pre-Raphaelites there was to know, and could have been painted by one, as Ophelia or the Lady of Shalott. She slept in a carved wooden bed in a tall gothic bedroom, usually icy cold, with stained-glass windows. She was Keats's faery lady.

> O *what can ail thee, knight-at-arms,*
> *Alone and palely loitering? . . .*
> *I met a lady in the meads,*
> *Full beautiful – a faery's child . . .*

She fell in love with the palely romantic Clive Cullerne Bowne, a fellow-student at Oxford, and when her family tried to stop her, developed TB and had to be put in a sanatorium and barely survived. Her family were so horrified they withdrew their objections at once, Flora married Clive, and they lived happily ever after, in so far as that is possible once you have children, and they had three. I still miss her. That's more than enough of that, she says, over my shoulder, Angel of the House, before fading out for a time.

My problem was, and I could see it, as other people's dramas circled round me, that I was too practical to be truly interesting. Living with a rat didn't seem to count. Asked to write an essay at school, a recipe with accurate instructions which could be followed step by step, I wrote one for making bread. It was read out in class, as an example of good clear lucid prose, and that was gratifying. But how dull!

Meanwhile back home the rat came out from time to time and stared pink-eyed at me. I'd walk back home alongside the bombed-out houses which lined the Finchley Road. They stood behind long wooden walls, made up of nailed together front doors, from the grandly solid to the flimsy and wretched. They kept their letterboxes, their brass handles, their carved knockers, the sense of secrets kept inside, although there was nothing behind but bomb sites. Front doors would survive when ruined houses, ruined lives, crumbled round them.

At 21 Marlborough Place we used the tradesmen's entrance at the side of the house. The servant classes did not even get to use a front door.

Sister-in-law

I had a good friend called Shirley Austin who lived in a vast house in Bishops Avenue, the most expensive street in all London. Her father made Austinsuite furniture, and her mother made tomato sandwiches out of soft white well-buttered bread. Rationing cut harder into some households than into others, I could see. They also had a farm in Sussex, and Shirley and I would go down in the summers to help with the harvest. I became a specialist in the making of haystacks, standing on a structure you carefully built beneath you, using a pitchfork and the sheaves of wheat others heaved up to you, placing them stalk side out, chaff side in. It was a skilled task, and I was good at it, until I fell off one and so damaged my knee that five decades later I had to be given a new one. There were two handsome agricultural students there, helping with the harvest, but I was so shy I could hardly raise my eyes to theirs.

That year I came back home from the farm to the tradesman's entrance and opened the door to pale faces and distraught looks. In my absence trouble had erupted. Holidays have been a source of anxiety to me ever since: being away from home longer than a few days feels dangerous. In one's absence things tend to leap out of control.

Jane too had been working on a farm, a summer work-camp – since the beginning of the war young people were expected to spend their summers bringing the harvest in – had fallen in love and come home announcing her impending marriage. I burst into tears on hearing this and my mother said, 'But

we were relying on you coming home to keep us cheerful.'
So I cheered up. This was my accepted role around this time,
and come to think of it, always has been, and still is.

Jane had met him cutting corn. His name was John Dodd,
and he was thirty-two. She was seventeen. He was quite short,
rather bald, a teacher in a secondary modern school and a
serious communist. He had the hollow-eyed gauntness that
goes with the over-political, earnest male. Nona said, 'I met
her when she got off the train and there were leaves and grass
stains on the back of her cardigan. Poor little girl!' No one
was in favour of this marriage except of course Jane and John
Dodd, and Jane needed my mother's permission, and my
mother didn't know what to do. And supposing Jane were
pregnant?

When Jane got undressed for bed in the boiler room we still
shared because of the rat, I became conscious of how beautiful
the human body could be, and how poetic a creature she
was. Some new secret knowledge, or the memory of some
overwhelming pleasure, now brimmed over into her face and
made her smile as if she couldn't help it. Whatever sex was,
I came to the conclusion, however pitifully it marked the
back of your cardigan, it turned you from something cloudily
defined into something clearly delineated and complete.

She did not confide in me but then it had been years since
she had; she just smiled and smiled and crawled into bed and
pulled the bedclothes over her head. She was resolute in the
face of opposition. She would do as she wished, there was
no doubt about that; Jane did the doing-as-she-wished for
the both of us. I had settled very much into doing what I
ought.

She was deserting me, but I could hardly blame her wanting out, wanting her own household, a man in her bed. I see her in my mind's eye, etched in time, the rosy, slim body with its new knowledge, framed in the rigmarole of pipes and plumbing that fed through the room to furnish hot water upstairs, to warm the fingers of the string quartets, and I wished then that I could paint and still do.

Tania and Selwyn united in uproar: Jane was not to be allowed to marry this man: it was unthinkable. My mother insisted that Jane should be allowed to do as she chose, but didn't tell them her reasons. Not only this, but she altogether lost her cool and spoke in such a way to Tania that she was barred from the Maddox Street door for ever, and Tania and Selwyn from ours. Not that they had ever actually stepped over the Marlborough Place threshold, come to think of it – they were not the kind to come in by the tradesman's entrance. Be that as it may, brother and sister did not speak to one another again for the rest of their long lives, thus causing distress to Nona, and awkwardness to Jane and myself.

I wonder what was said to cause such very great offence, and sometimes think the ghost of the third sibling, the tragic, unspoken of and unvisited Faith, came to stand between them. Some people just won't lie down peacefully in their graves. Sylvia Plath and Assia Wevill, victims or persecutors of the Poet Laureate Ted Hughes, depending on how you see it, roam to this day, demanding a proper hearing from the world, and never getting it. Ted Hughes the poet sleeps peacefully enough and haunts no one. But that triumvirate of tragedy is another story, and typical of another decade. My Aunt Faith and her fate continue to haunt the generations of our family, and won't lie down.

Poor Tania was to become prematurely senile and be institutionalized. Then it was her turn not to be visited by Selwyn, which raised the eyebrows of all who knew them, and had envied their closeness and the apparent perfection of their relationship. It does not surprise me: Selwyn was a man who needed to be flattered by his accessories: and the accessories included friends and family. If they failed to reflect glory upon him he failed to see them. And perhaps, who is to say, he inherited a non-visiting gene from Nona.

Nona died in 1977, aged ninety-nine, and is buried in the Quaker graveyard at Old Jordans in Buckinghamshire, where she spent the last years of her life. She played the piano rather less towards the end, but was still managing to do so for three hours a day when she was ninety-six. She seldom played for an audience: indeed she preferred not to. Music was for her a form of worship, and also of escape. I went through her little box of treasures the other day. A miniature dictionary, two miniature Omar Khayyams, the poems of Ovid in minuscule print, some affectionate letters from Edgar; 'Dear Lamb,' in his sparse, repressed hand – he went on writing to her long after they were divorced – a letter written to her by the eleven-year-old Faith, and the love-letter from the Berlin correspondent of the *Economist* in 1929.

Jane married John Dodd in a church in St John's Wood in a cheap pink dress. I don't think Nona came: she was too dependent on Selwyn's financial support. She had no money of her own other than a mysterious thing called an annuity which brought her in a few pounds every quarter. My mother was in no position to help her. Pride is what you can afford or think you can afford. My mother always thought she could afford a little more than she could. Attendance at the wedding was sparse. John Dodd managed a handful of strange East End relatives in flowered dresses. I daresay they thought we were pretty odd. And now home was just my mother, myself, and the rats.

But not for long. My mother found a new job within weeks of Jane's wedding. We escaped the doom of the tradesman's entrance. Houses are built without such entrances now, but they exist in our heads: they are the boundaries which the politically and socially ambitious do not cross, for fear of uneasiness now and trouble later. Nor were my Aunt Mary and Uncle Michael, to the left politically, she a leading light in the Workers' Educational Association, he a Labour MP, any more anxious to step over our threshold than were fastidious Uncle Selwyn and Aunt Tania. But then poor relations can be a worry: they so easily stop being grateful and become vengeful.

My mother now did clerical work for the Overseas League in St James's. I find myself there sometimes: it is leathery and imposing and a favourite venue for literary prizes. Then it seemed vast and unfriendly: unknowable, the land of the haves, not the have-nots.

With the new job came a new home. Now that Jane had gone the suitcase was more than ample for my possessions, though I was working for my matriculation and had books and papers to take with me. Now we lived centrally, in a redbrick mansion block in Victoria, in the shadow of the Roman Catholic Cathedral. We shared a vast, dark, ground-floor flat with a bachelor teacher, who really liked my mother – but she had no time for him. I had a little room with bars, only slightly underground, which looked on to the main street and I could see the legs of passers-by in all their variety. No pair was ever the same.

When my husband Ron became an antique dealer in 1963 one of the first things he bought was a job-lot of glass eyes from a closed-down truss factory. I washed them free of a hundred years of dust – an alarming task – and this being the Sixties he prepared to sell them off as ear-rings. It was a problem to find two eyes even remotely the same, since nature, in search of the betterment of the species by way of variation, was clearly determined that they should not be. The same thing applied to the legs, let alone shoes and trouser widths and skirt lengths, which scissored along the other side of the bars which stood between the regular world and me in the late Forties. Mostly of course, shoes then were a sensible brown or black. Coloured shoes came along in the Sixties, along with decorated plastic bags and the permissive wearing of blue with green and other hitherto forbidden frivolities.

I was fifteen. Men lurched into me in the street, or hissed peculiar things in my ear, or rubbed their trousers oddly as they sat next to me on the Underground. There is a certain age – when a positive physical development converges with a nega- tive degree of self-awareness – when young females attract the sexually disturbed. I can't say it upset me particularly. It was just the future pressing in, trying to explain itself to me.

Then, without warning, Jane came home. She had been mar- ried for eight weeks. It turned out she didn't like sex. She wanted a divorce at once. She shut herself in a room and wouldn't talk about it, other than to say he wouldn't leave her alone, he was at it all the time, even on the kitchen table. John Dodd turned up in a state of baffled distress. He seemed to think I was an ally. What on earth was going on? He had no idea what was in Jane's head: she had wanted to marry, had seemed perfectly happy, then suddenly, this. How could I explain that our family had values which didn't quite accord with anyone else's? How little self-interested we were, how because we were poor didn't mean we were humble or down-trodden, or without whimsicality, especially if we were Jane? And how little we knew of what went on in Jane's head? She probably just wanted to know what marriage was like, was my guess, and now she knew, she had come home. I really liked him and felt sorry for him and would have been very happy if he had taken me as a swap for Jane but he didn't suggest it, just stalked off into the fog and didn't come back.

The fogs in those days were thick and yellow and murderous, full of sulphur, but we breathed the stuff in as deeply as we did normal air: we were so little conscious of our health. I stood on a needle in the middle of the night, getting out of bed to let the cat in: the needle drove right in up to its eye and I went to St George's hospital up the road to have it drawn out by a great electro-magnet operated by a handsome young doctor. So began my love affair with hospital emergency rooms. I have been to them all over the world, from Sarajevo to Reykjavik, when my heartbeat goes into frantic overtime, and needs an injection to return it to its normal level: a frightening but not life-threatening occurrence, which began when I was twenty-five and has continued to occur a few times a year ever since. Others take to drink or drugs in their search for the extreme: I just go to A and E and gaze at handsome doctors.

I was sorry to see John Dodd go from our lives, he had seemed so very sane. Jane applied for a divorce on the grounds of cruelty and was accepted to study English at the University of Exeter. The latest correspondence course had done her very well. She hadn't even had to leave the house for a year or so, other than to get married for a few weeks the better to find out what went on outside her own front door – or at any rate her own tradesman's entrance.

Rejected

But shadows were closing in at school. Narrow-eyed neurosis, paranoia, was overwhelming me. I hadn't been made a prefect, and all my friends had, and I suffered. Off they went to the prefects' room to drink their superior cups of coffee and I was left on my own in the classroom reading a book and pretending not to mind. I felt abandoned and betrayed by them, and by fate. How had this happened? I was told it was because I was new to the school and the younger pupils didn't know me: I had been left behind in the vote. I didn't believe this. It occurred to me that I was left behind because my name went up on the school notice board every day as eligible for a free lunch, which marked me out as a scholarship girl, one of the children of the poor. Perhaps I had been altogether too blithe: perhaps I was indeed marked as a fitting recipient of pity and charity. I was humiliated. Instead of looking forward to going to school, now I dreaded it. I did not mention the matter to my mother: I did not want to burden her with my troubles. I just told her that I was sick of school and wanted to be a nurse and could I go to Nurses' Training School now, now, now.

I had made a mess of things anyway. I'd told the school I wanted to be a doctor and they'd switched me in the sixth form to doing the sciences rather than the arts, I having sworn I could catch up in the two years before matriculation. But I'd found the going too hard. The chemistry teacher was eighty-three and couldn't hear. She retired suddenly and a bright young thing came to take over and made me empty unlabelled jars of viscous liquids down the sink with the tap on. The school had to be evacuated because of the fumes, and there was a minor explosion of which I took the brunt. Nor, retiring in terror from the sciences, was I welcomed back to the humanities. The Latin teacher had gone into a sulk because I had abandoned her: the English teacher, with whom she lived, accused me of having a shallow personality. I was a disaster at English Literature. Asked what a writer 'meant' by a sentence I could only reply, 'Why, what is said.' I could never make an answer stretch to more than half a page. And I'd never really wanted to be a doctor in the first place but what else was a girl to say? I wanted to do nothing. I was back in limbo, in the grey featureless landscape.

The matron of the nursing college said I was too young to train as a nurse but why didn't I become a doctor? Rejected again! I was asked to a party by a school-friend. Long dresses and dancing! There would be boys, men, not just brothers, those strange rare things! I had nothing to wear but my mother scraped money together and sent me out to buy some material at Selfridges so she could make a dress for me. I came back with some flimsy gauzy material, pinky greeny, and while unwrapping it she actually swore. Hopeless. She did her best but the dress, when made, turned me into a foam mountain. She said I'd better say I was ill and not go, so I didn't. I went to bed and lay there with my head under the pillows, while ordinary people walked to and fro outside the bars of my bedroom, and I thought my life was probably unsustainable. In the morning, oddly, I was still alive, though I had to take the day off school to keep up the fiction of an illness. I still believe that if only I had chosen some different material I would have met my true love at that party and my whole life would have turned out differently. Goodness, I was cross.

Bad, bad, bad. Limbo lava time again. My friends had forgotten me. Jean Francis, the beautiful girl without doubt and the bottomless purse, whom I loved without reason, no longer even walked with me to the bus. I lay down in the sick-room and a teacher asked me if there was anything the matter with my home life and I said no. Once you began, where would it end? I'd been thrown out of the English class on some trumped-up charge to do with my defiant attitude – I wouldn't sit at their feet and worship, I wouldn't find fault with Tennyson, my essays were stubbornly too short – and was now being told I was too late to take the special entrance classes for Oxbridge, because of my rash flirtation with the sciences. I would have to go to some common or garden provincial university. They really had it in for me, I could see that.

But I now had a splendid new young English teacher, Miss Lutz, who seemed to understand what I was saying. I became enraptured with T. S. Eliot's *Murder in the Cathedral*. '*Seven years since the Archbishop left us –*' I understood that. The loss of the father. I still did not write to mine, but then he had not written to me. I wrote to Molly Banks and she wrote back, but that other life was so far away and long ago. I vowed to know more Roman History than any of my teachers – let them fault me if they could on that – and succeeded.

We moved to a cutesy little cottage on the edge of Hampstead Heath owned by Flora's mother and I could at last ask people home to tea. I was beginning to feel better. I applied to St Andrews University because it was a long way away and I could start again and Jean Francis was going there, and she always seemed to know what she was doing. Moreover, students wore a red flannel gown under which all sartorial errors could be hidden. The London County Council said that if I passed the exams they would pay my tuition fees and give me £167 a term. My mother assured me this represented riches and comfort. I could see that any minute now my proper life was going to begin.

I stayed with Shirley Austin in the country, went swimming at Brighton and got jaundice. I had to do my exams sitting up in my sick-bed with an invigilator on the chair beside the bed. It was rather satisfying to have this special attention. I decided there was no reason to suppose that an anonymous poet quoted in the English exam paper was male and not female, so referred to him or her as 'she' throughout. It was whimsical and unlikely, there being so few female poets around, and exams are no place for whimsy and wishful thinking. I knew that, and worried. And as I found out later I was wrong, and the poet was male. Nevertheless I was forgiven and passed, with credit if not distinction.

St Andrews accepted me, believing I was male, because of my name, Franklin. When I filled in forms for a female hall of residence they queried my gender and discovering I was female said they wouldn't take me: their female quota was full. It was at the time something like one woman to every five men. My mother protested, and the university relented. I would be slipped in under the net. Shirley was going to

Cambridge, Flora to Oxford, but I was going somewhere rich, strange, distant and even older than Oxbridge, and further away. It was okay.

Among the Dispossessed

In the summer of 1949 Shirley and I were packed off by her father to help at a Youth Aliyah camp in France. Youth Aliyah was an organization set up during the war to collect lost Jewish children from all over Europe and establish them in Israel. Three years after the end of the war they were still emerging from hiding, mostly orphaned, many ill, all distressed, but at least alive. Now they were to be returned to health, educated, and taught the beliefs and rituals of Judaism. They were the lucky ones: from being the accursed they were now the chosen, they were to reach the Promised Land. So I was a Christian, so what, said Shirley's father Frank, I could be an honorary Jew: I struck him as one of the persecuted. If I didn't say they wouldn't know, and I could learn something and be of some use. It was time we made ourselves useful, Shirley and I, we spoilt young members of British Jewry and quasi-Jewry. I was seventeen, Shirley eighteen.

The camp was in a chateau near the village of Vierzon, in the Loire. It was a long hot summer: the landscape dreamt. Swallows flew in and out of the eaves. At night there were fireflies in the ferny woods all around. The chateau crumbled, all ruined gables and pinnacles like a palace in a fairy-tale. It reminded me for some reason of Burgess Hill School, a place dedicated to sopping up the disarray of past and present.

But here if the children drooped it was because they were ill: if they ran round like mad things it was because the burden of desperation and danger had suddenly been lifted. This one's mother had been lost to medical experiments, that one had lived with the goats for five years, this eight-year-old girl had syphilis. But next year in Jerusalem! Just after we arrived, to a groan from those in charge, who saw us as little better than sightseers endured for the sake of funding – Frank Austin was a generous patron – another group turned up unannounced at the chateau gates. A young woman teacher, a German, a Christian, bringing in six Jewish teenagers. She had led them into hiding, out of her infant school classroom, in 1940, one step ahead of the Gestapo, pupils listed to go with their families to the camps. None of them had ever gone home again: it was too dangerous. She had kept them together and safe all through the war, over this border, over that: and after the war in the refugee camps. She had come to the conclusion their best hope was in Israel. Now she was here, she could see her job was done. She sat on a chair in the hall and cried. She apologized: she had tried to keep her charges in the knowledge of their religion but they'd grown rusty with the years. Now she would go back to Germany, or what was left of it, to see what had happened to her own family. I hope Yad Vashem eventually traced her and recognized her, and named her one of the Righteous among Nations.

Here was the world at the end of its tether: Youth Aliyah still picking up pieces, and how were they doing it? Why, by murmuring prayers, dancing horas, providing history and keeping rituals. Staff and children seemed caught up in a magic net of restoration, hovering like the fireflies in the space between realities, curing the past, learning forgetfulness. I went out into the woods in the moonlight on my own and sang a Christian hymn, 'Oh God our help in ages past', right through, though quite why I didn't know, except I felt God's presence hovering there, regardless as to how He was categorized.

I got tired of doing nothing and worked with the nurse, swabbing skinny arms for injections, nit-combing, doling out pills. On Fridays we laundered, by hand, so that on Saturday everyone could be dressed in clean clothes, albeit communal, and feel renewed. My French improved: I learned a smattering of Yiddish. Nobody found out I wasn't Jewish. Shirley's father came over to see us and lent me five pounds which stayed on my conscience until the Eighties, when I repaid it. He came in an open Rolls-Royce with a charming French lady friend by his side and took us out to a local restaurant where we had steak béarnaise, the like of which I did not know existed. I had never tasted garlic before, let alone olive oil. Few had, way back then. Then back to the iron institutional beds and stale bread. How the high life kept flitting in and out of the everyday. I felt born to it. You didn't even have to do anything – just hang around and it happened. I thought I would write to my father since at last there was something to say, and started a letter, but didn't finish it.

One Sunday night a coach came to collect a batch of children for shipment to Israel via Marseilles. It was a moonlit night. There was great excitement. The small suitcases were ready and packed. The children sang their happy-mournful folk songs. A fiddler played. One nine-year-old who was meant to be going off with her friends was kept back: she was still testing positive for syphilis. She cried for her sorrow, everyone cried with her, and I realized that until that moment I had seen no one, not even the youngest child, cry at all. The bus went off into the night and was gone into the future, and the nurse said to me, 'So long as the British don't blow up their ship they'll be all right.'

Orphan

When I got back to London the dinky little house on the Heath had been handed back to Louise Goodwin. My mother, with both children starting university and finally out of the home and off her hands, had decided now was the time to start again. She had shut up shop: she had her life back. Now she lived in one of Louise's single-bed-sitting rooms at 1, Belsize Park, but she had all my belongings safely in the suitcase.

There was a week's gap before I started at St Andrews. I would need a dressing-gown, she said, it would be cold up there, and she was making me one, out of a length of nice green woollen cloth. In the meantime I was to stay with my Aunt Mary and Uncle Michael in Amen Court behind St Paul's. It was as if the enduring respectability and permanence of my new surroundings – Amen Court stood ancient but intact among a bomb-blasted landscape – was to compensate for the way home shifted and changed if you so much as looked away. And so indeed it did.

My political relatives were most affable, and pleased I was going to university and had some kind of future, and looked a little less like being a liability than hitherto. They told me my father and Edna had another daughter now, and her name was Barbara. They told me to beware the Socialist Students' Union, it had been infiltrated by Marxists, but to join the Labour Party. Aunt Mary bought us all tickets to *Oklahoma!*

But she came into the dining-room the morning of *Oklahoma!* with a telegram which said my father was dead. He had had a stroke. The world went dead to keep him company. If he was dead to me already, as I realized I had supposed, why was I crying? Aunt Mary was crying too. Well, she was his sister. We discussed whether we should or should not go to *Oklahoma!* and decided we would. *Poor Judd is dead, that lonely soul has fled.* That got to me. The next day I cried some more, on the top of a bus, in public. I wanted to say to people 'my father is dead', but what would they care? I developed a nasty boil under my right armpit and had to go to have it lanced. My mother came to collect me from my Aunt Mary's and took me along. Pus flew all over the place. The doctor, who was Jewish, looked at me with slow, kind eyes and said, 'Is there anything else the matter with you?' and my mother replied for me, smartly – 'There's absolutely nothing wrong with her.' So I didn't even tell him. She never reckoned fathers much, and didn't approve of grieving anyway, it smacked of self-pity. My ears blocked with wax and I couldn't hear for a time.

I actually had a new suitcase, and a nice new sensible green woollen dressing-gown inside and I stood with it on the platform at King's Cross Station on the night of my eighteenth birthday, 22 September 1949, and my mother waved me goodbye. She was free at last to go her own way. Jane was already in Exeter, so I didn't know what she thought about my father dying. I wore a black armband as people did in those days, there being so little money or time for full mourning. Jean Francis, who was going up to St Andrews at the same time, saw the band and expressed sympathy. I took it off during the journey because what was the point? It just seemed a stupid kind of ostentation, relating to an age so long ago and far away it didn't matter. Jean Francis sat in another carriage, anyway. I was alone, and back in limbo.

The custom of wearing full black when members of the family, friends or royalty die has fallen into abeyance. Nowadays most people wear black most of the time anyway: go to a literary party and one would imagine everyone there was in perpetual mourning for their lives. A glimmer of pink or a bright striped stocking but mostly black, black, black, and I am the worst offender.

I find I never buy the stations when playing Monopoly. They seem so desolate: centres from which you launch yourself into the unknown and no good will come, let alone profit. I buy Kentish Town and Islington and the cheaper brownish properties, because I feel at home there, and avoid the utilities because they make me think of bills. I love Mayfair, though, and Regent Street. They seem so glamorous, though it's mostly other players land on them. Some people just have the knack of it: the dice fall in accordance with their self-image.

Student

St Andrews is a small mediaeval town which perches on the edge of the cold North Sea a very long way from anywhere. It has a famous golf course and a university, some cobbled streets with crosses etched into them to mark the bonfires in which Protestants and Catholics burned each other alive, and a ruined castle, with black stone crags to set against the wild sky. It looks very fine indeed as the sun sets over the ruins and filters pink into the town. There is usually a bitterly cold east wind, and in my day the grey streets were bright with red-gowned students running for the shelter of houses scarcely warmer in than out.

I lived at first, in my newly half-orphaned and friendless state, in a boarding-house which overlooked the sea, run by a Polish ex-airman. A Polish squadron had been stationed at Leuchars airport, just outside the town, during the war, and many airmen had preferred to stay than to go back to their now communist homeland. There was thin flabby white toast for breakfast: everything was thin and strange, including the ex-army blankets so ubiquitous at the time. They were made of some kind of stiff dark grey compacted fibre, rather than wool, and had a red stripe running through them. They were not cosy. The sea from my window was strangely colourless and flat: a limbo sea. Sound stayed muted although my ears were clear of wax.

I made an effort to join in student life. I went to Chapel with the others on Sundays, wearing my red gown and a mortarboard and felt silly. We walked down to the pier after the service to meet the visiting pastor, as was the custom, who was never to appear, having been drowned in a storm on his way from Dundee one Sunday several hundred years ago, and felt sillier. I was to encounter his ghost later.

I went to a hop at the Students' Union and was asked to dance by a plain redheaded Scot in glasses who had an erection under his kilt. I thought in the time-honoured way perhaps it was his pipe, but where does a man in a kilt keep his pipe? I had no idea how difficult dancing was, since I had not done it before – in those days it was waltzes and foxtrots, with the body held still – and kept treading on his toes. What with one thing and another I felt embarrassed and confused, and when he asked me to go walking with him on the sands I broke away and ran for the boarding-house, and never went to another student hop. A hop! It was a silly, dismissive kind of word, anyway, as if those who went amounted to nothing, and hoped for nothing.

I had lost all interest in Jean Francis, who lived safely in a hall of residence where you were allowed to have men in your room up to nine o'clock at night but only if you had pulled the bed out first and put it in the corridor. I made three good friends, Serena, Hilda and Ellen, all from what now would be called dysfunctional families – like appeals to like, it was clear from the start – who preferred to live a life unprotected by wardens.

We rented a whole great stone house, 12 Queens Gardens, from a trusting elderly widow who was off to New Zealand for a year. She was not wise. We did not understand house-work, nor I'm afraid had any desire to. We let candle wax fall on polished mahogany surfaces: we did not realize that coffee cups leave rings and cigarette stubs leave burns, or that un-removed orange peel and sweet papers lead to sticky growths in the wastepaper basket: that if you leave plates on the floor people step on them, and break them.

We could see nothing but the inside of our heads, as we tried to deduce the nature of the universe from our books, our teachers, and each other, and what was reflected back from our mirrors and the eyes of men. It was 1950: we were into the second half of the twentieth century, and the nation's universities were still full of ex-servicemen, whose education the war had postponed. These were men, not boys, some had killed, and nearly been killed: they did not put up with nonsense, from girls or from their tutors.

Now there was a war in Korea and the nation's young men were still not free of their martial obligations: they were conscripted as National Servicemen. What did we girls care, what did we know? We were very social: we gave parties. It was the age of dating and petting, pre-pill, pre-Dutch cap. Contraception and war was what men did. We lay around on the floor on cushions and drank cheap red Chianti from half-wickered bottles, which served when empty as candlesticks, and tried to lose our virginities.

This was not so easy as we had supposed, partly because we were not quite sure, in our pictureless, windowless, wordless world when it came to sex, how to set about it. Men were more gentlemanly than you might ever have supposed. We were too young, too trusting and too virginal to offer much temptation to decent men and the thought of pregnancy, in the days when abortion was illegal and dangerous, was even more daunting to the boys than the girls.

One by one my friends managed to steer the back-seat kissing and hugging into actual sexual congress, and joined the selective ranks of those who monthly feared being 'late' – and anxiety was famous for making you so – and wished they were virgins again, but I didn't for a long time, long enough to decide it was my fate to be unattractive to men.

Ellen said I was too clever, and it put men off. My mother had always implied much the same thing: that men preferred women who were restful, and not too bright: they didn't want to be made to laugh for fear of being laughed at. It was in any case generally held that the way to condemn women to spinsterhood was to send them to university, give them careers, and allow them an opinion on public affairs. Common wisdom also had it that the way to get a man to marry you was not to have sex with him, but to claim the right to be married as a virgin. In the end the man would capitulate and marry you. It was the same wisdom offered to Polly Peachum in the eighteenth century, back in the days of *The Beggar's Opera*.

> *Oh Polly you might have toyed and kissed,*
> *Been wooed at length but never won.*
> *By keeping men off, you keep them on.*

It was not a wisdom which appealed to me and my friends: we would not stoop to anything so low and cheap. But it was essential to have a suitor to make these decisions *about*, and I simply didn't have one and they did. My preoccupation as to how a woman was expected to win a man and keep him, and yet retain her human dignity was to emerge seventeen years later in novel form, in *The Fat Woman's Joke*. Today's young woman, looking for Mr Right, her self-esteem much elevated compared to ours, is a great deal choosier than we ever were. But then our Mr Darcys had feet of gold, hers has feet of clay.

I was not sophisticated in my search for Mr Right. I didn't know enough. I looked what I was – a nice, non-sexy English eighteen-year-old virgin. I dressed in shapeless twinsets and wore a shirt underneath the jumper with its little white collar sticking out and wrapped my red gown around me, hiding attributes and imperfections equally.

So much is a matter of presentation, but I didn't know that then, and it never came instinctively to me as it did to some women. I was bad at adornment and still am. Girls who grow up without fathers are said to be bad at flirting. I did not know how to set about it. It was not for ten years further down the non-virginal line that I gained any sexual self-confidence at all. And that was only because I worked as a hostess in a strip club and observed that it wasn't beauty men were after but availability, and their own certainty of not being rejected or humiliated. Sit on a barstool in a skimpy dress and swing your legs and look as if you charged for your favours and perfection of leg simply does not matter. Male enthusiasm for you knows no bounds, at least for the next hour or so of drinking and consorting, and they will even offer to marry you, if only to take you away from all this, before going home to their wives.

But I didn't know any of this at the time. The women's magazines of the day were no help: they consisted of page after page of knitting, recipes and how to treat arthritis. And they featured the Horlicks ads. '*Darling, you look tired, he said. A man in his kindness can strike to the depths of a woman's heart.*' For tired read old, for old read short of sleep, for short of sleep read Horlicks. I read the ads carefully, since they seemed to know rather more about what went on in the real world than the body text, and searched for truth in the pages of novels, Evelyn Waugh, Aldous Huxley, Orwell, L. P. Hartley. But no woman I met in their pages ever seemed to apply to me. Nor, oddly, did those written by the few women writers around. Their emotions were all: the

199

practicalities of life were not attended to: how did you make a living, who cleaned the floors, who ever lost a ration book? The domestic was evidently not a fit subject for literature. Madame Bovary and Anna Karenina seemed to me objects of envy, unreasonably condemned to misery and death by their writers.

Men with Feet of Gold

The first man to whom I accorded feet of gold was – naturally enough – Ellen's boyfriend, Ray Barnes. Well I would, wouldn't I, after her dismissal of me as any worthy rival. Oh, the dark, male, saturnine-ness of it all. He rode a Harley-Davidson. He wore a leather jacket; he smoked French cigarettes, Gauloises. He was working class, in his mid-twenties; he had done his National Service. He was handsome, angry and chippy: he was James Dean-ish, inciting in others the feeling that he was dangerous and didn't quite know how to behave. I thought he was wonderful: I blushed and stumbled when he came into a room. The sound of a motorbike coming up the street at night still turns my heart over. He was coming to visit Ellen but when Ellen was away he would come to visit me.

Ellen's father disapproved of him as a suitor for his daughter. She had no mother to disapprove: her name was never mentioned in the house and Ellen had no idea what had become of her. One night when Ellen was away he and I sat in front of the gas fire drinking Cointreau and talking about our families. He was an only child: his parents put great hope in him. He suggested I change into something more comfortable.

'What sort of thing?' I asked, puzzled. My clothes were perfectly comfortable, and in any case mostly hidden by the red flannel gown which students wore to keep out the northern cold.

'A dressing-gown,' he suggested. 'Or whatever it is that women wear.' So I went to my bedroom and came down in the green woollen dressing-gown my mother had made as a goodbye present, and he laughed quite a lot and said it wasn't quite what he'd had in mind but never mind.

He turned off the light and we rolled around on the floor in the dark, one limb exchangeable with another and before I knew it spirit had split from body, I had in some way de-materialized, and was hovering in the top left-hand corner of the room looking down on a stirring, humping bundle on the floor in the glimmer of the gasfire, which was made by him and me. I had joined the ranks of the women. Though I still could not tell you – because it was dark, because of the Cointreau, because the experience was all sensation, un-blessed or uncursed by the naming of parts, and I was up there near the ceiling anyway – what exactly it was that went on. Other than that now, I assumed, I owned a bit of him and he owned a bit of me, and whatever was to happen next, and what happened next would be influenced by this event. I have never quite lost the sense, even leaving aside the begetting of children, that it is through our sexual associations that the fates work out their plans, no matter how trivial, neurotic or one-night-standish these comings-together may appear at the time.

Single acts of intercourse can topple governments. Single acts can break families, or in one way or another come bouncing back at us through our lives, changing their course. Forget the name, forget the face, but nothing is without result.

After the manner of the times we did not speak of what had occurred, to one another or to anyone else. I assumed that Ellen had first right to his attentions, she having been there first, and so forth, and being a proper woman and me not. Ray went on sleeping with Ellen in the top left bedroom, turning up late once or twice a week to spend the night, and went about with her to meetings and societies. If she was away – and she would go home to York from time to time – he would turn right instead of left and come into my bedroom. I would like to say I kept the sheets clean for him but I don't suppose I did. It was too early in the world's history for washing machines or detergents and everything had to be washed (if it ever was) by hand, with Sunlight soap, in the sink or the bath, and why would we bother? There were far more exciting things to be done with our time.

My mother came to visit me, all the way by coach to save money – 'It's like coming to the end of a long, flat, washed-out dishcloth,' she complained – and cleaned up for us. She continued to clean up after me until she was eighty-five, when she stopped feeling so responsible for me – seeing the things I never did; the dirt that collects behind taps, stains on the carpets so familiar you don't see them, crumbs in the cutlery drawer.

She was sorry but not surprised, on this first occasion of visiting an autonomous household of mine, to find me without a boyfriend. She was still convinced I was a lesbian. I could hardly tell her about my semi-involvement with Ray, let alone the monthly fear of pregnancy. In those days men were in charge of contraception. They practised coitus interruptus, if they could remember to, and so far as I know no man ever used a condom. They were deliberately punctured in their factories, the story went, by minions of the pope.

Anything other than the missionary position was perverse. Oral sex was simply not on the agenda, neither were female orgasms, since we didn't know they happened. It was our role to pleasure men – they would persuade and we would resist. Mutual desire could mount to intolerable levels. It was the girl's duty not to arouse a man unless she was prepared to satisfy him – it was bad for him to be thwarted. 'Being late' was a cause for panic. Illegitimate babies meant shame and disgrace. There were no benefits, no counsellors, no free housing. Abortion was illegal, and cost more money than anyone had. Two hundred pounds cash was the going rate and how were the likes of us to afford that? If abortion went wrong, medically, as it frequently did, and you ended up in hospital, you would be arrested and hauled off to prison even as you came out of the anaesthetic.

Even given all this, sex was worth it: it was an affirmation of trust in fate and trust in men. We were the five per cent of the nation's women who went to university, and though most of us would work only until we got married and had children, like anyone else – secretary at the Foreign Office was a favourite job – and then give up all academic aspirations, for the time being we were *special*. God would not let us get pregnant.

Ray of the golden feet, to everyone's shock and disappointment, married a girlfriend no one knew about and they went off to live in California. He worked as a psychologist for the

Douglas Aircraft Corporation, designing cockpit and warning system layouts. His wife died within ten years: he came back to London briefly in 1963, and found me married and pregnant, and Ellen in a state: she had been living with a car salesman, but had woken one morning to find that he had run off with her car, her bank balance and her typewriter. Her father had given her up as a bad job: she took after her mother. But Ray came to Ellen's rescue and married her. They went to live in Orange, California. Sometimes he wrote to me, which always moved me greatly: it was so very much the male habit then to discard the past and the women who had inhabited it, that I was surprised and pleased to be still included in his life. He was working on the new DC 10, one of which was to crash outside Paris twenty years later and kill my best friend Claire.

Claire and her sister Sandra were brought up in London's East End, and were of Jewish immigrant stock. They had been brutally evacuated when the war began: their mother had turned up as usual to collect them from the school gate and had found the school empty and closed. The caretaker refused to tell the mothers where the children had been taken, in case Hitler found out, and though the mothers stormed the Town Hall, the authorities did the same.

Some said this was rather less to do with fear of Hitler's bombs and the expected German invasion, than part of a social experiment – if you took the children out of the slums, separated them from their parents, and put them in the healthy English countryside they would pick up honest rural virtues and values. As well snatch today's children out of the sink estates, and despatch them all to live with Cumbrian hill farmers and hope they will end up shepherds.

It didn't work, of course. The parents could not find out where their children were, but the children knew where their parents were. Those who had access to telephones used them: those who hadn't simply set out to walk the hundreds of miles home, as if they were so many uprooted cats. Those who couldn't, or didn't, escape, for the most part had a hard time of it. The English countryside was as much filled with villains and opportunists as anywhere else: scandalous stories abounded of evacuees treated as skivvies and slaves, underfed, overworked, and leaping with lice. Claire's and Sandra's experiences turned up in the third novel I wrote – *Female Friends*. Both lived briefly, but with great aplomb, and made names for themselves in the London of the Sixties. It is the sum of the achievement of past lives which feeds into the future and makes it what it is. One evening Sandra wrote the lyrics to 'Sweet Georgie Fame', and whenever it's sung she's there, forget death. She died of asthma – or rather of the first of the inhalers which in those early days delivered far too massive a dose: just as the early female contraceptive pill went in for overkill, and sometimes did.

Claire lived quaintly in a little mediaeval house on the banks of the Thames facing St Paul's. It had not yet been defined as 'heritage', it was just where she lived. Catherine of Aragon, poor thing, disembarked here on her way to marry Henry VIII. In my mind their veiled and tragic fates become the same. Claire was not beautiful – indeed, my mother was once driven to ask why, since she had so plain a face, did she go round behaving as if she was the most attractive woman in the world? My mother's generation found it difficult to understand that personality and not just passive good looks contributed to a woman's attractions.

Claire collected artefacts, the quaint, the beautiful, the battered and the old. Every surface in her house, quaint enough as it was, so quaint that sightseers would peer in the window as we were having tea, or knock at the door and demand to be taken on a guided tour, was covered with beads, cards, bottles, shells, boxes, carvings, paintings, fairground trivia, embroideries, ships made out of matchsticks, funeral accessories, and so on: everything the river washed up and junkshops had to offer that took her fancy. There scarcely seemed room for people but Blossom Dearie the singer would stay with her, and sweet Georgie Fame would call by.

She had a difficult husband, a psychiatrist, and three sons. But I can see he would have had a difficult time of it too, if only finding somewhere to lie down in the house, what with the objets d'art, the guests and the music. They divorced, disagreeably, and when it was all but over she was asked by friends to go on holiday to Turkey. Claire asked me if I thought she should, at this particular juncture, and I said no, she ought to stay quietly at home and wait for the children to settle, but she took no notice. It was on the way home from the holiday that her DC 10, its cockpit and controls devised by golden-footed Ray, crashed. I saw her quaint Victorian style shoe on television, lying in the foreground of the gruesome wreckage in the forest.

Claire said to me once, 'I always thought by the time you were forty you had everything sorted out and could live happily ever after. But it's not like that, is it?' And I'd said no. Now there were no more years left to sort everything, and no Claire to talk to about how it was to be done. I don't get on an aircraft to this day without thinking of her and I always choose Cointreau if offered a liqueur, which people find very odd of me. It is not a sophisticated drink. But we owe these ceremonies to those we knew in the past.

The accident preyed on Ray's mind and he became depressed and a few months later Ellen came home with the shopping and found he had shot himself through the head in his study. I have always thought that suicide is catching: when we were students Ray's best friend had killed himself, taking poison one winter's morning in the fields outside St Andrew's. Those who are left behind seldom recover, and Ray hadn't, and didn't. No one should give back the gift of life, unless they are very old and full of tears, when the body outlives the spirit, when they should be allowed to join the others who've already gone.

So I lost two people in the Paris crash. Ellen came back to London, and we smudged Ray's death certificate so that it looked as if Ray had died of natural causes. We did this for his parents' sake. Ray had taken me to visit them once, trusting me not to look askance at the plaster ducks on their wall, the tropical aquarium in their parlour, as others of his new acquaintance might. I felt we were doing as he would have wished, forging away, almost as if Ray had foreseen his own end, taking me to see them out of the blue: and Claire, fleeing on holiday, had stepped on that aircraft to complete a circle.

Fiction never seems a patch on real life: so far-fetched, people will complain about novels, especially mine. But the objectors are often the ones whose own lives seem remarkable to everyone except themselves. Write the truth and no one believes you: it's too alarming. So you might as well make it up. I seldom do research. If you as a writer don't know already, or can't find out very quickly indeed, forget it. If you can think of something, someone or other in the real world is pretty soon going to do it if they haven't already. You only have to read the novels of Arthur C. Clarke, or Philip K. Dick, science-fiction writers, to know this to be true.

In Another Part of Town

My mother had moved to St Ives in Cornwall, which was about as far as you could get from St Andrews. She had shut her eyes and put a pin in the map and St Ives was where it landed, so that was where she went. It was a good pin, a good place to go, a haven for the artists and craftsmen of the Forties and Fifties. The climate was mild, the light transfiguring. The St Ives Group was in full swing. Peter Lanyon, Ben Nicholson, Alfred Wallis painted, Barbara Hepworth sculpted, Bernard Leach made pottery, Guido Morris printed, the Nance brothers handcrafted their shapely furniture. The St Ives Group, such was their talent and temperament, plotted, conspired, bad-mouthed each other, and grew world-famous though scarcely rich. The Tate Gallery now has an extension there, a glowing, translucent structure, perched equably between cliff and sea, though it can scarcely afford the once cheap and local, now astronomically priced and international, works of art it commemorates.

My mother lived at first in a little cottage at a crossroads called Boswednac, between St Ives and Penzance, in sight of the Eagles Nest, the house where D. H. Lawrence and Frieda lived during World War I, and not much else. Even the Eagles Nest was hidden in a grove of trees as if it had no right to be there. It is a bleak and ill-omened Wuthering Heights of a place.

The Lawrences were accused of being German spies – not perhaps surprisingly. Frieda was German and from the von Richthofen air-ace family, and made no secret of her hope that Germany would win the war. She liked to be contrary. The Lawrences lived a stormy life: friends would come down to stay and be kept awake all night by murderous rows and, terrified, would plan to flee – only to find David and Frieda sitting serene and peaceful at breakfast the next morning, sex having healed all wounds. No wonder he set such store by it.

I wrote a TV play about Frieda and Lawrence for the BBC in the early Eighties: it was beautifully cast and elegantly directed but it was never transmitted. I had – at the time still fairly ignorant of the laws of copyright – quoted something like six lines of Lawrence text and the Lawrence estate refused permission to release it. The full displeasure of the BBC landed upon me. Forget the script editor who had passed the screenplay without comment, the minimal length of the quote, the fact that the passage could easily be edited out – never, I was told, had a drama had to be withdrawn like this and it was all my fault.

The BBC sent me to a copyright barrister in the Inns of Court for scolding: he rocked up and down with his eyes closed and told me something I did believe, that the law of copyright was so complex the only thing to hold on to was that good faith was what mattered. Ignorance of the law, alas, did not count as good faith, and whether or not the passage I had quoted was in the public domain would have to be tested in a court of law, the Lawrence estate was being so adamant.

The row died down, the play did not go out: many were disappointed: acting careers which might have blossomed never did. A year later it became apparent that the play was the victim of an internal BBC row: the Series Department had bought up all the rights to the Lawrence estate because they intended to do a six-parter on Frieda and Lawrence; our hapless one-off play out of the Drama Department would have stolen Series' thunder: it could not be allowed to happen. I was just the fall guy; the whole matter of breached copyright was disingenuous.

Visit my beloved mother in Cornwall in the early Fifties and find a bleak, stunning, haunted landscape: criss-crossed by stone walls, stirred by rumours of goblins and mermaids, speaking stones, giants and curses, and scarcely a fit place for humans at all. Tourists were only just beginning to come, lured by Daphne du Maurier and tales of Manderley. The nearest noticeable village to where she lived was Zennor, a tiny fishing hamlet tucked into the coast by rocks, where it is said a mermaid once lured a young fisherman down to the sea to his death. (My husband's grandmother's family, quite coincidentally, came from Zennor and are buried in the churchyard there.) It was a romantic place, but not benign.

My mother picked reeds and flax, wove them into baskets and once a week walked into Penzance, seven miles away, to sell them at the market there. She'd buy her food supplies for the week and take the bus home. Other people, she had come to think, were absurdly fussy about their home comforts. Life could, and should, be lived minimally. And anyway, as ever, she had left herself no other option.

Jane and I, our grants spent, would hitchhike down from our universities when we could, to be with her during the vacations. It could take me three or four days to get there in those pre-motorway times, but it was always an adventure: you got to know your country well, if only by standing on the side of the road in the rain as darkness fell and staring at its stubborn immobility. I got to know the blowy wildness of Shap Fell, the dull peace of Grantham, the smoky blackness of the midland towns: to marvel at how a ridge of hills or a river would divide dialect from dialect. You could improve your hitchhiking technique as you could improve anything: you learned where to stand with your rucksack beside you, and how to look, respectable yet pitiful, girlish but not forward. The nation still trusted itself not to rape, pillage, serial-kill or take undue advantage of its young women.

Stand at the side of the road long enough and someone would always offer to help: the nation still felt like family: everyone looked pretty much like family, and spoke like family, and if the poor relation could afford another way of getting around obviously he or she would. 'No blame attached' as the *I Ching*, the Chinese Book of Oracles was to have it, but that was further on into the future, in the Sixties when it became popular, part of the New Age's excursions into wishful thinking, aromatherapy, karma, crystal healing and the rest.

Once arrived in St Ives for the summer, by courtesy of my fellow-citizens, I would go to my on-going job as a waitress at the Copper Kettle down on the waterfront, opened in the summer for the tourist business. The joy of pushing aside a plate and finding a tip was very great, though at the Copper kettle very rare: the view over St Ives bay was charming but the food was plain to the point of absurdity – for lunch and dinner all that was served was a bowl of watery tomato soup, followed by a thin slice of ham, three small boiled potatoes, a spoonful of canned peas, and then a scoop of ice cream. Customers would take their discontent out on the staff.

But behind the scenes we had a riveting time – the woman who peeled the hundreds of potatoes served daily was discovered to have active TB and had to go: I ran over my big toe with an industrial vacuum cleaner (and have had no feeling in it ever since). The owner insisted on driving me all the way home to Zennor every evening to the displeasure of his wife, while his daughter taught us student staff the practice of what is known now as bulimia, but then seemed just a sensible way of both eating what you wanted and staying thin. The words 'eating disorder', like 'racism' and 'sexism', were yet to be coined. The world seemed more full of subtle variation then, and oddly enough, more open to change. If you didn't know the word 'bulimic' or the word 'anorexic' it was hard to become one. It was just something you did, occasionally, and sometimes didn't, and no big deal. It is as if a net made up of pigeon-holes has been thrown over us, and the more we struggle against it, the more enmeshed and helpless we become.

My mother, her simple life palling – she was only after all in her forties – moved into St Ives and found a less arduous and more companionable job, running the Nance furniture showroom down on the quayside. Every graceful wooden line was exquisite, talked about, conspired over. The Nance brothers were gentlemen craftsmen in the William Morris tradition. During the war furniture sold had to have the Utility Kite Mark on it, to certify that it met basic government requirements and was no more lavish than was strictly necessary. It was stable, practical, and if plywood would do, it did. But now the nation was beginning to feel the need for the exotic, the luxurious and the aesthetically pleasing.

For a whole generation of intelligent women, the pursuit of 'austerity' as it was called, during the war and for five years after it, had been almost a pleasure. Unable to function outside the home, they at least had something to do inside it. Making do and mending, turning sheets to middle (when the middle became thin from wear you slit the sheet down the middle and sewed the firmer edges together). You ended up with a sheet with a seam down the middle but discomfort was seen as something which, albeit obscurely, helped the war effort. 'Doing without' was a virtue. 'Stretching food' was an exercise in skill and paying attention. The best underwear was made from the silk parachutes of downed airmen, which would vanish as soon as they hit the ground. Money did not come into it: in times of rationing and shortages all women started equal and those with the most functional and practical intelligence won. A repressed sexuality did, I think, come into it, especially in those with a puritan disposition – 'If I can't have that I won't have anything' – and gave the pursuit of austerity a sometimes manic flavour. For a generation of women, now fading into threadbare old age, these were the good days, and they lamented their passing.

We now lived in a little seaman's cottage on the cliffs in The Warren. It smelt of salt and seagulls, and in stormy weather sea spray was flung against the windows. To this day I dream about storms, tides, and ocean waves crashing against windows. At night I'd go down and swim in the sea in the moonlight: it was erotic in the extreme: how the ocean could embrace you if it had a mind to. Cornish waters were full of mermaids, luring men into the sea, hungry for them. I identified. I lay on the cliffs in the sun with a fellow-student, down to visit me from St Andrews, and knew that if I stretched out my hand to his, or he to mine, our whole lives would change, we would make babies, get married, our futures would go this way not that. Neither of us moved. Such pivotal moments haunt us for ever. I can still feel the sun, smell the heather, hear the larks: perhaps they happen at junctions in our lives when alternative universes intersect; where the parallels get a sense of each other, where what could be comes face to face with what is going to be. But then I've always had a weakness for science fiction. It is gratifying to know that the alternative universes one senses, from time to time, are now open to mathematical proof and quite serious scientific speculation.

It was in St Ives, in 1953, that my sister Jane, then aged twenty-four, met Guido Morris, a good twenty-five years older than she was, and nothing would do but they married. They met at a party up at the Smoke House – a rather crude structure originally used for smoking kippers – up on the cliffs above the North Shore. The Smoke House happened to be owned by Ina, the same Ina who once had an affair with my father. Ina would turn up in Jane's and my life from time to time, as if appointed by fate to be a rather unchancy guardian angel. Her mother Winifred was my mother's friend: where my mother went Winifred followed, and vice versa, and Ina tagged along behind, at any rate in the intervals between her many dramatic affairs and marriages.

When I was fifteen it was Ina who pointed out that I should be doing science not the arts if I wanted to be a doctor like my father, and that caused many problems. On the other hand, when it was my shift to be married to a man twenty-five years older than me, Ina turned up out of the blue to say, 'If your father could see you now he would turn in his grave,' so I was moved to run away. That was certainly for the best.

I do not know that this marriage between Jane and Guido could be said to have been for the best, although from it sprung three excellent and handsome children, all of whom took firsts at university, and now live settled, useful, entertaining and fruitful lives.

I cannot remember what Jane wore to this wedding, but all the now-celebrated artists of the St Ives Group came along to it. Guido, born Douglas, was the son of a West Country clergyman. He was an artist of no mean quality – handprinting volumes of poetry, catalogues of art exhibitions, and so on. His work can be seen in the Tate, or whenever the work of the St Ives Group goes on exhibition, as it does from time to time.

He had a classical education and a deep, rich, wonderful voice; there was a time when, as a guard on the London Underground, he worked as an announcer at Victoria Station, and rush-hour passengers would stop in their tracks just to listen to him. He was driven out of St Ives by his debts: as my mother was the first to point out, it is hard to support a family if you rely on handcrafts. It was a marriage which would spring apart and come together again, over and over, with another child every time, and was simply not lived as most marriages are.

But then neither were Jane and Guido as most people are. Both were visionaries. As with John Dodd I rather wished sometimes that Guido would invite me to take Jane's place, but as with John Dodd, the thought did not occur to him. I was far too sensible and sane for their liking. And besides, I wrote prose, not poetry. I have never written poetry, though I can write just about anything else, to order. It seems to me to be forbidden territory. Siblings tend to divide the talents up among themselves when young: Jane took poetry, and drawing, I took prose fiction, both of us left music to Nona and morality to our mother. I quote from 'The Poet to His Wife', which Jane was to write a few years later. She saw Guido, rather than herself, as the poet: women were destined to be the muse, not the creator, no matter what they put on canvas, wrote on the page.

> *Money-and-law,*
> *Stands at the nursery door.*
> *You married me – what for?*
> *My love was not to get you clothes or bread,*
> *But make more poems in my head.*
>
> *I've fathered children*
> *God!*
> *Am I to die*
> *To turn them out as fits a mother's eye?*
>
> *I wanted mothering and they, this brood,*
> *Step in and take my daily food.*
>
> *Money-and-law*
> *Stands at the nursery door.*
> *Money-and-law, money-and-law,*
> *Had the world in its maw.*

Or as Cyril Connolly said, there is no more sombre enemy of good art than the pram in the hall. The modern world is kinder to poets than it used to be: a man or woman can have a family and be a poet too, now we live in a welfare state and women can earn a living and look after their own children well enough. But the poetry is perhaps not as good as it used to be. Many good things come out of sacrifice.

A Sentimental Education

St Ives was a glimpse of the adult world: the great advantage it had over the child's world was that you could leave it when you wanted. Later on husbands, children and duty would keep one rooted to the spot, but twenty just seemed a good age to be: where your feet moved, you moved too, without guilt or remorse to keep you in more than one place at a time, headwise.

It was time to get back to St Andrews and the students. I cannot say that I took my education seriously. It was my ambition to get through the three-year course without once speaking to a member of the academic staff, and I almost succeeded. The system of tuition was lecture-based: we went to vast lecture halls and slept away our drunken and sexual excesses, read the books on the reading list and went to the library to write essays. At the end of three years we would get an MA. Classwork would be graded but not the final degree itself. I got a First in Economics two years running, and it was in Economics that my system hit the rocks: the modern notion of seminars was introduced and I had to speak quite often to Professor Nisbet. He once told me that money supply had no more effect on the trade cycle (as boom and bust was then called) than sunspots. A clutch of my successors under Professor Nisbet, who were to become Mrs Thatcher's advisors, went so far in defiance of him that they became the most Hayekaan of free marketeers. Oh, nest of vipers!

There was no problem in failing to address Professor Knox of Moral Philosophy, since he would not speak to or even acknowledge the presence of women – there were four of us – in his class. He spoke exclusively to the male students, maintaining that women were incapable of moral judgement or objectivity. We female students did not object: it was just another of the widely held views of the time. (Henry James had already explained earlier that this was why women could not write drama. They would never be able to achieve the ping-pong effect of conflicting views: their emotions would keep getting in the way.) Knox was a remarkable teacher and we considered ourselves privileged to be allowed to attend his classes at all. Young men of today who wish to attend classes in gender studies suffer the same kind of dis-crimination at the hands of their female professors, I believe. I for one took it as some kind of extra sign – along with my apparent inability to attract the men I fancied but only the ones I didn't – that I wasn't a proper woman. What else was to be concluded?

Professor Knox had been forced to accept women into his classes by some kind of convocation degree, as the world moved on and required women in the labour market (let us not suppose that 'progress' is anything other than the converging dynamics of the needs of capitalism and changing technology), but resisted fiercely. He refused to mark our essays and failed us on principle. But the marking of essays is not so important as the writing of them, and grades were of little importance in those heady days when education was for its own sake, and not to get you a job. There were precious few jobs for women to get anyway, in which a degree made any difference, unless you were a scientist, or meant to give up your personal life and go into the Civil Service. So pottering along behind the men, I learned from Knox how to tackle vast and impenetrable subjects on the page – 'What is the nature of good?' for example, or 'Is it legitimate to break a promise?' – by the method quite popular at the time, much used by Professor Joad of BBC Radio's *Brains Trust*, then in its Reithian way also, if only inadvertently, doing its best to educate women as they went about their housewifely tasks. That is to say, you first demanded of the examiner what he meant by 'good', or 'promise', and having decided for him, then began to make your answer.

Husbands complain that I am argumentative: critics complain that I am over the top in my assertions. I blame St Andrews. We had an agreeable way of conducting dialectic: it goes thus. I say something extreme, you say something equally extreme in denial: I listen to what you say and amend my view a little: you do the same for me: thus in the end compromise is reached: we are both nearer the other's views than when we started. It is like a successful trade-union negotiation: you go in asking for a third more than you know you will get: management goes in offering a third less. Both sides settle satisfactorily. But these days I say my over-the-top thing, wait for the comeback, and there is none. Or else silence, and then uproar. I suppose it is true: I expect an argument, like a child: others prefer to receive balanced and authoritative adult statements.

Psychology obliged me to struggle with the laws of probability, and it was Cyril Burt's work on twins which gave me an enduring interest in identity and the uses of nature and nurture, which was to surface again and again in novel form. Burt's work turned out to be more speculation than science – he had rigged his results, it was later alleged – but his guesses were more apt, interesting and true, I always thought, than anything anyone else was prepared to offer for decades to come and I personally never held his creative science against him.

I was reduced to doing the same thing in one of the only jobs I ever had which related in any way to my having of a degree, when a proficiency was assumed of me that I simply didn't have, at the headquarters of a market research agency. I was to work out the statistical basis for prospective field trials, compose the appropriate questions, and collate the results when they came through. It was, as so often before computer technology came along, what would now be seen as the work of ten plus a computer. The developed world is in search of occupation and goes to great lengths to find it.

I realized one day that I had based a few million pounds' worth of research, now ongoing all over the country – customer response to the new hair conditioners, I seem to remember, and how much extra they would be prepared to pay for what degree of silky hair – on a statistical error. What was I to do? Own up? To whom? I was the only one in the office who even vaguely understood the technicalities of what I was doing. Too late to recall the research teams. So when the results came in, like Cyril Burt, I re-jigged the figures to fit what I reckoned ought to be the case, even if I had no real evidence. My employers were mean, overlooked the offices from a glass box to make sure no one was slacking, wouldn't let you stop to have a coffee, read the newspaper or rest your brain, and I thought they deserved no better. I knew in any case, having been obliged to stand on street corners and accost total strangers myself, just how much misinformation got into the system anyway.

Women would pay as much for the conditioner as they would for the shampoo, I told them. Even a little bit more. Shampoo is to do with cleanliness, conditioner is to do with beauty. The future was to bear me out.

But I shouldn't have done it, I should have confessed, and I've never believed a poll result since. There's always someone like me back in the office, disaffected or prone to error, or both.

Dreams, Ghosts, Places and Terrors

I still have nightmares that I am faced by a statistical examination and can't cope: it ranks in disagreeableness with the other one when I am on stage, with an elaborate role to play and don't know the lines, or the one where I sit in the audience, second row extreme right of the stage, and I have written the play and everyone boos and I realize I have no clothes on. Though these dreams are as nothing compared to the supernatural horror ones, when I am confronted by evil in its purer forms: these are rare and get rarer, but they plagued my childhood. I remember being pursued by a vending machine when I was six: I know that sounds absurd; but the fear remains with me to this day. This was in a house built on a site in Akaroa, just north of Christchurch, where there had been a massacre during the Maori wars. Jane and

I spent a lot of time with our heads under the bedclothes too scared to come downstairs, until a lady in white came and sat on our bed, after which we wouldn't go upstairs. These are the nightmares which come from outside, and don't just brew up like a storm in the inside of the head – not just bad dreams, anxiety dreams; about exams, stage performances and so forth – and pity the child who suffers from them.

I had another batch of such dreams of evil in the last days of my life in Orchardleigh in tranquil Somerset, when it seemed to me something bulky, ugly and terrible had come to live upon the stairs and I dreamed the taps spewed blood: I would have assumed they were just extreme versions of inside-the-head dreams, if the dog hadn't managed to break the banisters in his efforts to avoid whatever he too had decided was there, and the electricity board didn't have to be called because whenever anyone touched the taps they got an electric shock, and since there was no reason for it advised us to wear rubber boots when we washed the dishes. (Even horror films, which always seem to me to be too near actuality for comfort, allow the occasional flash of humour.) I think something dreadful had indeed come to live with us – just as soft drugs lead inexorably on to hard, in popular myth – so the odd poltergeist and inexplicable footsteps in the house which we lived with happy enough, had hardened into something more extreme, and dangerous.

St Andrews was a comparatively benign place. People may have been put to the fire for believing what others had decided was a heresy, but at least they died willingly: if you recanted you were spared the bonfire. Though I did once meet a ghost on the pier, a lonely stone jetty that stretched out into the cold North Sea. I could only suppose him to be the pastor who'd drowned centuries back, on his way to preach to the students. I was walking out to the end of the jetty on my own, in some tear-streaked mood or other, when I saw a tall man walking towards me. He was wearing a large flat black hat. He hadn't been there a moment before: I wouldn't have started walking out if he had been: too embarrassed at eighteen to know how to meet a stranger graciously.

I didn't think, there's the pastor, that's a ghost, there's a man who wasn't there a moment ago, I simply thought I don't want to meet this man, and turned back and walked towards the land. I looked back and he was walking faster and catching up with me. I ran. And once I was off the jetty I looked round and he was gone, nothing but the flat pier and the empty sea and nowhere for him to have got to at all. I went and complained to friends and Kate Rose, daughter of Professor Rose, the then professor of classics, said she and her boyfriend had seen him too. They'd been walking down the pier at sunset, and they realized the two of them were throwing three long shadows, not two, the extra being of a man with a large flat hat. He'd walked with them quite a way and then was gone. I report this fact: make of it what you will.

But that end of the town, the ruined castle end, complete with bottle dungeon – its shape such that once they'd lowered you in there, there was physically no way you could ever be got out – was always more desolate than the golf course end, and to see a ghost was not so remarkable. Some places pull you back and weigh your spirit down, others don't.

Love, Money and Other Practicalities

But my main preoccupation, only slightly relieved by the increasing excitements of the life of the mind and problems with the immutable laws of nature which I kept finding so strangely mutable, was my inability to find any kind of permanent sexual partner. I had found out how to go to bed with men but now how to have a conversation with them afterwards. How did you turn a bed partner into a proper boyfriend of the kind others had no trouble in serially accumulating: someone who would go to the cinema with you, canoodle in cars on some kind of permanent basis with you, whom you introduced to your parents, and ho would eventually propose marriage. Others had family easier to pin down than mine, it was true, but it was the idea which counted. I was doing something wrong, but had no idea what. No sooner had I met someone who seemed to appreciate me, than one or other of my girlfriends snaffled him from beneath my nose. I let it be known that I had a regular boyfriend back in London: it was the best I could do for my injured pride.

My self-esteem improved a little when I was asked to edit the student magazine, *Saltire*, for a few issues, if only while the regular editor was away. There was so little to say I ran a banner headline saying '*Man Bites Dog*', and thought myself very clever but only confused most of my fellows. If you pleased yourself you were unlikely to please others, I realized. The Young Conservatives took exception to something in the text and stole one whole edition and dumped it in the sea, off the end of the jetty: nor did the pastor appear to frighten them off. It took me a long time to regain any faith in the Tories. An ex-service student, a political activist from Poland, took great exception to a frivolous, politically ignorant female student such as myself being allowed to edit a student magazine – there was a real world out there: a hot war in Korea, a cold war in Europe, and I didn't even seem to realize – and called a public meeting to say as much. I was obliged to agree with him, since what he said was true, and asked him to take over the editorship from me, but he wouldn't.

I was alarmed to discover that I had a reputation for 'putting out'. It hadn't occurred to me that men talked about their sexual exploits in the same way that girls did. I had thought I was among friends, and here they were, talking about me behind my back. I discovered this when one of the regular boyfriends, a fine-featured, handsome lad, whose fiancée insisted on staying a virgin until their wedding night two years hence, knocked on my door in the middle of the night, begging to be let into my bed. Word was at Joe's coffee shop that I would happily oblige. Hoity-toity, I declined to let him in, but I have always regretted it, as one does tend to regret the things one doesn't do rather than the things one does. Perhaps I might so have worked upon his imagination that he abandoned her and took to me? A likely tale. But he became as upset as I was: he wept, what was the matter with him? Why wouldn't I with him when I would with others? Was there something wrong with him? We parted in a state of mutual anxiety and dissatisfaction. I do not know why this particular memory sits so stubbornly in my mind: perhaps it was the first occasion when it dawned on me that men had feelings too. I had believed they were demi-gods, all-powerful in emotional matters, which I daresay is what happens when you are brought up mostly among women.

Reputations were important in those days. Good girls got married, bad girls didn't. It was now too late to be a good girl, I could see that, but I didn't want to be so bad as to be dismissed altogether. I don't know whether the sum of human happiness was increased or diminished by the strange court-ship rituals of the time: I do know the disgrace of being partnerless is not what it was. 'Who wants a man anyway?' is the young girl's defiant cry, and I am glad she is saved from the doom of the wallflower.

Joe's was the student coffeehouse where I worked nightly to supplement my grant. Far more money was needed than the State would provide. I paid a fellow-student to read Walter Scott for me and report back, when I needed to know about his novels the better to pass an examination. I could not bear to be told what to read: my mind fragmented at once: the C-drive on my (faulty) computer tells me every morning that it has spent the night de-fragmenting, and I feel sympathy with it. I came to be very fond of Walter Scott: he wrote so much because he had to support a large family and in the end failed and went bankrupt, but at the time there seemed something perverse about his fiction. I loved his essays, but we were not to be examined on those. My general feeling is that no one should ever be obliged to read fiction other than of their own free-will: I even wrote a book on the subject, *Letters to Alice*, which is now used as a vehicle for teaching fiction to students. You can't win.

Joe's coffee shop served waffles as well as coffee, cocoa, buns and toast. Touch the waffle iron and it gave you an electric shock. Any complaint to the management resulted in a shrug. Eventually, all someone at the counter had to do was say 'waffle' and I would jump, before I even touched the machine. A Pavlovian response, I told myself, proudly. The proof of education lies in the shocks thereof.

I took a vacation job at Rusacks, then a four-star hotel, which was as good as you get, at the cheerful golf course end of town. Princes and politicians came to stay to enjoy the golf. The place was Fawlty Towers with stars on: the trust of the rich is amazing. The manager came down to scenes of mayhem every morning, twirling an RAF moustache and saying 'Everything tickety-boo, chaps?' The head waiter gave parties every night in the kitchens, at which he and his local friends drank the cellars out. The guests would come down in the morning to find themselves locked out of the breakfast room. The pastry chef would wash his hands in tubs of whipped cream and blow his nose into it if he felt annoyed, and almost anything would annoy him. Steaks returned from the dining room as too tough to eat would be stamped upon and returned to the complainant tenderized, in traditional mode.

I was an untrained, unsupervised chambermaid. I left a hot water bottle in the bed of a rajah without putting the lid on tightly and when he went to bed it was soaked with water. He was very good about it. Guests complained remarkably little, and paid enormously. I never got a single tip, though. More ruthless maids than I put themselves in the way of departing guests and held out their hands while I was still dithering. They would give me false information if necessary just to make sure I was busy somewhere else at the critical time. I always fell for it. As a chambermaid, I was a lightweight.

But those nice Scottish girls let me into a trick or two of the trade; if you see a garment or a piece of jewellery you like and want, hide it under an unlikely cushion or so far under the bed it's not observable to the casual eye: the guest departs without it. Wait a week to make sure no one's noticed its absence: if they have, and contact the hotel, 'find' the article and return it. If there's no enquiry – keep it. I never did such a thing, but when leaving hotels I take care to look under every cushion, in every dark corner, right under the bed, and it's amazing what you find of your own property, somehow landed there. I am not surprised, all the same, or particularly shocked, when the poor steal from the rich. There is such a shortage of nice things at the bottom end of the ladder, and such a plethora at the top.

Much of the pleasure of work in those days came from the weekly wage packet. It was rare for anyone in the working classes to have a bank account. The wage packet was a little brown envelope filled with notes and coins, on the outside of which your national insurance contribution and your PAYE was noted and deducted, and that was that. No one did accounts, no one kept receipts, no one had credit cards and to buy something on hire purchase was barely respectable. If you wanted something, you saved for it, and you paid in cash. It kept prices down and possessions few. It was not customary for men to tell their wives how much was in their wage packet: they gave them a certain amount weekly for the housekeeping and that was that. For the most part only personal letters came through the letterbox: men called to collect the rent and take the gas and electricity money: it was a cash economy and worked smoothly enough.

The Real World

I left St Andrews in the July of 1952, when I was twenty, with an MA in Economics and Psychology, some good friends, one suitcase, what was in my head, and that was all. Ellen and I set off for London in her little unheated car, leaving the grey haunted towers and the crosses of the martyrs behind, we thought for ever. London seemed the obvious place to go though it was no more home than any other place. But there were jobs, or rumours of jobs.

I was exhausted. I had stayed on after my flatmates had left to clean up the old lady's house before she returned. They were conscienceless: I was not. I was my mother's daughter. I beat the rugs and polished the furniture, hid the cigarette burns as best I could, weeded the garden and got rid of the crumbs in the knife box, and tried to scare off the mice who had turned up to feed off our debris. I cleaned a bath which had not been cleaned since we took up residence, and removed the crud from behind the taps and the cooker. There was no refrigerator – they were not standard – or I would have cleaned that. It occurs to me that the sheer filth of the way we lived may have been what put potential fiancés off – but no, the others did all right. It was only me.

The St Andrews scarlet gown left with me and in the days of my domesticity it came in very handy as Father Christmas's red robe. It wasn't until the early Nineties that it finally collapsed from dust and moth, as did the domesticity. I left the green dressing-gown behind. Also in the suitcase was my make-up – a lipstick, some blue eye-shadow, some Nivea all-purpose cream, and a comb – and such of my wardrobe that I wasn't wearing. I owned as I remember two much-worn knee-length tweed skirts, two twinsets, a string of pearls, and for parties a full blue and white polka-dotted skirt, a V-neck black T-shirt which pulled down low over the shoulders and a cinch belt. Underwear was one white conical pointy bra done up with a safety pin, a suspender belt likewise fastened to hold up the beige non-run stockings, and two pairs of old white knickers, one to be washed out while the other was drying. A very few smart shops sold black underwear: it was considered outré and unhygienic. Who could ever tell how recently it had been washed?

Keeping one's underwear together with safety pins was a practice frowned upon by mothers – 'Supposing you were run down in the street and taken to hospital, what would they think?' – but widely practised. A twinset for those who don't know was a short-sleeved woollen jumper with a matching cardigan in a pastel colour, and was worn with the single string of pearls to convey extreme gentility, or with hoop ear-rings to show a certain wildness of disposition. I also owned two books, Eliot's *Murder in the Cathedral* and *The Waste Land*, more I think from affectation than from any profound love of the poet.

> *When lovely woman stoops to folly and*
> *Paces about her room again, alone,*
> *She smooths her hair with automatic hand,*
> *And puts a record on the gramophone.*

Not in my neck of the woods she didn't. She wasn't nearly so melancholic and lonely in the absence of men as male poets liked to think. And Eliot might have thought of sex in terms of stooping to folly, but the women I knew tended to succumb to its pleasures rather than stoop, yet how the words stuck in the mind. Poetry, I thought then, and still do, is a matter of space on the page interrupted by a few well-chosen words, to give them importance. Prose is a less grand affair which has to stretch to the edges of the page to be convincing.

I didn't stay for the formal awarding of degrees: I couldn't afford to. I was told I could describe myself as a graduate for the purpose of obtaining employment, and could come back at my leisure to graduate officially. Years passed, but I never graduated; at first I couldn't afford the fair, then I couldn't afford the time, then I forgot.

In the late Eighties I received a tetchy letter from St Andrews asking why I described myself as a graduate of the university since there was no record of my having attended, let alone graduated. I pointed out that if they looked me up under Birkinshaw not Weldon they might find some trace of me, and there thankfully I was, in their files, Franklin and all. I seemed so different a person by then I almost doubted they would find me. Some other age, some other me. The university insisted that I could put it off no longer and required me to come up to graduate and I stood in a row with a great many beardless youths and bright-eyed lasses and went up to be tapped on the head with a mortarboard and handed my scroll. I felt very foolish. The next year they invited me back and gave me an honorary doctorate, and I felt flattered and honoured.

It is both gratifying and alarming when the society of which you were once so sceptical and so intimidated by, steps back, takes a look at you, and welcomes you in as one of its own after all. 'If my friends could see me now,' you think. Once a delinquent, you had assumed, always a delinquent, but it is not so. Whether this counts as success or failure it is hard to determine. I remember the shock when A. J. P. Taylor the historian and man of many wives, then a neighbour, suggested I became a magistrate. I had always assumed I would be in the dock, never on the bench: always a tenant, never a landlord: but hang around for long enough, and little by little roles reverse. I don't know what I had said sufficiently censorious for A. J. P. Taylor to decide I was fit to pass judgments on others but it must have been quite extreme.

Lost Girl

I shared a basement flat with my friend Hilda in Chalcot Gardens off England's Lane, in Belsize Park. Much of my London life seems to have been lived in concentric circles around Belsize Park, as if fate had decided to link itself to those initial blasts of hot air from the Underground that had once saved Jane and me from hypothermia. The landlord saw himself as our moral guardian and we were not allowed to have men on the premises, though of course we did. This too was fairly standard for the time.

I looked for jobs but no one seemed to want to employ me. I had ten pounds in the world and rent was three pounds a week. I could have joined Marks and Spencer, who had a scheme for trainee women graduates, but that meant living in Newcastle. I could have become a teacher but the thought of facing a classful of children was too intimidating. I had no stamps on my card for the last three years and to run-of-the-mill employers my having been in prison was more likely a story than that I had been to university. Hilda, once head girl of Roedean, had sensibly done a secretarial course after her degree and was able to join the Foreign Office as a secretary. I had no such skills, and could not afford to gain them. My mother was in St Ives, my friends were scattered and Jane was lost to me again, married to Guido. The real world seemed a fearful place. How did people manage?

I went to the local doctor: I had a pain in my kidneys. He examined me and noting the fact that I was not a virgin sent me to St George's Hospital for tests. Here nurses put my legs in stirrups and my private parts were scrutinized by a dozen clustering medical students: it was a clinic for venereal disease, and the other patients were prostitutes. I was, I think, traumatized, though the word was not used at the time. This may of course be one of the reasons for my aversion to the Lanesborough Hotel. Forget its history as a hospital for the wounded of the Napoleonic Wars, what about my personal history? I saw myself stripped of all dignity, forget modesty, and there seemed no way I could ever re-enter the steady, composed, and reasonable world of ordinary expectation which others seemed to inhabit as of right.

There was of course nothing wrong with me but a mild case of cystitis, which three doses of cetrimide powders put right. I have no doubt but that the doctor knew it, and saw it as his duty to frighten me back into virtue. He was a power freak, one of those who like to humiliate the helpless. The expression is of recent origin, but seems a very useful addition to the language, there are so many about: from the girl in the call centre to the guard who shuts the gates when you are running for the train, from the traffic warden to the arts

233

administrator who will or will not fund your film. Doctors are far less power freaky than they were, but in the days when I was a lost girl I came across a fair number, and it was the initial assault on my sensibilities at the St George's clinic, I do believe, which far from returning me to respectability, was what turned me into one. Lost girls change their habits through the decades: they're the ones who horrify parents, sleep rough, take drugs, get drunk, tattoo themselves, body-pierce, cut, drive therapists to despair, risk prison and seem in general bent on self-destruction. Calmed down in later years they look back on their former selves in amazement.

I read a piece of research once that said that the daughters of doctors had a far more troubled relationship with their family doctors than non-doctors' daughters. They either experienced or reported more indecent assaults, rapes, and unwarranted interference with their clothing than the norm. From which you could only conclude that doctors' daughters unconsciously set up some form of sexual tension with their medical advisors: otherwise how can these things be? Certainly, of the many doctors I have consulted in my time, I have been indecently assaulted by two (shady, saggy, elderly creatures both, scraping a living doing medicals for insurance companies), had a true romance with a third, slept with another on the ground of mutual comfort and concern, as we both wept during a home visit, and was obliged to pay another in kind, in return for the offer of a free (illegal) abortion – which never transpired since he told me I was pregnant when I wasn't. Well, he would, wouldn't he. And I am sure this is not par for the course; I don't have similar experiences with accountants, lawyers or other professionals. It can only be me.

One of the seldom-mentioned objections to keeping abortion illegal and therefore expensive was the number of girls who used to have to pay in kind to obtain them. Not that it seemed too bad a trade-off – his skill and concern in return for her virtue, which was obviously lost already. It was disconcerting, all the same, to see on this particular doctor's list of appointments that he was a medical officer for the Society for the Protection of Unmarried Mothers, or SPUM, as it was affectionately known at the time.

But all this was lost girl land – with the exception of the insurance company doctors: lost girls do not take out life insurance: but those doctors, poor things, were lost old men, unduly tempted by the unconscious pheromones that mark the doctor's daughter. Down in the lower depths of society murky things always stir. These days, of course, doctors are beyond reproach, or at any rate more likely to be working in health centres, where eccentricity and despair are less likely to flourish than in the lonely corner surgeries they once used to inhabit. Mind you, these days it is much harder to get an appointment. As ever, something's lost and something's gained.

I woke to my unnoticed and uncelebrated twenty-first birthday alone – Hilda had been transferred to Cairo – and I cried all day, overcome by self-pity. Nothing has been as bad since. But then I got a job as a ward orderly in New End hospital up the road: I cleaned the wards and ran errands for the patients. I used a heavy, noisy, industrial polisher to clean under the beds of the dying who wanted peace but were not allowed to have it. Hospitals are dirtier places now but the dying are (usually) offered more respect. Then they just untidied the ward, not being able to sit up straight for

Doctor's rounds, and were a nuisance to Matron. I got accustomed to the smell of gangrene and was allowed to sort out the prosthetic limb cupboard by way of compensation. I got paid five pounds a week and cheered up. That was enough for rent, food and even a pair of hoop ear-rings.

I had a desultory relationship with a Cambridge undergraduate, a young man with a titled mother. I kissed him in a doorway and the silence of the infinite fell, as if we kissed in a sacred grove, not an alley, but such signs from the gods can be deceptive. It became obvious he thought he was slumming, going around with me, and I was not introduced to his mother: he was just temporarily charmed by the idea that I came from the demi-monde, and he wanted desperately not to be dull, which he was, though I loved his Cambridge college and his digs and the shock of his friends when it became clear I stayed with him overnight. He shocked me by telephoning to break it to me that he had become engaged to a girl I knew from school, a rather plain girl but the daughter of a well-known economist. It was his use of the phrase 'breaking it to me' that cured me of him even as he left my life. The conceit! But they lived, I believe, happily ever after.

I had a dream that the top half of my grandmother drifted towards me smiling and saying goodbye, goodbye, then fading out. It was so vivid I rang my mother in St Ives to see if Nona, who was staying with her at the time, was all right. She was, but only just. The night before, my mother said, she had gone into Nona's bedroom and found her lying as if dead, without a heartbeat. She had swung Nona's legs into the air, instinctively, and Nona's heart, my mother said, had started beating again. 'I was sure she was dead,' said my mother, 'but I brought her back to life again.' Of course there is telepathy between members of a family: I have never doubted it.

Even as I wrote this last paragraph I wondered how my son Daniel – I have four sons and he is the second – was getting on. He is on holiday in Cornwall. The telephone on my desk promptly rang. I picked it up and said hello. No one answered but I heard the sounds of a motorway and my six-year-old grandchild Ella saying, 'My feet are very wet. My feet are so wet I am going to cry.' I heard Daniel suggest to Ella that that being the case she should take her shoes off, and I heard him remark that he thought there was a hole in the car exhaust. I put the phone down on this unexpected snapshot of family life. All that had happened, of course, was that his mobile had fallen, and had put itself through to one of its own stored numbers, which happened to be mine. That is mere coincidence, I know. I just report it.

Ever ambitious, I was lured away from the hospital by the offer of more pay as a waitress, in a restaurant called the Dorice, at the Swiss Cottage end of Finchley Road. On the other side of the road was its rival restaurant the Cosmo. Both were the haunt of refugees and intellectuals. But the Cosmo was the classier, where Elias Canetti, who wrote *Crowds and Power*, and won the Nobel Prize, used to hang out. The young Iris Murdoch was one of his disciples, I later found, as was Bernice Rubens. But I was on the wrong side of the road.

This was no amateur Copper Kettle, but a Berlin-style restaurant where no one but me spoke English, the orders were for dishes I did not understand, Königsberg Klops, and such like, and I couldn't tell a dessert from an entrée. You had to

237

go downstairs to the hell-hole of the kitchens to holler your orders at the overworked, sweaty, furious chefs, who would ignore you if you couldn't out-yell and out-bad-temper the other waitresses, and in German too. Management despised me, and would pat my pockets as I left, in case I'd stolen something: they were suspicious of my lack of employment record. The customers sneered at my inefficiencies and once again I hardly ever got any tips. I was better off at the hospital.

Earlier, my mother had worked for a time at the Cosmo as a cook: she was not very happy there either, I think, but happier than I was at the Dorice. I would go in and help her prepare the sauerkraut sometimes, but was never allowed out of the kitchens and into the café proper. I was not sorry because I did not want to be seen by my school-friends from South Hampstead down the road. I minded for my mother, not for me, that she, who had once lived round the corner in Adelaide Road, with a cook, a nanny and a maid of her own, should now be the cook. But such are the fortunes of families in which freedom is preferred to convention.

Hilda having gone abroad I could no longer afford the Chalcot Gardens flat, and found a bed-sitting-room on a corner of Finchley Road, above a hairdresser's shop. I live a few hundred yards from it today, but up the hill, and I sometimes wonder whether I would rather be me now, in this residential road, lived in mostly by bankers and oil-company executives, or me, then, at twenty-one. How much is youth worth?

Youth gives a sense of new days dawning bright, going on for ever, and a kind of tamped-down excitement which keeps breaking through even the worst days of poverty, depression and loneliness. But then youth is something which only exists in retrospect: you are barely conscious of it while you have it. I can scarcely go into mourning for it now. What would be the point?

I was never one for regretting major decisions, which always seemed to me to be laid down by fate anyway: you married this person not that, took this job not the other, had this baby or that, wrote this novel not that play, without taking much thought about it. It simply seemed what you were going to do next. It was the trivial decisions that hung around to reproach one. The occasional man I didn't sleep with: silly things: if I'd chosen netball instead of hockey I might have ended up a prefect: if I'd bought a different fabric I could have gone to the ball. The endemic if-only's which we all have to live with when it comes to property: if only I'd bought this house and not sold that one, how rich I would be; more painfully, if only I'd responded to Jackie Gillot's phone call she mightn't have ended her life: ditto, with Assia Wevill: if only I'd been fiercer with Claire she mightn't have gone to Turkey and died in the Paris air crash – but these if-only's merely serve as a mirror to one's own vanity and solipsism.

It is not so easy to influence the course of events. I should have been with Nona the night she died and not left her alone with strangers. The same with my sister Jane. But that's enough of this, other than to observe that in 1976 I wrote a stage play, *Action Replay*, about this question of life-changing decisions. Six friends progress through life, given the opportunity to replay the scene they later regret, and to act differently: all that happens is that one replayed scene then cancels out the other and everything ends up the same anyway. I am not sure I actually believe this. But I'd certainly like to believe it, and audiences liked it and if I had the time I would re-write it in the light of twenty-five years' more life knowledge, and see how it falls out now.

Security Risk

I escaped the Dorice – it has always been my experience of employers that when you tell them you are going they are shocked, surprised and hurt by your ingratitude, no matter what their attitude to you to date. In much the same way teachers will punish a child who dares to run away from an institution, to make them like it better. On Flora's advice I visited the Marlborough Street Labour Exchange – what would now be known as a Job Centre – where there was a kindly and sensible woman who made it her business to filter needy girl graduates into appropriate jobs.

She had already found Flora a job on the Russian desk of the Information Research Department of the Foreign Office. Now she found one for me on the Polish desk, and another good friend from St Andrews, Judy, was attached to the Balkans. IRD was then housed in Carlton House Terrace at the top of the Duke of York steps – a row of very grand eighteenth-century houses looking out over The Mall. I was finally where I thought I ought to be, if only as a temporary assistant clerk earning six pounds a week; barely enough, as they once used to say, to keep body and soul together, scurrying up the great steps with my scuffed shoes, jerseys worn thin at the elbows and darned stockings – too early for tights: we were harnessed up with suspender belts, which though sexy now, when worn as a necessity tend to end up as grubby strings kept together with an array of safety pins – and the thrusting conical Jane Russell bras fashionable at the time and designed, I believe, by Howard Hughes, then an aircraft designer.

Our Carlton House Terrace mansion at number twelve – which now houses the Institute of Contemporary Arts – had been requisitioned by the Foreign Office during the war and was only barely converted to office use, as had the good ship *Rangitoto* barely been converted to peacetime use. At least this one did not pitch and sway, and there were plentiful bathrooms – with splendid early plumbing, and massive taps – where we kept the files. Sometimes at lunchtime I would lock myself in and take a bath, and shake myself dry. Our staff canteen was a ballroom and Flora, Judy and I lunched under dusty chandeliers between muralled walls, trestle-tables set out on marble floors. I was back among friends and happy.

The Cold War was at its iciest; Russia was indeed suffering mightily under Stalin, but the liberal intelligentsia of the time was reluctant to give up its view of Russian communism as the hope of the world. The idea took a long, long time dying: only North Korea and Cuba cling to it today. If you were to consider life and times in North Korea, you could say, well, a brilliant idea in theory, like comprehensive schools, just hopeless in practice. At that time both Burgess and Maclean were in its grip, passing secrets – many of which flowed from IRD – to those whom others considered the enemy. Churchill was still PM, though fading fast, and an eventual war with Russia still very much on the cards.

IRD served both as the propaganda arm of the Foreign Office and its intelligence gatherers. We girl graduates had only a vague idea of what was going on. The day-to-day running of the offices was left to us. Our visible heads of department were mostly out to lunch, or engaged in the conspiracies to which they were prone – that is to say the overthrow of the Soviet Empire. The visible heads were, for Flora, White Russians: for myself, Free Poles, and for Judy, Hungarian aristocrats. The unseen heads moved silently and meaningfully behind closed doors; it was the world of *The Spy Who Came in from the Cold*.

It was our function to keep tabs on what went on behind the Iron Curtain, the other side of the wall of secrecy. We kept card files on politicians, who was in and who was out, who had died and who had disappeared, who was moving into the scene, and who was suddenly on the scene. We kept our clever if politically innocent eyes on social change. We were Miss Moneypenny's girls in the back office. We supplied the tacticians of the Cold War with what they needed to know, and had close links with Radio Free Europe – in theory a US private organization.

For our source material we used newspapers – always sensitive to the bottom right-hand corner of page two – which is where under dictatorships the real news is usually to be found – radio broadcasts, monitored at Caversham, and the debriefing sessions of those who had 'chosen freedom', jumped ship, slipped their minders, or in one way or another escaped to the West. All these were translated for our benefit by real adults, for Flora, Judy and Fay, none of them older than twenty-two, who took baths among the top-secret documents.

I wrote pamphlets for RFE to be dropped over Poland by air and distributed there by Boy Scouts, ever lackeys of the capitalists, poor little things, to keep the spirit of resistance alive. The implicit promise – never kept, of course, because RFE was not America – that if there were an armed uprising the West would come to their aid. I wrote papers for my masters on the state of coal-mining, housing, education and so on behind the Iron Curtain, and understood that it was my task to present the worst picture and not the best of what was going on.

No one wanted the good news, only the bad. They wanted to know about unsafe mines, badly educated teachers, unseasoned wood – not, what to me was extraordinary – that the mines were working at all, that schools were opening everywhere, that people at least had somewhere to live, even if the windows didn't fit and the cold winter blast blew in. But wherever I have been it is the same: very few people are interested in the truth, most would rather have their preconceptions confirmed than bother to alter them: the guiltier people feel the more secrets they keep.

Sometimes my papers would be presented to Churchill himself, and would come back marked like a school essay, with a tick and an 'Exc.' or a 'V.G.', and his initials, but I was told not to make too much of it, he was no longer very acute in his judgements.

From time to time, security men would come round and change our desks so they faced the walls and not the glass windows which let light in from the corridors. There would be people coming down them they would rather we did not see. We could only assume it was James Bond and his like: spies, field workers in espionage, undercover agents. 'Watch the wall, my darling, while the gentlemen go by.'

Those poetic gentlemen on horseback on a moonlit night were on their way to fetch contraband: these men in their Homburg hats pulled low over their brows were probably only coming in to get their pay. When Salman Rushdie came to dinner decades later he was rushed the few yards from the security cars into the house disguised as a football supporter, woolly scarves and all. All my brushes with security have been faintly ridiculous, though often frightening.

Security, all agreed, was something of a joke. We girls were not security-checked before we began work. Enough that Flora, Judy and I had English names and had been to good girls' schools. Hilda, on the other hand, ex-head girl of Roedean as she was, was nearly barred from the Foreign Office because her father – child of a Scottish oil engineer – had been born in Moscow. In the nature/nurture debate the Foreign Office came down very heavily on the side of nature. We pooled our top-secret documents with the Balkan desk and locked them in their safe overnight. We kept hats and umbrellas and personal articles in ours and didn't bother to lock it. We got to work one morning to find our empty safe bound with red tape and sealed with red sealing wax, and disciplinary action being taken against us for a class-one breach of security. How these things rankle through the decades. Wouldn't they have been better employed detecting Burgess and Maclean?

I may be being unfair. Decades later, and many changes of name too, back from Moscow and at a debriefing party for the members of a cultural delegation, one of whom I was, I remarked to one of the benign old men from the Foreign Office that I once worked for IRD. 'Oh, we know all about that,' he said. Perhaps they always knew more than I thought. And I always loved my country, and still do.

Pregnant

The young Queen's coronation came and went. We had ring-side views from Carlton House Terrace, and I was happy, other than for my ongoing feeling that I ought to be partnered, that nights spent alone were wasted nights.

I was paid six pounds a week. Three pounds a week was rent for the room in Finchley Road. I would walk the long way home to save the fares to buy the new pair of shoes I needed because I walked instead of taking the bus. Poverty is a kind of perpetual-motion machine which provides its own energy.

Then by a stroke of luck and friendship I found myself living on the houseboat *Eagle* down on the Thames on the Chelsea Embankment, under the clouds of smoke which belched from the Lotts Road power station. The boat belonged to Janice, then the girlfriend of Jimmy Wells, once the boyfriend of Serena, who was now the girlfriend of Russell the man I loved. My St Andrews friends had re-grouped in London, with new attachments, and taken on their customary *La Ronde* patterns of behaviour. I was happy.

The *Eagle* was a rickety structure, which took rather a lot of water, but it was a very social place. The boats were strung out along the embankment, and the only way of getting from boat to boat was along planks which were strung from one deck to the next, and all night long partygoers and random wanderers would stumble along my deck, inches from the bunk where I slept. I felt no fear, as I remember. I certainly would now. I loved the river: the passage of the boats, the sense of perpetual movement, the fullness of its floods, the baring of its muddy soul at low tide, the wildlife struggling for survival on its smoggy, Dickensian embankments. I came to love London properly then, escaped for once from the concentric rings of Belsize Park.

Jimmy Wells had a boat anchored a little way off shore. Not so much a boat as a box which floated: he was too frugal to pay for anything as unnecessary as a prow for a boat which was never going to go anywhere, let alone a porthole which let in light, but he was generous with his friendship and his gossip and his wit; he was, is, the archetype of the eternal student: he never washed an article of clothing, rinsed out a milk bottle or parted with a penny if there was any other way out, and ended up a Doctor of Philosophy and rather rich too, though you would never think it from looking at him. He was, is, the human equivalent to me of Belsize Park: my life has run in concentric rings around him.

He came round the other day with photographs of a baked-bean can with holes wrenched in it by the teeth of a grizzly bear he had just encountered while on a bike trip round Alaska with his girlfriend. It seemed par for a never-ending course. All his girlfriends through his life have had to be prepared to cycle the world, whatever their age or condition, or indeed his. What can heaven be, that it could contain the infinite variety and pleasures of this earth? When we are all dead – first he died, then she died: as with the Binswangers, so goes the story of all of us – what will become of us?

To lose identity and will, to merge with the oneness and float about with worshipping angels, as is the best that is suggested by most religions, seems such a waste it is almost as hard to credit as the notion that we simply cease to exist. I think we have to conceive of some sort of wrinkle in time, in which Jimmy and the bears and the bicycles exist for ever, always with minimal changes, always open to narration, working towards perfection but never quite getting there.

The universe in which the pastor didn't drown on his way to St Andrews keeps slipping through to ours for the very reason that the perpetual Sunday walking to the pier by the students prevents him making a proper separation. I always knew there was a good reason why I was made uneasy by the students' ritual walk: not just that even way back then it smacked of 'heritage', rather than the true legacy of history, but because it was the last thing the pastor needed. Better say prayers in the chapel for the resting of his soul, than go on insisting he might still turn up any minute. Be all that as it may, I felt safe enough on *Eagle*, in the knowledge that Jimmy was in a floating box not far away. Jimmy had gone off Janice in his floating box.

Janice left instructions that when the tide went out and the boat lay on the mud I was to open the bilge plug and let it drain, and remember to replace the plug before the tide came in again, otherwise the water would rise and the boat would stay on the bottom. That was alarming. I had to come back from the office sometimes, just to check I'd put the bilge plug back in, in the way others turn back to make sure they turned off the gas. I had taken up with Murray Sayle, an Australian journalist, then working for the *News of the World*, the one who coined the journalist cliché – 'I made my excuses and left,' when investigating a brothel or a call-girl ring, and push finally comes to shove: are you a client or a mere impostor?

He was, is, an immensely clever man and a fine and serious writer, deceptively bluff and hearty in appearance and with a musical taste that has never developed beyond *Iolanthe*. On the whole he preferred sailing and drinking to women, and always surprised himself, I think, with his liking for me, which was endemic over decades. He lives in Japan now, decorously, in that very decorous, delicate land, with his wife and children.

It was Murray who once told me that the difference between a columnist and a reporter was that a reporter could never get further than 2000 words, and even that was a struggle. I read an article by him on the Japanese economy in last week's *Spectator*, all of four pages, 6000 interesting words long, and thought there indeed is a columnist.

But I had another suitor, Colyn, doorman of the Mandrake Club in Soho's Meard Street, a folk singer, as lost a young man as I was a lost girl. His situation in the world was far worse than mine: he was the illegitimate son of a nurse and an unknown soldier and had been brought up in an orphanage where all the dreadful things that happen to children in care happened. He had been put in the navy when he was sixteen as a Boy Bandsman and had emerged ten years later to drift to Soho. Now he knew everyone and everything, was an expert in Victorian street ballads, which he would perform in a shabby top hat which embarrassed me greatly, did *The Times* crossword in five minutes flat, was David Low the cartoonist's best friend; and here and at the Gargoyle Club down the road, and round the corner at the French Club and Muriel's, kept the company of Quentin Crisp, Dylan Thomas, Lucian Freud, Francis Bacon, Elizabeth Smart, who wrote *By Grand Central Station I Sat Down and Wept*, Dan Farson and so on. How they drank – but seldom drugged, or I daresay they would not have been as productive as they were. The drugs on offer in the Fifties were mostly the remnants of those offered to the troops in such large quantities during the war, and still drifting on to the market, amphetamines to keep you awake and morphine to relieve pain.

Alcohol makes people incoherent, sometimes permanently, but at least seems to make them more human than human, not less so. With it Dylan Thomas wrote, and with it Freud and Bacon painted, and with it Elizabeth Smart wrote her sad, brilliant, lyrical memoir to her husband the poet George Barker, who seemed to make a habit of marrying Canadian heiresses, spending their money, dumping them, and marrying another – and then he died, and then she died, as my mother would say – but they did produce such beautiful, talented children between them.

A year earlier my friends had set off for Paris in a coach from St Andrews: rumours had reached them of fine philosophical times and living art in the cafés and garrets: there they could mix with Sartre, de Beauvoir, Giacometti, Cocteau, and the jazzmen from New York – and so they did – for this was the heyday of Paris in its Beat years. I'd stayed behind to work as a chambermaid at Rusacks: I had no money at all. I did not wish to be obliged to them. There they had encountered Colyn, working as a street busker, and had spoken of me and he had decided from afar that I was the girl for him. Once back in London he wrote to me and telephoned me, and sent me sentimental Victorian love poems with execrable rhymes, until I agreed to meet him. He told terrible jokes and wrote terrible, wonderful, rude, crude poems. Had he been born five years later the Education Act would have saved him, sent him to grammar school, to university, given him a formal career, and made sure his rhymes were properly metric. As it was, he was an inveterate hanger-outer and if he could do nothing rather than something, chose to do nothing.

This is the stubbornness of the child in care, and of the colonized, the survival strategy which defies the world to do its worst, while not lifting a finger to stop it. Now see what you've done, fate! He had not of course got a penny to his name, only what he had in his pocket from the evening's playing, and his job as a bouncer, and an early Lucian Freud upon his wall. He was a troubadour and I ran off with him, pitter-pat bare feet by night through the long hot summer streets to his place up at Belsize Park (where else?) and pretty soon I was pregnant.

So was my sister Jane, two months ahead of me, as it happened, living with her husband Guido in the Smoke House, overlooking St Ives bay, helping him print the nation's finest poetry on the Latin press. He was going bankrupt, not for the first time, and not for the last.

Finding out if you were pregnant was not a simple matter. Ten weeks without a period and you were fairly sure – dangerously near the twelve-week mark after which few even considered having an abortion. The soul had entered in and it was murder. Before twelve weeks and it was dangerous and illegal, and the penalty if you were discovered was still prison, but it was considered morally okay. Have a baby you can't provide for and all it does is keep the next one out – who might well have had a better start in life. You had a few days to make your choice.

But there was now a new pregnancy test out which could tell you when you were six weeks pregnant. If a laboratory toad injected with your urine developed signs of pregnancy and then died, the test was positive. If it went on hopping and croaking in an ordinary way it was negative. We felt badly for the toads but not badly enough not to take advantage of this. Off went the test. Five days for the response. Then it comes. Yes, you are pregnant – seven weeks pregnant. Poor sacrificial toad, dying to save you.

A woman's body works as if it knew something she didn't, and does not have her best interests at heart. If you need to look your best it will deliver you a pimple; if you don't want it to, your period will start early; if you want a baby badly your body refuses to give you one; if you are content in your life, lo, you are pregnant. Maternity wards are full of paradox: women lie weeping, some because they've had a baby, some because they haven't: the woman who wants fertility treatment lies next to the one who's had a termination. When it comes to our reproductive lives mind and body are at war: our species-nature drives us on – a baby, a baby, answer to all ills: our common sense holds us back: it can't be done, not now, soon, sometime, never.

The good civilized abortionists worked down near Half Moon Street in Mayfair, which was known cheerfully as whirling spray alley, after the technique then used, but they were expensive. The option for girls of slender means or religious convictions was to marry if you could, otherwise to carry the baby to term and then have it adopted. How could a working girl bring up a baby on her own, in the world before benefits, before equal pay? If you failed to provide properly, the State took the baby away and put it in an orphanage. There was

251

one on the 31 bus route in Maida Vale: you could see the crocodiles of children, in little brown capes, going in and out: destined for the army or domestic service. Look what that had done to Colyn.

Friends offered a whip-round to raise two hundred pounds for an abortion. I stood on the Albert Bridge, near where *Eagle* rocked up and down on a rising tide, and watched the sunset. It was not in my nature, I concluded, to deny another human being such a sight. Of course I would have this baby. God had given it to me. I would not throw the gift back.

I was twenty-two. I had no idea of what was entailed. Girls always like the thought of babies: little creatures who lie quietly in the arms and adore you and find no fault in you or you in them. It seems an exchange of perfect love. That babies grow into children, who run round your ankles and bite you, like as not, somehow escapes their putative mothers. That the love which seizes her will be so anxious, powerful and overwhelming, she does not understand. Standing on the bridge in the summer of 1953 with the dirty water tumbling below, I had no idea of how it was to be done but I would do it. I also had an inkling, true enough in retrospect, that I was still a lost girl: if I had a baby I would have no choice but to find myself again.

I wrote to Colyn, who at the time had a part in a play in Newcastle and he said he would marry me and look after me and that he had never been happier. Accommodation in London for young couples with babies was difficult – *no coloureds, no dogs, no babies* – but he had heard there were free houses for gas fitters in Luton New Town, one of the new satellite towns built in a ring round London to cope with the pressure of population in the city – and he would train as one, and we could live in Luton happily ever after. I said no, that was kind of him, but I wouldn't marry him. I should have, of course, as it transpired, but what was I to know? Haughty and disdainful, I did not see myself as a gas fitter's wife in Luton.

Flight

I wrote to my mother to tell her what had happened. Was there a slight element of 'now see what you've made me do!' in my heart as I posted the letter? Probably. If she had contrived her life differently wouldn't mine be more emotionally and practically comfortable? All children feel this about their parents, including my own about me. All mothers love their own children as best they can, according to their temperament and circumstances, and all mothers should have done better, in their children's eyes, when the going gets tough for the children.

My mother wrote back saying she would do everything she could to help me, though Jane, also pregnant and penniless, needed her too. But at least Jane was married. My mother saw my lack of marital status as the worst of my problems. Obviously women alone could bring up children – had she not done so – but the stigma attached to the unmarried mother and her bastard child was still very strong in society. Just because I hadn't noticed didn't mean it wasn't so. What I must do now, she wrote, was not let it be known that I was an unmarried mother. I must tell the Foreign Office that I was getting married and hand in my notice, and go to live somewhere I wasn't known – in went the pin: Cambridge! Now that was good, a university town, I had a degree, I could probably find work, I must start learning shorthand typing in the evenings: there could be no more gadding about now. I must change my name by deed poll to Colyn's, pretend to be married, have the baby and then let it be known that he had left me. Better an abandoned wife than an unmarried mother, if the baby and I were to have any kind of future. I could say goodbye to any prospect of marriage now, anyway: who was going to want to take on another man's child? But for the baby's sake, these things would have to be done. If you brought a child into the world, there could be no easy options.

So I did as I as told. I assumed my mother knew best. I supposed it was true that, like my father, I viewed the world with far too rosy an eye. I simply failed to notice the disapproval of others. I didn't mind in the least being described as an unmarried mother but I could see it would not be nice to be known as a bastard child.

I would have to leave the Foreign Office anyway. I would have to earn more. I could barely keep myself on six pounds a week, let alone a baby too, and promotion was not available to temporary assistant clerks. I said I was leaving to get married, and the staff did a whip-round and bought me a wedding present. I was mortified but how now could I tell them the truth? I had to flee the town and let time muddy the issue. And Janice was coming back from the States to claim *Eagle*, anyway.

My friends knew the true situation well enough. They thought I should just stay on at the Foreign Office. They did not share my instinct for flight, learnt or inherited from my mother. The Civil Service was a broadminded institution: it allowed you three children out of wedlock by two different fathers; only if any more children or any more fathers turned up did they fire you. But it was too late now.

Judy thought I was crazy, a) to propose to leave London, b) to leave the job. She lives in Sydney now and is a Professor of History. If all fails here – I keep the feeling that it will: I have little faith in the constancy of good fortune – I will go and live next door to her and listen to her advice.

Flora was in disgrace too. She was in a TB sanatorium, where she would have to stay for two years. There was something of a stigma attached to having tuberculosis – it was the disease of the poor, the hungry and the over-sexed – but nothing compared to being an unmarried mother. Her family had stood out against her marrying Clive, for reasons none of us could understand – and she had responded by doing this to them. They withdrew their objections very quickly, and when Flora's lungs were better the marriage went ahead. We sat on the healthy green grass outside the hospital – fresh air was considered the great cure for the illness – and considered the extraordinary fate that awaited girl graduates. Family took either too much interest in your life, as in Flora's case, or too little, as in mine. The aunts and uncles would only want to hear good news, not bad news, and any I could offer would be seen as bad. Selwyn and Tania abhorred misfortune, and Michael and Mary abhorred scandal, and I would be a source of both. I was on my own, at any rate until Jane stopped occupying my mother's attention. Having a baby was more complicated than one could ever have supposed.

Serena wrote, surprisingly, from St Ives. She was staying with my mother. She and Russell were having a baby. My heart broke, not that I had realized I had any left to break.

I was running out of money. The lady in the Marlborough Labour Exchange seemed more amused than shocked by my predicament and found me a job sitting down. It was in a workshop in Rathbone Place off Oxford Street where they manufactured pop-up books. It was piecework. You sat at your bench bending card this way along the dotted lines and that way along the unbroken lines, and when you had completed a sheet you folded it and sat on it. Twenty folded cards in, you were sitting quite high. When you had twenty you would take them up to the overseer who would count them, inspect them, reject a few and accept the rest. Wages depended upon speed and accuracy. Stop for a chat, a stretch, a joke and how your income fell! A couple of particularly dexterous workers were said to make sixteen pounds in the week, but I daresay that was a rumour put about by management: I never managed more than about eight pounds, but it was better than six. Some of the cards were much easier than others, and were quickly done, but then the rate would be changed so management always won. Management usually does, changing the goalposts the minute the workers begin to score. Workers need unions: it was borne in on me in the course of that job.

My mother said she was coming up from Cornwall to see me. She would find somewhere for us all to live in Cambridge where the pin of fate had fallen.

I found among my papers the other day a little brown diary for 1953, in which, in the middle of emptiness, were a few entries. I must have thought there would come a time in my life such as the one I now live through, and wrote to myself in this future. I have certainly not written in a diary before or since. This is how it goes.

Saturday, October 3rd. *Left London with Mummy and came to Cambridge: we walked into a flat, but no light, no heat. Meals out.*
Sunday 4th. *Meals out. Went to pictures. Dull.*
Monday 5th. *Saw solicitor about Deed Poll – now Mrs Davies. (Ugh!) Changed name at Insurance Office, registered at Labour Exchange, looked for the doctor's in the evening. Wrote to Judy to tell FO I am married.*
Tuesday 6th. *Went to doctor in morning, quite well, he says, explained my state and status which upsets me rather always. Letter from Judy at FO saying Colin keeps ringing her at work, not to be put off, so I say I'll meet him. Oh heavens what do I say to him, am I to have him about for the rest of my life? Write to Russell – he said get in touch with him, saying dull here, come over.* (Russell as it happens lived not twenty miles from Cambridge).
Wednesday 7th. *Go to antenatal clinic, wept on sister in charge who is sympathetic but thought me an idiot. Well, I daresay I am. Mummy out at Newport* (where Winifred and Ina were living; ten miles from Cambridge) *got very depressed and keep on crying. Nothing to read. Lonely. Go to pictures. Oh yes, registered for unemployment benefit. Feel so ashamed.*

I went with Russell to Saffron Walden, a small town in Essex, for the day. The name sounded so pretty, as indeed was the place: a market town, with a wealth of plastered and pargeted houses from the seventeenth century and earlier, the remnants of a twelfth-century castle and a maze which a writer friend of mine, Eric Paice, who was later to live in the town, swore was haunted. I have never been in a haunted maze myself but I can see that the desire to get out would be very great and one's ability to do so very limited.

Market Hill was the short road which ran down from the Sun Inn where Cromwell had his headquarters in 1647, in the Civil War, to the old market square. On the corner facing the Sun Inn, from whence hung the earliest extant insurance sign in the country, the first in a row of lattice-windowed shops leading down to the market, was a half-timbered house, lathed and plastered, and crooked with age. Very early houses were built out of green oak, which shifts and changes as centuries pass, and it seasons in situ, which is why beams creak and floors slope, and there is seldom a right angle to be seen inside or outside. The house was for sale. We fetched the key from the agent. Forget the dank courtyard to the back, the smell of damp and empty houses, the lack of bathroom, the cold water tap, the peeling layers of wallpaper inside, which served to keep back the crumbling lime plaster between the interior oak beams, I fell in love with it. I was always falling in love with disastrous people: now the propensity extended to buildings. Russell's presence lent it grace: his golden feet were glittering. The walls caved in and crumbled, the roof leaked, the floors curved, who cared? Not me. The price? Nine hundred pounds. Why was that sum familiar? Of course, my mother's legacy. It seemed like a message from heaven, like the silence when I kissed my Cambridge friend, I had forgotten how deceptive that had been. A shop! Surely one could make a living from a shop?

But how was I to buy a house, start a business? Michael Allen, a good friend from St Andrews, offered to lend me nine hundred pounds interest-free. I accepted. The fates were in convulsion, giving with one hand, snatching away with the the other. I could hardly keep up.

More entries from the diary.

Saturday 10th: *Is one willing to live one's life out in Saffron Walden?* Apparently, yes. I go to a free lecture on Mental Mechanisms (*interesting if bitty*), go out with Russell again. *Two teas, no lunch, very amicable: supper in Cambridge. Says he'll marry Serena in the end.* At least Serena is now staying with her mother, not mine. Jane has left Guido or perhaps he has left her. The failing is in money, not love.

By the thirteenth I'm in London seeing Colyn. *Bought a pair of shoes, meet Colin for lunch, home with him, find I've left my bag behind so stayed the night . . . was very sick all night, tummy upset.* It is not easy to brush people out of your life: they have an external reality. Young women find this hard to take on board. I insisted on spelling his name wrong, I notice, refusing him the 'y' his mother gave him to improve his lot in life. Meanwhile I'm negotiating with Michael to borrow the money to buy the Saffron Walden house, and it's working out. On the seventeenth I go to the Council Offices in Saffron Walden to see about a catering licence. *Can we do it as a delicatessen? Don't see why not. Work out plot for a radio play. Don't like it.* On Saturday the eighteenth I get really busy. *Write to M saying see him Tuesday with details. Ring Russell and tell him to write to J Walter Thomson and go into advertising.* ('Going into advertising' was the worst kind of selling out: what can I have been thinking of?) *Ring*

Judy who has sent telegram saying can't come over, it won't work (I must have asked her to come and help set up a delicatessen with me). *Tell her to give my love to the FO. Contemplate writing a novel. I wonder.*

There it stops. I wish I could feel closer to this twenty-two-year-old. I don't. She's too far away and long ago. Though clearly she feels close to me, writing to me like this from the past. Pregnant by one man, hankering after another, crying one moment, bent on self-improvement the next. I had crisp and shiny wavy hair, I remember that, and scarcely ever took the time to comb it. I seem competent enough, when I'm not crying. I don't let the grass grow under my feet.

Fay Davies

But I'm not her, not pregnant weepy Fay Birkinshaw any more, send messages to me though she may. Those who don't change their names enjoy a straight line from their past to their future, stay the same person, for good or bad. Children change you too: you absorb their characteristics as they grow in the womb, it isn't all a one-way street. Is that a reason to have children or a reason not to? I don't know. But perhaps the feeling of alienation is only because I had changed my name, nothing to do with pregnancy: I just wasn't Fay Birkinshaw any longer, but Fay Davies – a name acquired by Deed Poll, not the solemnization of marriage or even the regular cleaving of the flesh – a neutral name with which I seldom felt at home – and indeed didn't have for long. I'd try using Fay Franklin Davies for a time, to add the gravitas

I felt I so badly needed, but that seemed dishonourable, cheating.

Soon I was to become Bateman, then Weldon, now Fox. I am still sometimes tempted to throw in the Franklin for good measure. Fay Franklin Fox would be a good name for a writer.

A month later we were all living at Market Hill, Saffron Walden, my mother, Jane, Serena and I, we three girls all in advanced stages of pregnancy, and not a live-in man in sight, let alone a married one. Forget all aspirations to married respectability, name changes and so forth, it hardly mattered now. The neighbours were polite but distant: I think they scarcely knew what to make of us. Other than that perhaps we were some kind of charitable institution; perhaps my mother was running a reformatory for fallen girls.

My poor mother; so much for her hopes of setting out in life again, so much for the belief, endemic in so many parents, that when the youngest child is seventeen you will be free. It is not so. Jane and I had allowed her five years and now we were back to claim her, and had thrown in Serena for good measure. Serena disclaimed her own family, or they disclaimed her: they were a scattered collection of old Etonians and well-born women: they had no central point of focus, as it were, as so many families did not, after the war. There was nowhere for her to *go*, as there had not been for us, until now by the skin of our teeth we finally had a family home.

It was a cold winter and there was no hot water and no heating, other than by Valor stove. A Valor stove ran off paraffin: it was a tall, pale green, rather unsafe thing you could carry around by a handle: it worked on the principle of an oil lamp. You lit the wick and instead of light it gave forth a rather fumy, smelly, damp heat: droplets of water condensed as soon as it was turned off and left the room colder than before. We slept on camp beds under army surplus blankets, and we had no furniture other than a table and four chairs. Slats showed through crumbling lime plaster to the outside world. But there was a big cooker in the shed in the yard which never got the sun, and the downstairs front room was low and oak-beamed as a Ye Olde Tea Shoppe ought to be, and the little shop, once you had cleaned the leaded windows and removed generations of dead flies and scrubbed the wooden shelves, was almost inviting.

We replastered, painted, and listened with disbelief when my mother explained that washing nappies – since you had to heat up the water by the kettleful, use Sunlight soap and rinse a minimum of three times before putting through the wringer and pegging out on the line – could take up to two hours a day per baby. Surely she was just trying to frighten us, in an attempt to calm us down.

Russell came to visit quite often, and it was clear that sooner or later he would marry Serena. Well, she was having his baby. Jane wrote long letters to Guido and he came to visit once or twice, but not to leave any money. It became my experience that men were always happy to give their children toys and treats, but were always reluctant to buy socks, or shoes, to pay rent. I would not let Colyn visit. Luton!

Mind you, hot water was beginning to seem remarkably attractive, and a gas fire would not have gone amiss, which

Colyn could have fitted. The idea of a delicatessen was attractive but how did you start one? The food regulations were strict: you needed capital for equipment. And though central London was ready for garlic and salami, was Saffron Walden? The longer we were there the more unlikely it seemed. A cake shop seemed a better idea: you could bake almost to order. Couldn't you? If only we were better cooks.

And now a ghost was beginning to trouble us. I bet they didn't have those in Luton. My mother thought we had probably unleashed it by taking off at least three hundred years' worth of wallpaper. She refused to let us take off any more, which meant that the idea of a tea shoppe was postponed. We were running out of our small savings, my unemployment benefit would finish soon.

This suspicion of an apparition stood about unseen in corridors, weeping, and the cat – a pregnant stray who had claimed us, naturally – would stand staring and spitting at something we couldn't see and it certainly did. But we really had no time to give it much thought. If we didn't want to linger in some of the rooms, because of the dark chilliness which now seemed to pervade them, there were enough others to be worked upon.

My mother waxed the old oak beams with margarine to feed and darken them. It was cheaper than proper wax and served the same purpose, or so she maintained. Our hands were red and rough with lime plaster dust as well as chilblains, and it got into our hair and made it brittle. But mostly we glowed in the full flood of shared oestrogen.

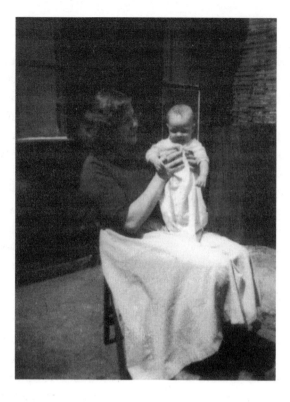

New Mothers

And then of course the babies came, and took us by surprise, as babies do. First, how much you love them, second, how much work they are, third, how difficult it is to leave them. We would rather sit and sing to them than get on with running a business.

Jane's baby was the first to come, in January. A boy, Christopher. Then came mine in March, a boy, Nicolas. Then in

April, Serena's, a boy, Michael. An ambulance drove us, in turn, to Addenbrooke's in Cambridge. Fathers weren't allowed into delivery rooms, even if you had one to boast of. Jane's was an easy delivery and I thought all births would be like that. But no. I knew practically nothing about the processes of giving birth, assumed I was dying and, classically, wondering where the screaming came from, realized it was me. But we survived, Nicolas and I, he at a good eight pounds.

In those days they kept you in for two weeks after delivery, three if it was a difficult birth, and they were good enough to concede that of mine, though how would they know, since no one had been around at all until the last five minutes, I couldn't imagine.

Colyn came to visit me, in spite of my requests for him to stay away, and I found I was pleased and proud to be able to produce a father for the baby. I was learning. I was moved to a side ward and nursed in isolation, apparently the victim of the highly infectious and often fatal puerperal fever, but they had the test tubes mixed and I was fine: it was one of the other patients in the ward who had it, and died. The ward was closed and we were all sent home, ready or not. The National Health Service, in spite of what they say, is in a better state now than it ever was then.

But back home, in the midst of the sea of unwashed nappies, leaking breasts, soapy babies and the general fuzzy crooning maternity, we were beginning to pull apart. When the shop finally opened it was a cake shop. We had difficulty deciding what kind to put in our sparkling shop windows: my mother won out against our fancy cream ideas and made very plain ones indeed. I think we sold four in all. Perhaps the customers thought they contained some kind of fertility drug.

Serena wanted Russell, Jane wanted Guido, the group endeavour fell apart. We were falling into the gap between the dream and reality; what we would have liked to happen and what happens. In the rosy glow in your head others do as you want: in real life they stubbornly do as they will, whether they are lovers, or the buying public, or rose bushes. It's a hard lesson to learn, but not too terrible, and settles down with maturity into the boring understanding that, by and large, nothing is as bad as you fear, or as good as you hope. Judy was right: it wasn't going to work.

Had we persisted we might have made the cake shop work and the tea rooms too: we could have hung burnished copper kettles on the walls, worn little white aprons and caps, presented ourselves as Thomas Hardy heroines, and even learned that there was such a thing as buying wholesale – we were running down to the corner shop to buy a half-pound of margarine here, a pound of sugar there: what price now my degree in Economics – and become the cosiest tea shop in all Essex (there's an ambition!) but we did not persist. It would have been nice if it was in our natures, but it wasn't.

Six months later Russell had claimed Serena and little Michael, Guido had claimed Jane and little Christopher, and they had moved out to live in less eccentric domesticity in villages outside Saffron Walden. Reality had overtaken us, as reality will.

For my mother and myself, left behind, the ghost became very active. We had it exorcized by the local vicar but it took no notice, and kept us awake at night with its weeping: the cat just ran away. Spring came, and summer, but the house never seemed to get brighter or warmer. At night I would be woken by the noise of the deathwatch beetle, tap tap tapping with his scissored teeth into the old oak beams. They work by night and sleep by day.

We moved upstairs to the haunted part of the house and let the downstairs to an ambitious young man who said it was his intention to flood the market with cheap chocolate gateaux. The phrase was lovely, and seemed enticing and exotic in the mid-Fifties, and we shared his enthusiasm, but it didn't work. No one wanted chocolate gateaux from his van. The world of failed enterprises is a dismal place, a little tucked-away section of limbo, where everything that happens seems to be happening a little way off, a little muffled.

But then our tenant began to sell fish and chips from the outhouse. He had at last found Saffron Walden's culinary button and pressed it. The yard had never been busier; after the pubs shut the smell of vinegar and the cries of amorous louts filled the house. We were horrified; claims to past gentility still assailed us. Living above a fish and chip shop, albeit one built in the fifteenth century or earlier! But Baby Nicolas crowed and laughed and sang and thought everything was just fine. It was in his nature, and still is. People are much the same at three months old as they are grown up. He had bright blue eyes, pink cheeks and a shock of almost white hair. He was very, very clever and astonishingly handsome: he was Colyn, given a second chance at life, and me, ditto, only a male version.

Cheques for Jane and me, for two hundred pounds each, came through the post – Edna had sold the house in New

Zealand and thought Frank would have wanted us to have a share, though of course he had died without making a will. This was manna from heaven. I spent a hundred pounds on a typewriter and wrote a hundred letters to various firms in London asking for a job.

I received one reply, from the *Daily Mirror* in London. They had been impressed by my letter. So much so that they were offering me a job on the Readers' Advice pages. I was to answer hire purchase problems. Hire purchase had only recently become a feature of domestic life, and people easily misunderstood what was going on. It seemed to them outrageous, and outrageous it was, that they should be expected to pay a third more, or double, or two-thirds again, on the list price, just to have it now instead of later. But they would keep signing these forms, because they looked so official that it was bound to be all right. And most people trust anyone who comes to the door wearing a suit and tie. I soon mastered the hire purchase law but that was the least of the job. Some twenty of us sat at our desks sharing four typists between us answering readers' queries – I was the hire purchase and credit expert, very dull. The plum job was Personal Problems. There is a belief that these are made up in the offices, but there was no need. Problems came flooding in by the sackful, unstoppable. Readers would send me pieces of frayed carpet and rotten meat pies and wormy chair legs, and I would do something about it if I could.

The power of the Press is behind you! I told them. The *Mirror*, the People's Friend! We will protect you from your wrongs and increase our circulation while we do it! It was a horrible job – there was a suicide while I was there and the union had to step in to have the boss's mistress fired: she believed in

Efficiency Through Humiliation, and made our lives a misery – but I got about nine pounds a week, and could almost live on it. Fares took up three pounds, and I had to travel five hours a day – from Saffron Walden station at 7 a.m. to Audley End, change for Liverpool Street – but they were peaceful hours. One day I bought an *Amazing* magazine on impulse, running for the train, and became a science-fiction addict and have been one ever since. Those original magazines, with their lurid covers, now fetch fantastic prices: I'd take the covers off: they were embarrassing. But those early writers – Heinlein, Asimov, Kornbluth, Pohl, Simak – were a joy, and oh, the pleasures of the bug-eyed monster, and the alien civilizations, when the ghost was lurking in the old oak beams of here and now, and the deathwatch beetle would go crack, crack, crack all night long, eating away the floorboards your bed rested upon. 'Alienation' in space and time was how my rather disapproving psychoanalyst, Miss Rowlands, was to describe my craving for science fiction a decade later, and no doubt there is something in that. It seldom relates to the personal: it is infinite joyous speculation and what can be wrong with that?

But hey, I was now in the world of riches: I could buy a magazine on the newsstand like anyone else and one lunch-hour I even went to Gamages in High Holborn, cutting through from Fleet Street and the *Mirror* offices, and bought a toy for Nicolas, an Andy Pandy doll, based on the TV show. Not that we had a TV. I practically ran from the station up the hill to the haunted house, that evening, to hand this silly thing to this beaming one-year-old child, with his firm, strong, solid limbs – little boys at this age are a miracle of compactness – rolling and tumbling over uneven floors to meet me. I was grown up at last.

From time to time, running like a thread through my life, I would become conscious of a glittering excitement, a stir of possibility, which came in the oddest places, a playground in New Zealand, a forest in France, now in Gamages, that long-gone department store, which specialized in job-lots of tropical helmets, galvanized buckets, men's braces, gardeners' kneeling pads, floral dresses, and things which increasingly nobody wanted, and just happened to have a pile of cut-price Andy Pandy toys on display. As if my mother's angels were waving at me through some almost transparent, but not quite, carapace of worldly affairs.

My mother, my poor mother, was left to look after the baby by day, but I think she thought she was a whole lot better at it than me. I tended to use only two rinses instead of three for the nappies and he'd get nappy rash. I missed Jane and I missed Serena: I wanted to go to parties, I wanted to meet men, I wanted adventures. I chafed. I met some interesting men on the train, but they always seemed to have wives to meet them. And my mother was decidedly against men and adventures: look where they'd got me. No. Sit tight, keep quiet, gather strength for the next attack from fate.

She was right, but it wasn't me. In the evenings, when Nicolas had gone to sleep, which was late, because he had so little interest in sleeping, I would pace, and pace, and the walls would seem to slope inwards on me and the floor up towards me: perhaps I was my own ghost, or was it that Jane had left hers behind?

The boss's mistress called me in and asked me why I was so slovenly and said I would be fired if I didn't smarten myself up a bit. It seemed to me I had a perfectly respectable grey

270

twinset, though it did stretch a bit over the bosom and was rather over-washed, because babies will be sick down your back when you hold them up to wind them, and a black skirt, which I always wore but how was anyone to know it was the same one? It was usually dark when I left the house, admittedly, and there was the normal shortage of mirrors – just the one propped up over the bathroom basin. And the bathroom was one of the spooky rooms – you didn't linger. But it wasn't as if I was on show to the public: I was very much in the back office. No, the boss's mistress was just having a good time at my expense. This was her pleasure.

She had a tiny waist and wore a full red skirt, tightly belted, and a crisp white blouse. She had flat black hair in carefully organized curls pressed against her forehead and bright black button eyes and a slash of a red mouth. She looked like a witch and we hated her but the boss loved her.

And I was going to be in trouble soon. I knew it. I'd thrown out a piece of smelly stained blanket a reader had sent me, and we weren't meant to throw anything out. I'd told the reader that since the blanket was six years old and bought in a sale anyway, the holing he complained of was not unreasonable and the *Daily Mirror* wasn't going to take up his case. But now he was asking for his patch of blanket back to send it to our rival bureau at the *News of the World* and if he didn't get it he would take the matter further. There would be no end to this, I could tell. I started looking for another job. My, she was a horrid woman! She, and her like, surfaces in my novels from time to time.

Commercial television was about to start. But practically no one in Britain knew how to write the TV commercials which were to fund the new programmes. In the States they were screened live, and then disappeared for ever, unless someone bothered to film the screen and thus kept a record. I answered a Pearl and Dean ad in the back pages of *Campaign*, or its equivalent at the time, to join a team embarking on a new venture in TV advertising, and to my astonishment I was taken on board. My wages went up some more. I bought some new clothes. There were five men in the department and me, which suited me very well. None of us had the slightest idea what we were doing. A man came over from New York to explain what a TV commercial looked like on the page, but he was soon fired. We struggled on, on our own, re-inventing TV advertising from first principles.

There was uproar in the country when commercial television was first mooted. The BBC was considered bad enough: at the time it was obliged to close down every evening between six and seven to allow the nation's children to be put to bed. Television, the gloomy said, would be the end of family life, regular mealtimes, conversation, reading, piano-playing and proper bedtimes. People would sit in front of the screen and eat their dinner on their knees. The children would become delinquent, class envy would be stirred, the nation would lose its respect for its leaders. (All these horrors came about, of course.) But ITV! Advertising! The vulgarity of it! We would turn into a consumer culture. Good God, before we knew it, programmes would be chosen for their popularity, not for their merit. More could only mean worse. The prophets of doom, in my experience, are generally ignored and usually right.

We in our department at Pearl and Dean, traitors to the cause of academia and decency though we were seen to be, also thought hard sell was very vulgar and wouldn't go down well with the British market. I wrote a Black and Decker commercial which went on for a whole two minutes before mentioning the product in the very last line. The commercials were to be done live, on TV – this was not film – so there was no record of what anyone had done before. And ITV hadn't actually started yet, so there was no way of seeing what other people were doing. Meanwhile tape was coming in: it was possible to record, but what was recorded still had to be done 'as-live', because it couldn't be cut.

The general lack of direction bothered my colleagues, who being men wanted to have some kind of specific aim to attend to, but I just loved inventing characters and fitting them into mini-sagas – that being my personal take on the problem of the TV ad – in which the product not the character came out best. One of my very agreeable fellow-workers was Anthony, Shaffer, who wrote *Sleuth*, identical twin to Peter Shaffer, who wrote *Equus*. They were in many ways so different. Same genes, same environment; what would my hero Cyril Burt have made of it?

On 22 September 1955, my twenty-fourth birthday, ITV began. There was a variety show and drama excerpts linked by Robert Morley, and a boxing match. There were six minutes of advertising screened during the variety show, and they were generally acclaimed as tasteful, that is to say there was no real risk of them shifting product. The toothpaste advertisement was ours. We were very proud. The BBC tried to steal our thunder by killing off Grace in *The Archers*. She went into a burning stable alive and never came out. The BBC denied that there was any connection, but then they would, wouldn't they, even then. It was also said she was the one chosen to die because she'd just asked for a rise. It was to set the pattern for the ratings war to come, and the BBC made the first move.

Haunted

With the money left over from my own family's needs, and there was now just a little, I would take food parcels over to Jane's cottage, since Guido came down only at weekends and left her without money for food during the week. He usually brought a parcel of marrowbones, though, which he truly believed could keep anyone nourished for a week, when boiled up with celery. But I think Jane just wanted to live unobserved by her family and I could understand that, so I didn't go often. And Serena didn't want me hanging around, and I could understand that too. She was pregnant again. She had four boys in as many years, and eventually became a lecturer in mediaeval social history, and is as a sister to me still.

We wild, lost girls were just rather too clever for our own good, I think. Ray had married the wrong person and gone to California and Ellen was now an advertising executive having a good time, and trying to *forget*, as the women's magazines would have it, going round with rich men in smart cars. Judy had taken up with Jimmy Wells.

But oh the ghost. It made its presence increasingly felt. At the other end of the line out of Liverpool Street was a different world; Saffron Walden seemed set in some other dimension where you could never be quite sure what was real and what wasn't, what was sane and what was simply mad. It was like moving from the waking world to the sleeping one, where dreams come, only you did it not by putting your head upon a pillow and shutting your eyes, but by getting on a train. Yet Nicolas seemed solid and cheerful enough, and in no way doubtful about the reality of the sloping floors and the beamed walls, and what went on between them. He smiled and held out his arms when I got home – seldom before eight, and then away the next morning at seven.

Crunch time came one weekend when I was alone in the house with Nicolas. My mother was away for a few days. Night fell: the desultory sounds from the fish and chip shop in the yard faded away, and so did the smell of salt and vinegar. My bedroom was in the front room above the shop. Nicolas had a cot in the corner: my bed was a mattress on the floor. Nicolas slept, I couldn't. The street outside was empty. The row of ancient shop fronts opposite were blank and closed. I became convinced there was someone waiting in the corridor the other side of the door. I heard it snuffle and sob a little. Nicolas woke and began to cry. He had finished his bottle. He needed his dummy. The dummy was in the bathroom. I didn't have the courage to leave the room and get it.

The baby set up the most tremendous roar, as was his wont, but when he paused for breath I could hear the sobs outside, getting stronger, as if vying for an attention that was not mine to give. The hungry ghost. There was no curing it, only catching its own fiendish distress. I took the baby into bed and tried to persuade him to suck my finger: he wouldn't. Eventually he exhausted himself and fell asleep, little limbs flung anywhere.

I lay sleepless all night in a state of increasing terror. The fear is absolute, free-floating: it attaches itself, like anxiety, like love, to this, that or the other: rarer than anxiety, rarer than love, but always lurking, waiting to be stirred into life. Yet it seems to be an invasion from outside, and not self-generated at all. Mine was in full roaring flood now, paralysing. I understand why in horror stories the man locked in the haunted room comes out in the morning with white hair. In the early hours whatever it was went away, or at any rate the pressure eased, there was birdsong outside. Someone opened up a shop across the road. The terror faded.

In the morning my mother came back and I told her I wasn't going to stay another night in the house, and she said neither was she. We packed – the meagreness of our belongings always making for a quick getaway – though the baby managed to have an awful lot of gear, by our standards – and we walked up to the station, got on a train, and left Saffron Walden and never went back. We were good at running away. There are always demons to run from, I suppose, though mostly of our own making and I daresay this one was as well.

Ask me if I believe in ghosts and I will say no: they're just the 'cold spot' phenomena researchers say they are, unexpected drops in temperature which create goose pimples and are associated in the mind with the emotion of fear. Pre-menstrual tension, water retention, others will say, causing excitations in the frontal lobes and reproducible in the laboratory. Or the hysteria of the gullible. Sure, I'll believe it, and with gratitude. But then I haven't experienced a ghost for at least thirty years: these days I live with the seen, not the unseen, awake even in my dreams. Not prone to terror from the unreal world, only the real one. I cross my fingers even as I say this.

I can't watch horror films on TV if I'm alone in the house. Yet what is there to fear? Whatever it is seems worse than death, but how can that be?

Orchardleigh, the family house in Somerset where I was to live decades later, was old enough (it was registered in the Domesday Book) to bump and thump rather on the top floor, for no apparent reason. Just enough for us to say 'Oh, is the dog upstairs? He shouldn't be!' And then when it became apparent the dog was sleeping innocently at our feet, to forget about it, since it was inconvenient and troubling to investigate further. Once in the early years books hurled themselves through the air to hit the shoulders of a child guest sleeping peacefully in his bed, but none of us reacted much, more than to say, 'Are you sure someone didn't run upstairs and throw the books?' when there was no one around to run. Really it was little more than a random phenomenon, and mildly benign, until it left the door open for the bleeding, hulking thing upon the stairs.

Happenings such as the water from the kitchen taps giving electric shocks count as the inexplicable rather than the supernatural: the pain is physical, not emotional, and fills you with the ambition to render it explicable and stop it: the supernatural is accompanied by terror and the desire to run away.

I had my own exorcism ceremony at Orchardleigh: I simply burned the house down to the ground in a novel, *Worst Fears*, leaving it to dwell in peace and tranquillity in the real world. Obliged to drive by the place recently I was surprised to find it still standing: in my head it was just a square of black ashes on the ground. A story of mine, *Angel All Innocence*, about unhappy wives and hauntings, the result of so many over-heard footsteps in the attic, suggested that ghosts are like repeating dreams, just yourself trying to tell yourself something you'd rather not know. That's the most plausible.

An art-dealer friend, going recently to visit a painter who knew my mother in the Saffron Walden days, had 12 Market Hill pointed out to him as somewhere I had lived. Apparently the house had just been exorcized, the dealer friend remarked to me, apropos of nothing. Which struck me as rather good news: perhaps the experiences I had there were more than the sum of my neuroses, after all. There is something vulgar about seeing ghosts, or acknowledging their presence, more vulgar than contracting TB, or having babies out of wedlock, let alone running away because of them, more especially if it's all in your own head. Though the Church of England was never averse to going out with bell, book and candle to try to bring peace to the unpeaceful.

Out of the Frying-pan

My mother went to Cornwall, with great relief, and Nicolas and I stayed with Colyn who now had a room in Belsize Park Gardens (where else?). But we had dreadful rows – I wasn't accustomed to arguments. Colyn was actually human and had feet of clay, not the gold I was accustomed to – and living in one room with a man who is not accustomed to living with women, let alone a baby too, and who would rather buy a secondhand book than a loaf of bread, was difficult for both of us. In theory Colyn looked after Nicolas while I earned but it was too early in the world's history for that to work smoothly. Nicolas stopped looking happy, so I moved out, in search of space as much as happiness, and I think Colyn was not sorry to see me go.

My mother came to the rescue again and we found a dull flat a million miles from anywhere that I called anywhere, in Chiswick. Finding accommodation was never easy, once you had a child. *No coloureds, no animals, no children.* You took what you could find. We sold Market Hill to the tenant – by post, because I did not have the courage ever to go in its doors again – paid back Michael, and made a profit of some fifty pounds. The tenant started a small electrical shop, a fly-blown affair. When on occasion I have had to go to Saffron Walden my heart beats very fast. It goes into overload. You can get a physical aversion to places if enough troubling things have happened there, enough to outweigh the good.

Our department at Pearl and Dean closed down a month before Christmas. Soft sell wasn't working and the firm backed out of TV advertising and so far as I know never went back, though their logo continued to dominate big screen advertising in a very impressive way. I would have fired me too, had I been management.

But it is never nice to be told one is inadequate, even leaving aside the financial implications. You slink away like the outcast from the pack, the one who doesn't measure up to expectation. Management has good reason to fear the disgruntled employee – the ones who are assumed to be to blame for contaminating the product or burning down the factory – they have been dealt a fearful blow to their self-esteem and do not take it lightly. And forget redundancy payments or unfair dismissal – such concepts were still twinkles in the legislature's eye. The employer had it all his own whimsical way.

So here I was, unemployed, jobs in short supply, even in the city. I could not afford to be unemployed longer than the one week's pay in lieu of notice would last. The terror of being Nicolas's sole support was borne in upon me. I heard of a vacancy for a receptionist/barmaid in a club in the West End, and took it with gratitude. It turned out to be the Folio Society, a members-only club for those who appreciated beautifully bound and illustrated books, with a tinge of erotica about them. Just a tinge, in the *Fanny Hill*, *Clarissa* school of writing: classics if possible, because what is inexcusable to the present is often excusable in the past. A degree of raciness in their reading kept some of the clergymen members – of whom there seemed to be many – happy, but that was as far as club land went.

What impressed me most was the leisured life so many men of the cultured classes seemed to live compared to their wives. They had time to go to Lord's and watch cricket, sit in their studies in the evenings reading the classics and being vaguely titillated by *Clarissa*. They had time to develop theories about the universe, take offence at other nations and wage war, only because women kept them fed, clothed and clean. Even at work they had secretaries to do the tricky work of actual communication – in those typewriter and pre-Tipp-Ex days getting a single perfect letter out could take a good hour.

When I was a student I had taken a holiday job as a help in a clergyman's household outside Oxford, because his wife 'needed a rest'. The house was an old country rectory. There were bicycles in the hall, polished copper in the kitchen, chintz sofas in the living-room, and croquet on the lawn: another England altogether. There were five sons between fifteen and twenty-five and their mother stayed in her room all the time I was there. I was not surprised. She was evidently on strike. I had been called in as the strike-breaker. None of the men lifted a finger in the house or saw it as their business to do so. The one woman present, me, had to do it all: shopping, cooking, cleaning, laundry, oiling cricket bats and whitening sports shoes. I started at six in the morning and finished at ten at night, during which I prepared their favourite meals and unknotted their stubborn laces and found their lost pencils. Their helplessness and ruthlessness struck me as extraordinary.

The father, whose income came from South American gold mines, stayed in his study most of the day and once a week wrote and delivered a sermon. Otherwise he seemed to do very little for his parishioners. But the family were all very amiable and kind and I was pleased when one Sunday – I did not have a day off: wives are not servants and being unpaid are not employees – they offered to take me to a cricket match with them.

I thought at least I could sit down in the sun for a couple of hours' rest, but when we got there I was handed a basket and asked to pick blackberries to make the summer pudding they so loved. It wasn't that I was a servant – they spoke to me with respect and said please and thank you – but that I was a woman. I felt the first stirrings in my heart of what became known later as 'feminism'. They rather thought I could do for the eldest son, who needed a wife. Perhaps they thought that being a hard worker I would make good breeding material.

My slowness at the typewriter suggested to the Folio Society that I should spend more time behind the bar and less in the office, which suited me. But I was asked to read piles of potential publications – the classical slush pile – and make recommendations as to what should be published. Alas, almost the most important job in publishing, because it is tedious, is the one often passed to the most junior and inexperienced of the staff. But I got through great quantities of eighteenth-century novels, and realized that things stopped around 1860, after which you had to choose between Samuel Smiles and his ilk, or outright pornography. I'd had no idea, I began to see, of what went on in the world, or how delicately I had been reared.

A Royal Academician asked me to model for him and I went to his studio: but once I was there I was affected by a sudden reluctance to take off my clothes, and fled. Fay Davies was a very different creature from Fay Birkinshaw: Davies was a mother. She didn't sleep around, waste time and was for ever having to get back to the baby, anyway.

The next name was to be Bateman, and Fay Bateman turned out to be more neurotic and masochistic than the comparatively responsible and hard working Fay Davies persona could have anticipated. As it was, Fay Davies felt very foolish and that she had probably missed out on a good career as an artist's model, which paid comparatively well, and could be done part-time.

The baby was beginning to suffer from her absence, or she was from his: he would wrap his arms round her legs to try to stop

her leaving the house in the morning. She had to re-think her situation: she must resort to desperate measures.

Davies/Bateman

It is around this juncture that the first person begins to seem inappropriate to the tale and changes into the third. An 'I' for Davies/Bateman is not possible to incorporate into the current Weldon at all. Franklin Birkinshaw can be osmosed, Fay Franklin Davies acknowledged, but Fay Bateman is more than the current 'I' can bear.

The Fay Davies structure broke down under the influence of alcohol on Christmas Eve, 1956: she lost the Fay and became simply Davies hovering on the cusp of Bateman. I will refer to her as Davies. It seemed to Davies to be party time, and though she was meant to take money for the drinks she poured out from behind the bar, she forgot, and soon all the dry sherry and the fine whisky was gone and the bar was drunk dry. And she was fired again. It may just have been that the job was temporary, but she felt fired. She got another job within the week as a researcher for a Gallup poll, standing on street corners stopping men passers-by, asking them why they chose the ties they did. It was very cold, and most men hurried by and those who stopped assumed she was accosting them, and responded accordingly.

So she made the answers up, or most of them, inventing names and addresses, matching the reasons given with likely name, age and address, correctly assuming that if she got it about right no one back at the office would check up. She was promoted to head office on disclosing her qualifications and sat from nine to five, fined an hour's pay if she came in five minutes late, setting up polls single-handed, realizing how much truer to life fiction is than life itself. But you know about that already: I have told you.

The wages were not good. Women's wages were pin-money. She could not support her mother and the baby and herself on what she earned: there were often not two pennies to spare to work the immersion heater which fed the bath, and besides, nobody was happy. Her mother was not well and exhausted from looking after the robust and energetic two-year-old that Nicolas had suddenly become, and her mother, frankly, wanted out. Davies wasn't facing up to her responsibilities: she'd let her mother baby-sit all day and then all night as well. Davies would go to pubs, parties, and goodness knows what. Davies was man-crazy. Davies's mother was frankly pissed off with her. It was time Davies grew up, which in her mind still meant giving up. But not quite yet.

Davies managed to get another job as a junior copywriter in a tiny advertising agency in Dover Street called Scott Turner Limited, which specialized in small ads. She wrote copy for a foot product. '*Did you know that there are 200 tiny bones in every foot, and every one can be a pain?*'

The newly started Institute of Contemporary Arts was in the offices below, and the first ever 'happening' – forerunner of those cultural events which were so to entertain the Sixties – took place in the room below. Naked girls bounced up and down on trampolines in the name of art, which later Davies realized was mostly by men and for men. Davies sat opposite a nice-looking and attractive if rather melancholy man named Michael Birmingham and thought perhaps he was the answer to her prayers but she introduced him to her friend Judy, who married him without delay. This was pretty much the pattern of Davies's life, living it as she did, as did so many at the time, as if the right man was the be-all and end-all of female happiness. Judy and Michael went to Australia and presently Judy divorced him because he was so profoundly melancholic. Not even the love of a good woman could save him, as everyone had hoped.

Davies's problem was that she had a good deal too much love to offer and nowhere for it to go. Davies's current answer to her problems was to eat. There was a café round the corner from Dover Street, below the brothels kept by the Maltese Mafia of the day, where she could buy for next to nothing wonderful crusty rolls filled with ham, cheese, pickles and so forth, which she remembers with delight to this day. Her attitude to food at the time is pretty much that of Esther in the novel *The Fat Woman's Joke*, the first one she ever wrote.

To Davies's mind all people now looked at her with revulsion, including her own mother, her child being the only exception. Babies were easier, mind you, when they just lay and gazed at you in adoration: children were not simple: they had passions, feelings, went right or wrong at your behest. Children suffered, just as you did. The rent was overdue: she had spent too much money on filled rolls for lunch and tea.

Her mother went on strike: no more childcare. This was beyond a joke: she had agreed to help out, not take on a lifetime's task. Davies found a nursery – there were a few available for unmarried mothers – and left Nicolas there for one day, but the faces of the other children were the faces of the poor: pale and strained and miserable, and when she collected her own he looked the same. She realized that she had become one of the poor, the pitiable. She saw the reality of it: that if she failed to look after this child properly he would simply be taken away, put in an orphanage. If she was ill, this was what would happen. There was no safety net at all. She'd been selfish, not wanting him taken away at birth, she should have had him adopted: society was right, it was the kindest option. He would have had a proper mother to look after him, security, a home that didn't keep changing, a father. She panicked.

She would have to get married, and fast. She would donate her sexual and domestic services in exchange for bed and board for herself and her child. It was really no more than what the good girls did: hadn't George Bernard Shaw likened marriage to slavery? The good girls could choose their masters, of course, and surround the bride sale with orange blossom and tulle, to cloud the issue of the transactional nature of what was going on, but that was about all. It was she and her friends, the bad girls, the wild girls, who did not see sex as trade: they waited for true love, and continued in the stubborn belief that though they lay down with wolves they would wake up with lovers. And sometimes, just sometimes, it happened. But the great majority married where self-interest lay: now she would do the same.

She could not hope for much: she would not be spoilt for choice: she had a child, which suggested incompetence as well as loose morals. Even leaving that aside, it was a rare man, in the days when fathers visited the nursery as a stranger, who was prepared to take on another man's child. Why should he? He wanted his wife to pay full attention to his own children, not some other man's: that was why he toiled and struggled to keep her.

Men and women, Davies could see, paired off in roughly equal groupings: the rich marrying the rich, the beautiful the beautiful, her virginity in exchange for his earning capacity, and so forth. Frankly, she did not have much to offer in the marriage stakes.

Davies did have a suitor, whom so far she had tended to ignore. He was a schoolmaster, Ronald Bateman, in his late forties, tall and thin and already rather stooped and grizzled. He'd had a wife and son, briefly, but was now divorced. The son had come ready-made, a stepchild. But they had vanished into the West Country, and there was no legal impediment to a marriage between herself and Davies. Would she consider it?

He was persuasive: she and her child needed the proper home and protection he could provide: his parents, who were devout, working-class Methodists, would be upset for a time by his choice of bride but were kind people. His was a success story: he was the very bright child born to humble people who had made good. He'd been to Oxford – that was a great plus in the status stakes – and had an MA in mathematics. He'd never, she thought, read a novel in his life, which was a kind of relief.

He confided in Davies that as a child he'd had to sleep with his hands tied every night for six months because his mother had once caught him masturbating in the bath. Davies was sorry for him and thought she could make him happy. She'd met him through another boyfriend, a depressive pharmacist who would have been a better bet, being at least rather younger, but he wasn't offering her and Nicolas a home, just an occasional weekend in his one-roomed flat in Belsize Square, and his surname was Willy, which was an even worse bet than Bateman.

The headmaster owned the top half of a house in Chatsworth Gardens, Acton: there was no garden, but it was a long time since she'd had one of those, anyway – in the old New Zealand days, in fact – and he said she could have a cat. He was to start the new term as headmaster of technical college. (These were pre-comprehensive days: there were grammar schools for the academically inclined, technical colleges for the practical, secondary moderns for the great majority who declined to be pigeon-holed; all were small enough schools to have a local and human face, and dedicated and enthusiastic teachers for all of them.)

Ronald Bateman was thrilled by the new direction his life was taking – he was ambitious, and meant to climb the career ladder of school-mastering – and wanted her to be thrilled too. He didn't think they should sleep together until they were married: scandal had to be avoided. This was a strange new world for Davies: but she was inquisitive: she wanted to step into it: she could not face the anxiety of single-parenting any longer. Besides, the rent was due and she didn't have it and Jane was on her own again, and pregnant, and needed her mother's help with Christopher. Poor man, poor Ronald Bateman; that Davies was a heartless, practical monster.

Mrs Bateman

They were married in Ealing Registy Office in 1957: she thinks it was in June: somewhere in her head is the idea that she married three times, all in June, once at Ealing and twice at St Pancras. She was very fat and wore a tight-fitting uncomfortable blue silk suit which he paid for. This was wonderful – you got married and thereafter your husband – your minder, your keeper – paid for everything. You had to ask, of course, but surely that was a small price to pay for freedom from anxiety?

There was a small party afterwards in a wine bar in central London: her idea. He'd worried about the price, and whether his family would feel at ease there: he'd have preferred the Excelsior tea rooms in Acton which could be booked for family functions, but conceded to her tastes. There is no photographic record, which is just as well.

The old Birkinshaw friends were invited and looked alarmed, and she thought horrified, though she could not tell if it was because of her size or her husband. His family likewise, though placid enough, managed to look disapproving: she hoped it was not something intrinsic in her, but just the age gap, which she realized was more than twenty years. She mostly forgot about this herself unless she saw him in his underpants when she realized just how skinny and tired his flanks were. He was a Mason: he seemed to have any number of single male friends of his own age, all of whom looked at her curiously, for some reason, and who were shopkeepers, electricians or slightly seedy-looking business men.

There was no honeymoon, and since her husband complained of feeling unwell there was no sex either, on the wedding night or thereafter, though he did like to share a bed. It was a situation which she could see seemed set to be permanent. If she thought about it too much, which she tried not to do, this was something of a facer: either she was to live sexless for the length of her days, or she would have to be unfaithful, which she had hoped not to be, or she would have to find some reason for divorcing him, which she did not see that she had. Many couples, he assured her, did not have sex. Most of the couples he knew, anyway. She decided, as was her way, not to think about it, but to get on with what there was under her nose.

It was wonderful for Bateman, at first, not to have to get to work: it was wonderful to stay home and be able to build your life around your child's needs, and prepare an evening meal for a returning husband like all the other mothers down the street. She was given a housekeeping allowance, and was without anxiety. It was annoying to have to ask for a new pair of shoes and be told that there was nothing wrong with the ones you had and that they could be re-heeled yet again, but she could endure it. He was a kind stepfather. And she was Bateman, no longer Davies. She wondered if her character would change, and it did.

At first it was merely housewifely, though within the year it was to become delinquent. Mr Bateman gave her some money so she could buy new curtains, and she bought some more of the wrong fabric: a pale shiny green with a kind of Chinesy pattern of dragons on it, popular at the time. Mrs Bateman sewed the curtains and put them up and they made the front room with its bow-windows look worse than ever. She should have bought some of the bold peasanty striped fabrics about at the time and done what she could to overwhelm the old sofa and the cream and brown paint which filled the house, but she lacked nerve. Her mother had always had strong opinions about taste – whether it applied to wallpaper, furniture, hair or clothes, and one way and another she had not managed to develop any of her own. But Doris Day sang '*Que sera, sera!*' on the radio and Mrs Bateman had the house to herself in the day and could dance around with Nicolas to its tune as much as she pleased. What will be, will be!

They bought a television set. It occurred to her to write a television play. She sent it in to the BBC who sent it promptly back saying however well written it was, they could not possibly take a drama dealing with such a subject. It was about a prostitute living as a married woman in a suburb rather like Acton. Mrs Bateman wondered if they meant the play was well written but even so, or even had the play been well written, forget it. Not a particularly self-confident person at the best of times – and something about living in Chatsworth Gardens, this long winding row of similar houses, each lived in by a pinnied woman with curlers in her hair, depleted her sense of singularity – she decided it was the latter and gave up. Mrs Bateman even wrote a novel and sent it to a publisher but the report came back that the dialogue was very bad, no thank you. She threw the manuscripts in the dustbin. Writing novels was too like her mother winding raffia baskets with Ottie Binswanger: it was the home handcraft that got you nowhere.

She gave up and wrote letters to the local council instead, and managed to get a bus stop shifted, a pavement ramped to allow buggy access, and a hole in the road mended. Those were the true days of people power, and she hopes Acton is grateful to this day.

A rather bad-tempered woman had the bottom half of the house: they shared a front door so Mrs Bateman could not do anything without everyone knowing, which she found irksome. Her friends did not come to visit – later they said they simply didn't know what to say – but there was a public library round the corner and she read a lot of books. She secreted enough from the housekeeping to be able to buy a second-hand copy of a first edition of Wyndham Lewis's *The Apes of God*.

Once the novelty of Acton had worn off Mrs Bateman began to get restless. She felt she was getting very old and had achieved nothing nor was ever likely to now. But Nicolas was there and could already read the numbers and destination of the buses that crawled up and down the Acton High Street, on their way to Goldhawk Road, Shepherd's Bush, Notting Hill – distant, far away, exotic places. At least he could have a life even if it looked as if hers was over.

She was lonely, no doubt at all about that. Her mother had taken a job as an elderly lady's companion and was hard to contact. Her sister had gone to live (again without Guido) in the country, where she was beginning to hear voices and had the feeling people were watching her. Mrs Bateman couldn't even talk over the garden fence to her neighbour. She tried but was frowned off. It was considered vulgar: this wasn't the working class, this was the lower middle class and people had their aspirations. Husbands discouraged women from gossiping and out of loyalty to their husbands women refrained from doing so. If a woman happened to be in a neighbour's kitchen when the husband came home, she would melt away through the back door.

The boredom was punctuated by bursts of terror. Her husband liked to go on drives at the weekend. They would go long-distance, for the sake of clocking up miles on the dial. Mrs Bateman would sit in the front seat with little Nicolas on her lap. In those days everyone did it. There were no seat belts and little sense of danger. Mind you, the roads were comparatively empty.

Mr Bateman had bought a new pale blue Ford Popular, an upright four-seater, and had it souped up. The car was famous for its slow and steady dullness and reliability, but this one was capable of sudden bursts of unexpected power. It became Mr Bateman's habit to startle oncoming traffic by overtaking the car in front of him and managing to pull in at the very last minute, just when a head-on collision seemed unavoidable. Onlookers would imagine instant death was on the way, and so would Mrs Bateman. Mrs Bateman begged her husband not to, but as so often characterizes men when driving, if you ask them not to do something they do it more. She would get home from these outings a wreck, though Nicolas loved them and crowed for more.

It was not that Mr Bateman's sexuality was non-existent – on the contrary, it was just thwarted. She could see that the way he drove the Ford Popular was part of its natural expression, and forgave him. Other things were harder to understand. There was some mystery here. He boasted how in his previous job he had supplied the names of communist teachers and student activists to MI5. That shocked her. It smacked of betrayal from within, an abuse of the loyalty others expected. When she wanted to join the local Labour Party he became very agitated: he said a headteacher had to be above politics. She protested, he became hysterical, she desisted. Mind you, when she'd said that now Nicolas was in nursery school perhaps she could take a part-time job and pay for her own shoes, he'd come back at her with 'No wife of mine works'. A working wife was synonymous up and down the street with male failure to provide. So 'No wife of mine joins the Labour Party' was perhaps not so strange.

Nevertheless she was packed off to a couple of weekend courses in Holland Park, now alleged to have been financed by the CIA, on the rule of law. She was allowed a new dress for the occasion: a green poplin shirtwaister. She thought the place was wonderfully grand, the weather was sunny, she made friends. They ate delicious sandwiches on the lawn and had glasses of wine. The lectures were interesting and convincing, though she knew most of the theory from her time at IRD: she did not need convincing that communism was not so hot on personal liberty, why had Mr Bateman been so anxious for her to go? Did he have masters he did not tell her about? Was his ardent anti-communism practical as well as theoretical? Perhaps the way to become a head-master in those Cold War days was to tell tales out of school and go on telling them in the bigger and bigger schools which they would obligingly provide for you?

It would not surprise me: twelve years later, in 1968, when Nicolas was at grammar school, his headmaster provoked a riot at Warwick University, when admission forms were found to have been annotated – 'political activist, do not admit'. It seems unlikely that the forces of reaction, or con-servatism, or the CIA who had in a previous decade funded the literary magazine *Encounter* over here, and Jackson Pollock and his friends on their own side of the Atlantic (on the grounds that content-free art was at least harmless) – would stand by and let the extreme take over the schools and universities. The least they could do was help their friends.

The previous Mrs Bateman, who sounded rather pleasant, telephoned the current wife out of the blue, to say she'd thought she should be warned that the reason Mr Bateman had married her, and quickly, was to achieve consistency on Mr Bateman's application forms for headships: he'd described himself as a man with a wife and son and that was how he meant to stay. He did not want to be found out as a divorced man. It made a kind of terrible sense. Wives were interchange-able. Had she not married her husband on the same principle: that one was much like another? And it was perhaps the kind of thing ex-wives tended to say; not that this one had sounded bitter or resentful, just rather helpful and concerned. She did not take it up with her husband. She had not married him for love, why should she expect anything different from him?

He was full of secrets: he kept his Masonic vestments and regalia in a small suitcase under the bed in their small back bedroom, with its view of vegetable patches, clothes lines and tool sheds. She was forbidden to open the case. It contained secrets women weren't meant to know about. She waited until he went out to open it but could see nothing but a lot of braided garments and a few embroidered hieroglyphics.

She was finding the lack of sex onerous, and tended to snap at him although she tried not to. But nor did she go to any great efforts to mend the situation. She could see the benefits of occupying the moral high ground.

She took Nicolas for long walks, and to the South Kensington Museums. By now she knew the top floors of the Natural History and Science museums by heart. The lower floors had more attendants, and since Nicolas liked to fling his arms in the air and run along the aisles shrieking with pleasure, she avoided meeting them if possible, in case they were asked to leave. Or she would sit on the lawns outside and watch while he ran into flocks of birds and shooed them up into the air. It was such a wonderful example of cause and effect. You ran: they rose. You waited: they returned. You ran – it was never-ending. Sometimes Jimmy Wells would meet her, but more out of pity, she felt, than anything else. She had very little to say. She worried that time was passing by.

An event in Acton! Her husband was elected Master of his Masonic Lodge. He was thrilled. He loved to be master of this and that. This promotion meant she would have to be mistress of the annual Masonic Ladies' Night, the occasion, as it was put to her, when the ladies were rewarded for putting up with their husbands' mysterious absences. She was to choose the menu, stand to welcome the guests as they came in, sit in pride of place at the top table and see that everything ran smoothly. She felt unfit for the task. She hired a dress for the occasion: another of her gauzy mauve efforts which they swore at the shop was fine; but she thought other guests looked askance. Or was it just that they were mostly the grey-permed wives of local business men with strings of pearls around their necks, and she just somehow didn't fit, being younger by far than any of them, and yet the one in charge. She thought the women looked at her husband with new eyes. It felt vaguely exhibitionist of her just to be there, and oddly exciting. Little did they know the secrets of the marriage, or rather the lack of them, at least sexually.

The menu she chose was tomato soup, roast chicken and ice cream and peaches. She tried to deliver something more exotic but in the end there wasn't any choice. She could have served prawn cocktail or half a grapefruit with a cherry in the middle for starters, or roast lamb and mint sauce for the main course, and chocolate gateau for the pudding, but that was the limit of the hotel's expertise. She chose the free gifts from a catalogue, and that was exciting. Everyone was given silver cake-servers. She had never used a cake-server in her life, and now was able to keep an extra four, which the guests neglected to take home with them.

Sent Out

Dangerous driving was no longer enough for her husband. After Ladies' Night his interest in his wife seemed to take a different form. He let it be known that he understood that as a young woman she might feel the need of sex, though again he cited the many couples he knew who never 'did it'. He did know a couple of friends whom he could ask over to oblige: she hoped he was joking, but he did not seem to be. She wondered which of his friends he had in mind. The friends would drop by from time to time, to eat a meal or share a beer, but they'd seemed so respectable, though, it was true, mostly single and in their forties: stamp collectors, churchgoers, members of the amateur operatic society of which Mr Bateman was musical director. She had assumed they were simply not interested in sex.

She thanked him for the offer but said no, it was not wise: supposing word got round: it would not be good for his job prospects. He took the point but said in that case if she felt inclined to go out and find a lover he would have no trouble with that, so long as she was discreet. She would need to tell him all about it, keep him properly in the picture. They were married, there should be no secrets between them.

She took him at his word and would go over to visit Ellen in her little flat in South Kensington on Wednesday evenings. Ellen was now a junior executive at a large central advertising agency, through whose halls passed a flow of visiting executives from sister companies and clients from up-country. They needed to be kept entertained and happy while staying over in London. Mrs Bateman joined Ellen in showing them a good time, as the phrase then had it, sometimes in foursomes in the flat, if the clients felt very daring and wicked, after dinner and champagne: or more discreetly in lay-bys outside London, in those days lined with cars occupied by sex-bent couples with nowhere else to go. Landladies still felt entitled to ban visitors of the opposite sex, either out of a surfeit of respectability or because they genuinely feared being taken to court for running an immoral house.

It was quite dangerous, out on the lay-bys, because the police would come raiding and shine torches into the cars and arrest those inside for indecent behaviour – in the same spirit that today's parking attendants clamp cars, both for the fun of it and to get their daily quota. But fear of discovery added to the danger, and danger, as ever, added to the experience.

No money changed hands, of course, or none that ever came Mrs Bateman's way, though it would not surprise her, thinking about it in retrospect, if advertising campaigns were accepted, or advertising budgets increased, as a result of her and Ellen's efforts to oil the wheels of industry. And the brave, she thought, deserved the fair. She refrained from telling her husband the details he by now so desperately wanted to know, which was mean of her, but she felt he was behaving badly in encouraging her to behave badly, and did not want to gratify him. What was the point of marrying a man old enough to be your father if he did not behave like one?

Part of Mrs Bateman's problem, other than her irrationality, was her curiosity: at that age she thought the only way to know a man properly was to know what he was like in bed.

For example, had she only known more about Mr Bateman, or what there was to know, she might not have married him, but some things were just not destined to be. *Que sera, sera.* She enjoyed having dinner with the clients: she really wanted to know about the problems of manufacturing the products represented by Ellen's advertising agency, how you balance the salt levels in a packet soup newly on the market, and what made the foam in the new generation of washing powders, and what men thought of their wives, and what they hoped for in life, and why coming up to London and having a good time played so important a part in their lives. She wanted to know how the fallout from A-tests had affected the price of milk.

She concluded that for many people sex was the means to an improved self-image, and the need to make money served as an excuse for people who just liked doing what they did. If you heard someone say 'I only do it for the money' it was usually a lie. They did it because they liked it. And most people settled for what they could get – as she had done – and then looked vaguely for ways out, as she was doing.

She met a very pale and handsome Dane in a pub, a Viking, Pers Neilsen, who told her she had the most beautiful shoulders he had ever seen on a woman. He had written a novel: he read books. He sailed boats and worked in an advertising agency as a copywriter. He had coined the slogan of the moment, which was fame indeed. She had forgotten that there were men as desirable as this in the world. He said he was in love with her, but he was a married man, and had usually had a great deal to drink when he said it. So she didn't pursue the matter. But he counted as a real human being, not a Wednesday-night as-if, the quasi men, as she and Ellen called

300

them, the men on a spree, looking for a story they couldn't take home to their wives.

The Batemans went on holiday in Europe, and mother-in-law came too. It was a horrendous event. The husband and the mother did not get on, and Richard was in charge. He drove the car, chose the routes, and decided on the food. Mother-in-law would be booked into the little back room while the married couple had the big front room, and he treated her as the baby-sitter: he had paid for her holiday, after all. She felt the indignity and her daughter felt it too. But they did get to the Dolomites, and to Hitler's Berchtesgarden and to the little town of Innsbruck perched high in the mountains, and Acton seemed a long, long way away, down in a ditch where she wouldn't have to crawl for ever.

In Innsbruck Richard insisted that Mrs Bateman order a speciality of the region: a hot soup into which was dropped a raw egg. When the soup came it was barely warm, and greasy, and the egg was slimy, and Mrs Bateman was disgusted, but Mr Bateman was adamant that his wife eat it, since he would be charged for it. Mother-in-law's jaw set hard and firm. This small incident, the daughter knew, one among so many, would not be forgotten: nor was it to be. In Mrs Bateman's experience men always behaved worse than usual in the presence of their mothers-in-law, and mothers always think their daughters are more happy than they actually are. Mr Bateman tapped his foot. Mrs Bateman gave in and ate, and then went away and was sick. She began to think that perhaps she put up with too much in the interests of a quiet life. But unless she could earn, enough to keep herself and a child too, what choice did she have?

301

As they drove up a winding forest road on the evening after the egg incident, on their way to the next hotel – one booked well in advance: the logistics of the trip were meticulous – Mrs Bateman began to find the road familiar. She remembered a recurring dream which had once blighted the nights of Fay Birkinshaw, that all but forgotten stranger. This was the very road Fay would travel, in her childish dreams, before arriving at a turreted hotel where she would have to stay the night. Then strange clawed creatures would come scrabbling at the window to get her, and she'd wake up screaming: the scream coming out as a squeak, as they do out of nightmare.

The little souped-up Ford Popular reached the very same hotel she knew from the dream: the party was shown down long familiar corridors to the very room she feared – and there were the branches she knew would be there, pressed up against the window – and what Mrs Bateman did, in her terror, was settle her mother and her child in that particular room, and put herself and her husband in the one opposite. She slept soundly and undisturbed all night, and so did mother-in-law and child: no apparitions came, no fearful accidents befell. But she has never forgiven herself, and in what trepidation did she not travel until the little, dysfunctional family were out of the mountains, and home again: surely fate had simply missed a beat and would catch up with them? But no. Nor did she have the dream again, not even when she became Weldon, the continuation of Birkinshaw by other means. If there's a moral or a message here she can't detect it – other than that in some instances cowardice can stand you in good stead.

Mrs Bateman's mother, thoroughly depressed after this inside view of her daughter's marriage, took a job as a guard on the London Underground. Winter was coming on: a free top-coat was offered as part of the uniform, famous throughout London for keeping the cold out. In pre-central heating days survival was more significant than fashion.

Her mother worked with the influx of West Indian immigrant labour brought in to man the Underground, because the native British were too lazy, or so it was said: that is to say they wouldn't work for the pitiful wages offered, and who could blame them? She became fond of a station manager, a lawyer back home in Trinidad, but as ever nothing came of it. 'Who, me? Wash a man's socks? Never!' She earned recognition for various acts of bravery: she alone was prepared to go down the tracks with the live rail still on, to do the various tasks which needed to be done. Automatically, she took on the worries and responsibilities of management, though she did not earn their pay.

The safety devices at some stations, built at the turn of the century, had never yet been tested, she had found to her alarm. They were designed to work only once. Coiled on the top of every lift, perhaps even today, is a grappling iron on the end of a rope, which in the event of a sudden fall whirls upwards, by sheer force of gravity, to claw into the side of the tunnel and arrest the lift's descent. They have been there for more than a hundred years, some of them, and who is to say the mice haven't nibbled the rope, or time has frayed it? But what can you do? And what can you do about a daughter who has deliberately disappointed you? Thrown away her life on babies and loose living? Married a man who makes her eat raw egg in warm greasy soup?

Mrs Bateman encountered her mother, then a guard on South Kensington station, and her mother refused to recognize her – cut her dead, in fact. Her mother had had enough. Mrs Bateman had not, however. Not quite.

The technical college was running well and efficiently. Pupils passed their exams. Mr Bateman, as Musical Director of the Amateur Dramatic Society, put on a performance of *The Vagabond King* for the local dramatic society. Like many mathematicians he was musical, though his taste tended to lie towards Gilbert and Sullivan rather than Wagner. *Love for sale, love for sale!* He was obsessed by the notion of prostitutes. Mrs Bateman tended to blame his mother: though the mother, tying her son's hands together to prevent self-abuse, was merely trying to save her son from going blind or mad. Everyone does the best they can for their children, according to the fashion of the day.

Her husband was applying for jobs at other bigger, grander colleges. He meant to get them, come what may. He was trying to buy a house up in Ealing, a better address. They saw a really nice house for two thousand pounds, but he thought it was more than he could afford. She suggested again that she took a part-time job but he shook his head: it wouldn't look good on the forms. A headmaster, like a doctor or a clergyman, needed a full-time wife. His pockets were full of bits of string, and *objets trouvés*: everything short of white mice. He was a schoolboy at heart, she realized, still going through a prurient phase: he had innocent round eyes and a gentle, surprised expression and still quite a lot of hair. She'd moved on to the sofa in the living-room out of the marital bed: it was easier that way. The silk Chinese curtains were too thin to keep the light out. She woke early and read Kerouac, Sinclair Lewis and Henry Miller. She had a terrible sense of time passing, and wasted: irretrievable.

Mrs Bateman foolishly happened to mention to Mr Bateman that one of the stall holders in the local market kept trying to chat her up. A hard-sell merchant, broadly built, powerful-voiced, good-looking if mean-eyed, fast on his feet. Mr Bateman went down to take a look at him, though Mrs Bateman couldn't quite think why. On his return Mr Bateman said, 'Next time he tries it on, ask him how much he pays.' *Love for sale!* Mrs Bateman did as her husband suggested. Some things are easier to do if you are instructed to do them than if you have to proceed on your own initiative. 'Pair of nylons?' murmured the market trader into her ear, in response to her question. Mrs Bateman returned the banter, feeling it would be undignified to bargain further, and the deal was clinched, and an assignation made for next Friday afternoon, at his place. A pair of nylons counted as a gift, rather than as payment. Anyway she fancied him. Acton was driving her mad.

Alas, the market trader enjoyed power, and his own strength, and liked to humiliate women. To the strains of 'Tammy's in Love' on the radio – a soppy tune she has never liked since – turned up to drown out any cries of protest, she found herself trapped in the front room of a respectable suburban house, empty but for him and her, thickly and pinkly carpeted in the new expensive deep nylon pile, stripped, humiliated and forced into painful and unwanted sex. Then, while she wept, he gave her the pair of nylons. Well, what did she expect? She could scarcely cry rape since she had freely put herself into this situation. She was to turn up the following Friday, he said, if she knew what was best for her. She had thought she was anonymous but now he said he knew who she was: none other than wife to the master of the local Masonic Lodge. Same time, same place, same treatment, no doubt. Blackmailed!

I am sorry to say that Mrs Bateman's neurotic appetite for drama, not to mention her free-floating masochism – she had begun to read the works of Karen Horney, the psychoanalyst, and now had a vocabulary for her own compulsive behaviour – made her almost sorry when he cried off the following Wednesday, telephoning her at home to do so, citing his wife's return, and all but apologizing, though saying in his defence that her selling herself so cheap had made him angry. He hated under-selling. It was pathetic.

She followed his career with some interest: he moved from the market to run a clothes shop in the West End – years later, when she would get out at the Underground station nearest her analyst for her early-morning session she would sometimes see him opening up the shutters – and thence to opening a chain of rather smart high street shops she liked to frequent. It gave her a sense of power – picking up garments, looking them over, deciding not to buy them.

'Did you enjoy yourself?' Mr Bateman had asked on her return, but again she refused to give him any detail, if only because she knew he would be upset to find out that he had been recognized and his reputation was at risk. She went on a diet, spurred by the fact that the market trader had remarked in his meanness that it was a good thing for her he liked fat women, since no one else was going to want her. It was not necessarily or observably true, but she did not like it said. She lost two stone in as many months. The more she lost weight the more restless she became.

There were no more Wednesday nights with the executive classes. Ellen had gone north to live with a car dealer who promised her the earth and was to leave her with nothing. Mrs Bateman looked up Pers again: they'd meet in Chiswick at the Black Horse pub, which looked out over the Thames. They'd embrace on its banks in the moonlight. He told her he loved her, that she had to leave home: he could find her a job in advertising, he would do anything he could to help. Then he'd go home to his wife.

Mr Bateman had a bright idea. If she wanted a part-time job and her own income so badly why didn't she apply for a job as a nightclub hostess? She was svelte enough by now. She could do it under a false name. (Mrs Bateman had a fleeting idea that perhaps the market trader had been one of Mr Bateman's 'friends', or had become one for the occasion, and that she had been set up. How otherwise had he found out her telephone number? She dismissed this at the time as too improbable. Now she is not so sure.) No one asked questions in clip joints, Mr Bateman assured her, she wouldn't be recognized, P45s weren't asked for and the fact that she worked needn't go down on his application forms.

Mr Bateman scoured the ads of the sleazier papers and found something he thought suitable. '*Wanted: attractive, experienced girl for bar work, busy West End nightclub, good tips*,' or words to this effect. He went with her to buy as revealing a dress as the fashions would allow, and drove her down in the little blue souped-up Ford Popular to a clip joint behind Piccadilly, not far from the Windmill Theatre. He drove decorously and without risking anyone's life: he was finding new ways of dealing with unconsummated desires. It would be exaggerating to say that inside many a respectable pillar of the community is a pimp waiting to get out: just as it would be to say that inside many a housewife is a tart: but the proportion is probably equal. They deserved one another. Mr Bateman left her outside, and waited until she had gone in before driving away.

Mrs Bateman usually went around most decorously dressed, with high collars and sleeves buttoned at the wrist, but she could see she would get a taste for exhibitionism, and for the sight of flesh and cleavage when she looked down, not sensible wool. She got the job and started that night. Management were flattering and said they appreciated her looks, her accent, and her manners. She would be an asset to them. It turned out to be as sufficiently respectable a job as you wanted it to be. You sat on a barstool waving your legs, wearing as few clothes as public decency allowed, encouraged men to buy drinks, danced with them if they wanted to but few did, being nervous about their dancing skills, and if you wanted to make any other arrangement, management said, that was up to you, nothing to do with them. Not on these premises though they did know of others.

One of Mrs Bateman's co-workers, Angel from the East End, who was eighteen and indeed had all the beauty and transparency of an angel, albeit one half-starved from birth, said that after a bit, if they trusted you, they'd send you off in a group to the criminal parties where the tips were very good, or the Arab ones, where the money was even better but you had to put up with stuff you didn't like. But these were optional extras. No obligation.

Mrs Bateman tended to drink the real champagne rather than the fake stuff the barman tried to give her and had rather a

308

good time. Men would offer to take her away from her life of shame, or at least to a quality club in St James, home-grown and not run by the Maltese, where she would find a better class of customer and earn more. A scientist from the Harwell Atomic Research Centre, hearing she had a degree in Economics and believing her – few did, and why would they? – offered to marry her. She quite saw herself as a scientist's wife, but alas he never came back to confirm the deal.

Nevertheless Mrs Bateman could see her way ahead to earning enough money to buy herself out of a marriage she had come to see as intolerable. She also knew that nothing was as simple as it seemed: what you anticipated seldom happened in the form you expected. The primrose path to independence by way of sex would be hedged about by pimps, criminals and smiling people with hidden agendas. It would not do. Sell your body and you sold your soul.

She did not mind taking wages for the dangling of the legs from barstools, the semi-baring of the bosom, the flirting and the dancing – it beat accosting men in the street on Gallup Poll's behalf and asking them questions about the colour of the ties they wore – even when minor liberties with body and dress were taken by enthusiastic punters. But when it came to actual sex Mrs Bateman would rather give it away for free than feel indebted to those who paid her.

This attitude was not popular either with management or the other girls. It was undercutting: the amateurs were trying to take over from the professionals. What was to become of the bad girls if the good girls began to do it for free? It was a question much asked through the Fifties and Sixties. As it transpired, with the arrival of easy contraception the good girls did indeed do it for free, and still the bad girls continued to earn.

Then Mrs Bateman frightened herself. She was followed to Piccadilly Underground in the early hours by one of her clients, a man with a metal hook instead of a hand, a gentleman farmer from the Shires, she having refused his earlier demands that she should come with him to the Strand Palace Hotel for the night. He claimed she was discriminating against him because of his hook, and she denied it, but alas it was true. She was terrified. He had seemed a pleasant enough man, and indeed handsome, just desperate with loneliness, as were so many who came to the club. Perhaps in the grander clubs in Piccadilly they were less sad, playboys and jet-setters, but she had come to doubt it. The farmer clawed into her coat with his hook so hard two police officers came to her rescue, and she ran for safety in her torn coat, down into the Underground for the last train, before she could be interviewed, named and possibly traced. She decided that was enough. She really could not bear to be the delinquent Mrs Bateman any longer. She would settle down to be the good Mrs Bateman, the headmaster's wife.

She phoned the club to say she wasn't coming back but would be calling to collect her outstanding wages, but they refused to pay: she hadn't given proper notice, and they would have to re-advertise the post. It was remarkable, thought Mrs Bateman, how self-righteous people could be when it suited them. No one seemed able to look at themselves, coolly, from the outside. Their reality was all that could be seen in the light cast ahead by their own wishful thinking.

Mr Bateman complained he would not have bought her such an expensive dress had he known how little use she would get out of it. He hoped she would at least return to work her month's notice out, but she did not. She told him tales of her experiences, much embellished, to placate him.

Running Away

She now had three children to look after. Ronald had been very good in letting them come to stay. Jane's children: Christopher aged four and Rachel aged two. Jane was looking for accommodation and work elsewhere. They were both wide-eyed, beautiful children. Rachel's fine blonde fringe fell into her eyes, which were open to infection and got sticky round the edges, so Mrs Bateman took it upon herself to cut the fringe. Guido called to see his children and afterwards wrote Mrs Bateman a long letter accusing her of infringing his parental rights by having his daughter's hair cut without his permission. He was disappointed with her.

Fay felt rather bitter about this, since he was contributing neither money nor time to their upbringing. But she was glad Guido cared, and he was after all an artist and she knew how hard it was for artists to earn a living. It emerged that he'd had another child called Christopher by a previous marriage. He liked Christopher as a name. Sometimes, when she compared it to that of other people, Mrs Bateman thought her own behaviour was not so remarkable. Then Jane moved in, having nowhere else to go, and Mrs Bateman had to move out of the living-room with the bow-windows and the stupid curtains and back into Mr Bateman's bed, where, like Scheherazade, she was obliged to tell him stories late into the night.

Then Guido moved in too, to be with his family. Ronald Bateman welcomed the company. Guido found the money to have a whole wall of bookshelves built in the front room for his books. There were so many books there was little space for the children to play. Mrs Bateman kept her copy of *The Apes of God* with the cookery books her husband bought her for birthdays and Christmas. This was another pattern Mrs Bateman began to see was typical of men. They must have their possessions around them, and they only occasionally saw these as including their children. Since she had stopped being Davies and become Bateman, Colyn had vanished from her life.

Sometimes she wished she were a housewife in Luton, not in Acton. Guido moved out again as soon as the bookshelves were built, leaving row upon row of empty shelves and Jane pregnant again. But Jane was cheerful and in good order and at least now Fay had someone female to talk to.

She went to a fortune-teller in Shepherd's Bush Market. He was a tall, thin, youngish man who stood in the open air with a crowd around him. You handed him an object you kept about yourself and he could tell everything about you. She waited her turn and handed him her diary. He all but dropped it, saying this was the unhappiest object he had ever touched, crossed himself and handed it back. She remembered a dog who had turned tail and fled in St Andrews at the sight of her, when she first arrived there. Ghost once more, and an even more miserable one at that! She had lost her identity, she might never get it back. She was really going to have to do something.

Ina, of all people, came walking up Chatsworth Gardens to visit the girls, looked around, looked appalled, and said their father would turn in his grave to see them living like this. That's all very well, thought the girls, but if Ina hadn't entered their father's life they mightn't be living like this in the first place. They might be happy New Zealand housewives, for all they knew. And what did Ina know about trying to look after three young children? The place was bound to be a mess. And their husbands might be elderly but at least they had them, and Ina did not.

But that did it, for the younger one, at any rate, the one to the left of the Rita Angus childhood painting, all hope and no experience. She had just had a message from her father after all this time: he was turning in his grave. The one to the right, the darker, older one, just went into her head and wrote poems. One day the older girl went to Barker's Store in Kensington High Street and came back with a fur coat she hadn't paid for and the younger sister had to take it back. The girl in the shop was nice and said it happened quite a lot, with girls who weren't quite right in the head. Mrs Bateman could see she was going to have to stop messing around and look after everyone.

Mrs Bateman decided the first thing was to leave. She would tuck Nicolas under her arm and run, anywhere. She couldn't announce her going because really she had nowhere to go and the authorities might move in and stop her. So she packed her suitcase secretly, stole four pounds from Mr Bateman's wallet while he slept to fund her flight into freedom, and without even telling Jane made her escape with Nicolas, who although it was midnight seemed quite agreeable to their departure.

She pushed his buggy with her suitcase hooked on to it all the way from Acton to South Kensington, where she stayed with friends from St Andrews. They were extremely good to her. She developed the most tremendous cold in the nose and it was five days before she was fit to leave the house, which was a studio in Yeoman's Row designed by Wells Coates, the Bauhaus architect from Canada. You had to climb up little ladders to get to the alcoves in the wall where the beds were: it was a house designed for proper adults, living in a world of surplus discrimination and taste, not women and children on the edges of necessity. It was a world she meant to join. She had no idea how, but she would. Nicolas was four: he had a positive view of life: he could read and write fluently and engage in a decent conversation. Mrs Bateman, previously Davies, née Birkinshaw, found herself able to resume the first person again. She was Fay Bateman, not Mrs Bateman any more. She could put her adventures as a married woman behind her and pick up where she left off.

Fay Bateman

Three months later I was living with my mother and Nicolas in a flat at 11 Stanley Gardens, Notting Hill. This was a large Edwardian terrace house owned by Rachman, the famous slum landlord. He was, by all accounts, a very pleasant and generous man, much loved and respected by the Polish community in London, of which he was a member, but ruthless when it came to business, and his tenants. He threatened, extorted, and bullied. How else could he afford to be so generous to those he knew but by being mean to those he didn't?

He certainly did not know us. We lived in one large room, divided into three by plasterboard partitions, and shared a bathroom on the stairs, which was lit by a ten-watt bulb – cheaper to keep this one burning day and night than risk the expense of one of a higher wattage left burning. The bath water was heated by a penny-in-the-slot geyser, which spurted soot over the naked body from time to time, but hey! the place wasn't haunted so the murk didn't matter. The furniture was nailed to the floor in case the tenants chose to burn it for warmth, and every Friday the rent collector came for his six pounds. He was a ruffian with a big Alsatian dog and had a wooden leg. Tap, tap, snuffle, snuffle, tap, up the stairs. The Portobello Road was round the corner and the world our oyster.

It was good to be free again, earning, recovered to a large extent from the anxiety that had driven me into my husband's arms. Mr Bateman had settled down well enough to my departure and even gave me fifty pounds to help me set up house, which was good of him. He was under no legal obligation to support me in any way, since I was a runaway wife and the house was not in our joint names. He seemed puzzled by the fact that I had run away and not just told him I was leaving, and so am I, in retrospect. I think perhaps women instinctively fear the wrath of the man they mean to run out on, and are frightened, often quite without cause, of his violence. As it was, I think my going was a relief to him: I had stirred up too many disturbing emotions in him: he had taken risks which were not in his nature: now all that could subside. He had Jane to cook his breakfast and evening meal, and again he had application forms for headships whizzing round the country.

Jane did not stay for long. Guido was sometimes there and sometimes not. She moved to a flat in Chelsea, in a house owned by Denys Val Baker, a writer from St Ives. There is, among his *oeuvre*, a novel called *Rose*, which is very much about her stay in his house. She becomes a figure of mystery, beauty, poetry and reproach, which is how I remember her.

Nicolas went to a near-by Montessori school around the corner from Stanley Gardens and began to learn Latin. He even came home claiming to be able to ride a horse. Now he was at school most of the day my mother was cheerful enough about looking after him: she had tried the outside world again and found it wanting. And I, I could provide properly at last. I had a job as a copywriter at Crawfords, in Holborn: once you had one job in advertising, in a big agency, you were likely to be able to find another. True, I was writing fashion accounts, which were simply not me, but I was too deeply in love with the married Pers to worry too much about what would now be called work-related problems.

It was Pers who found me the job, of course. How else did women get good jobs? It was current wisdom that you had to be four times better than a man to get any job and it didn't seem to me, certainly at that time, that I was better than anyone at anything. I had been hired by a Mr Mackenzie, a rather plain, small man, who told me that it was a woman's main duty to be attractive to men, especially in the office. This idea startled me and I made him rather cross by asking,

'Why?' He didn't answer, only snorted round for a bit but still gave me the job. I was lucky.

But what did I, out of Acton, know about the state of heels, the length of hems? In Paris Yves Saint Laurent had raised hemlines, though everyone else's stayed mid-calf, and had brought out some ridiculous puffed skirts, and Chanel kept producing the same dull old suits, that much I knew: and you would see girls around with beehive hair-dos, high scratchy edifices which made them look scared and nervous – but fashion was just not my scene.

In the Nineties I was to go to the Paris fashion shows with the editor of *Allure*, and finally discover what it was all about, and succumb to the hysteria of the annual ritual, which is, I decided, to do with the simultaneous worship and defilement of the female image, Paris being her original sacred grove, but it was never really my scene. Those involved fought and spat and sneered like cats. Fashion journalists stamped on each other's toes with their stilettos to get in to the most popular shows. The goddess always descended late. For all she looked so pretty, sweet and chic, the editress fired her chauffeur because he kept her waiting two minutes in the rain outside the fashion house Hermès. The gods moved over from Olympus to the Marais, that's all, the same whimsical, powerful, dangerous, exquisite creatures as ever, and go about in human guise. It's best to steer clear of them.

But I got by. I shared an office at Crawfords with Elizabeth Smart, mother of the poet George Barker's four children, and she taught me how it was done. She would fall into the office from time to time, dishevelled and beautiful and infinitely romantic, with her quivering mouth and distracted eyes, and would show me how to write fashion copy: all adjectives and no verbs. She explained to me that to suffer because of men was the most normal thing in the world.

She told me casually how once she had gone on holiday with George: they were driving down to the Riviera: she was very pregnant and they had with them two small children aged under three. They were in Spain, and marooned in a small hotel on a crossroads deep in the countryside. George had spent so much on drink there wasn't enough money to pay the hotel bill. So they had to stay where they were, unable to afford to leave, running up the bill day by day, not knowing what to do. One afternoon, she was up in their bedroom seeing to the children, and George was sitting outside drinking, when a big open car full of their friends screeched to a stop outside.

'George,' they cried, 'what are you doing here?'
'I'm on my way down to the Riviera,' he said.
'Do you want a ride down?' they asked.
'Yes,' he said, and simply got into the car there and then and they drove off in a cloud of dust.
'What happened?' I asked. Pers might be behaving badly, borrowing money from me to take his wife on holiday, so they could work it out, or going sailing round Malaga without warning, but he was not in this league. Elizabeth said it was the best thing George could have done: it turned out really well, the nuns looked after her and the children, and after the baby was born shipped the fatherless family back to England. 'And George?'
'George turned up after the trouble was over. He always did.'

I got a raise; once you had the all-adjectives, no-verbs trick it got easier. I was given a hair-conditioner and a bra account of my own. First hair-conditioner ever: a spin-off from the space race, they said – it was monkeys-into-space-and-back-alive time – and suddenly all the women in the country had shiny, manageable hair – manageable was one of the great adjectives of the time, as if everything was about to take off out of control, which it was. And I was taken round a bra factory by the client as if I was a person of importance – so much conical stitching and white fabric everywhere: but points were going out, I was told. The nation was wanting softer, more human shapes: here were some of the new underwired bras, to relieve the weight of the straps on your shoulders, and some in black and even scarlet, and in satin, not just puritanical scrub-clean cotton. You could get all this fascinating information from source, it seemed. You didn't have to resort to lay-bys and flashing police torches to get it.

An account executive went to great efforts to procure me for Perry Como, the singer, who was on tour and needed someone for his bed, but I declined. I said it was because I wasn't that kind of girl – and it was true, I no longer was – but mostly it was because I didn't have the right clothes or the time to buy them, if I was to give the occasion of my best. I have always regretted it: whenever I hear 'Catch a Falling Star' I lament my pusillanimity. Who is to say what might not have happened next? He was a falling star and I should have caught him, put him in my pocket and never let him fade away.

By the autumn Ronald Bateman had taken up with another unmarried mother and son, so his forms and his lifestyle continued to match, and taken over the headship of one of the biggest new comprehensives in the country. He wrote me kindly letters from time to time, over the years, and I would reply in similar vein. Jane had her baby, a boy, Benjamin. I took her to the hospital in the ambulance and when I called them later they said they could only disclose the sex of the child to the husband. He's not around, I said, but that made no difference: as much as their job was worth. Whatever changes?

Hopeless in Love

We moved to a top-floor flat in a giant corner house in Lexham Gardens, Earls Court. It was vast, unfurnished and on the sixth floor. I bought a round Chinese carpet, a total luxury, which for once looked right when I got it home, and was thrilled by myself. We had a television set. There were six flights of stairs but at least Nicolas didn't have to be carried up them any more. He went to a smart new primary school called Bousefield, meant to be the best in London, and came top in all his subjects. He started asking about his father, and as my mother pointed out, since at least I had one to offer, I really should provide one. I got in touch with Colyn and he came back into our lives, with alacrity, and took Nicolas swimming the day a new front tooth came through and Nicolas fell and cracked it and has had a crooked smile to this day. Fathers, I thought! But Nicolas evidently thought it was a small price to pay to have one.

I spent a lot of time with Pers in pubs: the late Fifties were their heyday. Homes were still cold and uncomfortable, the habit of dining with friends had not yet quite taken off – though the upper classes had always done it – stay-at-home wives were dull and reproachful and bored, and their magazines, still full of cookery and sewing tips, encouraged them to be so. Who'd want to go home? I never liked beer, though, and the wine was sour, and seldom drunk anyway – and it was only the love of Pers that kept me in there.

In the pub culture of the day the men kept an inside circle of noisy and drunken good cheer and the girls milled around the edges, comparing notes and going to the loo to fix their lipstick and their amazing beehive hair-dos, sustained by the occasional pinch on the bottom from their man, to show they hadn't been forgotten. When the pub closed the men and women would pair off and the girls would steer their menfolk home for drunken and ineffective lovemaking. The girls took a lot of Valium. Downers were the fashion, not uppers.

One morning we woke to find Pers's wife in my bedroom, crying, saying she had supposed he would be here, the children were missing him. But I didn't care a whit for her or her children. I was very offended by what I saw as her impertinence, turning up unannounced in my bedroom. I am appalled by my own bad behaviour now. I owe her and her children an apology. But young women in love are ruthless, and without conscience at the best of times: and these were not the best of times; it was before the concept of sisterhood had taken root and begun to grow, and though it's a sickly plant at least women now have a notion of it. They can think themselves into their sisters' heads. But then women were reared to be in a state of competition with one another: they were catty and bitchy in a way they are not now, but men are beginning to be. Divide and rule. The dominant gender always tries it on.

Pers gave her all his money, though, and borrowed a lot of mine, to assuage his guilt. He couldn't make up his mind, his marriage or me. He gave up his job and took to delivering yachts to the Mediterranean for rich hobby sailors, and was away a lot, trying to make up his mind, writing another novel. I would sing 'For those in peril on the sea', when I wasn't crying.

I cried so much I fell into Jimmy Wells's arms. He cheered me up a great deal: focused, organized and possessive in his passions as he was. But then Pers came back and Jimmy had to go, and when Pers and I looked out of the window in the morning there was Pers's car with 'adulterer' written in white paint all over it. I couldn't understand why Jimmy was so angry: he gave me up as a bad lot and took up with a girl who worked in the local supermarket, whom he later married. It is always easier to be dumped if the relationship one is dumped for turns out to be serious. I wasn't suitable for him anyway, since I didn't ride a bicycle and it was expected of his lovers that they would ride with him to the outermost limits of the earth, to be devoured by bears if necessary.

I think novelists may be like other professionals: astute when it comes to others, hopeless when it comes to themselves. Quite blind. In the same way that the accountant is baffled by his own accounts, the doctor fails to diagnose his own illness, and the shoemaker's children go shoeless, the writer, so clear about the conduct of others, misses some central part of the narrative while living through his own.

I was headhunted. I realized I must be good at copywriting. I could still not afford to have any moral qualms about what I was doing for a living. Necessity ruled. Advertising was still an innocent toddler, as was television: they had not

322

yet created the consumer society: we had no idea what these animated children were to grow up to be. I moved from Crawfords to Colman Prentice and Varley, where I was on the *News of the World* account and became the protégée of one of the wittiest men I have ever met, Maurice Smelt, who now lives quietly in the Scilly Isles, among flowers. He was a grammarian, a perfectionist and a father of four. He taught me the value of precision: he rejected nearly everything I wrote until in the end I understood why it would not do. It was he who, pacing up and down the office with the intense dedication of the churchwarden he was, hit upon the headline for Diana Dors's memoirs – *'I've been a naughty girl'* – which shook the bourgeois world at the time. He it was who invented the slogan *'All Human Life is There'* for the *News of the World*, or at least retrieved it from Henry James.

I was by now so established in the world that I even had time to take an interest in the misfortunes of others. Jimmy Wells asked me to help his new girlfriend, the one in the supermarket, to write a difficult letter. (He was allowed to take offence: I was not, but that's the way it is.) It was to an unknown young woman in a small village in Scotland, who had been sending desperate letters to her boyfriend at the shop's address. She was pregnant. She signed herself Chrissie. Someone had to write back to Chrissie and break it to her that her boyfriend had given her a false address and it was no use asking him for help, she would have to help herself. The sooner she knew she was betrayed the better, all agreed. It was decided that I was to be the one to write and sign the letter.

I sent back the letters with a suitable note, adding 'if I can be of any help', as one does – and six weeks later Chrissie was on my doorstep, out of breath from six flights of stairs, unannounced, a sweet, distracted girl. We took her in; she had nowhere else to go.

When she arrived she was straight up and down and scarcely looked pregnant at all. Two days later it was obvious that she was at least six months gone. Her body, allowed at last to give up the effort of concealment, relaxed, and swelled with gratitude. Her aim was to have the baby adopted in London and go back home and get back to college – she was training to be a nurse – and marry her steady boyfriend with no one knowing. She was a good Catholic. It had been a holiday romance: she'd gone to Spain with her parents – primary school teachers – and met a medical student from South Africa. He'd sworn he'd look after her if anything 'happened' and left his address. She'd told her parents she was taking a course in obstetrics down south: her boyfriend knew nothing; so far as he was concerned she was a virgin.

She'd been with us a week when she ran into trouble with the adoption people: she'd rashly put on her form that the putative father had once said he'd been 'depressed': the society thought this might indicate mental illness: they would not take the baby for adoption. Now she was denied a place in their mother-and-baby home. The custom of the time was that the mother moved in six weeks before the birth, gave birth, looked after it for six weeks in case she 'changed her mind' – in the unlikely event, that is to say, of the father turning up out of the blue to marry her or her parents relenting and taking her in – and only when she was well and truly bonded would the baby be removed. As it was, now Chrissie would have to stay with us: there was nowhere else for her to go. She went to St George's Hospital – now the Lanesborough Hotel – for the birth but came back failing to believe the

324

baby was hers, other than naming it Nicolas. She wouldn't hold it, feed it, or change its nappies: she denied the poor little thing's existence. My mother and I looked after it. One Sunday when the baby was six weeks old Chrissie put it in the nice new pram we had provided and took it for a walk. She came back an hour later with an empty pram. She'd left the baby with the priest who officiated in the Catholic church in, I think, Abingdon Road, round the corner from us.

I ran round to see him but the baby was already gone. The priest had given it to one of his parishioners, a nice lady with two children of her own, who lived in Pembroke Square (a good address) who needed something to fill the void now that her husband had died. It was perfectly legal, he assured me; what was called a third-party adoption. After discussing the matter with Chrissie he had decided it was the best solution for everyone. And so, I daresay, it was, though I sometimes wonder what became of that other little Nicolas.

Chrissie went back to Scotland the next day. The house felt very empty. We had a letter from her presently saying she was well, and had married her boyfriend and was pregnant, not mentioning the baby at all, but thanking us. I wrote a radio play later called *Run, Chrissie, Run*, in which she runs back to the church and reclaims the baby, but no one ever produced it. I think it seemed both unbelievable and sentimental.

Work Among the Poets

We kept to ourselves, we copywriters. We had our own pubs, restaurants, went to the same parties and seldom met anyone who wasn't in the trade, who might look at us askance and mock our enthusiasms. We were good at justifying ourselves: spoke about the valuable economic role of advertising in society, in increasing markets and so bringing down prices: the need for communication – how was the housewife to know that there were new, better products on the market if advertising didn't tell her so? Look at our posters, aren't these the new art? No, came the sour answer, they're nothing but commerce. And what is more, you are Americanizing this culture, with your short words and cheap ways.

All the same, when we met in the pub behind Berkeley Square – where the biggest agency of them all loomed, J. Walter Thompson, as did the eagle of the US embassy in the next block down, Grosvenor Square – there would be poets and artists enough. Peter Porter, Edward Lucie-Smith, Edwin Brock, Gavin Ewart, Peter Redgrove, David Wevill, his wife Assia; and novelists and playwrights too – William Trevor, Jill Neville, John Bowen, Julian Abercrombie, Jonnie Gathorn Hardy, all working as copywriters. Outsiders all, preparing for their great leap forward, learning the ways of the world. By which I mean they learned to write more persistently and fill up page after page with words, create books rather than booklets, plays rather than commercials, and wait for the applause, for years if necessary. Advertising is all small spaces and instant gratification; art takes for ever.

Stanhope Shelton, creative director of Ogilvie, Benson and Mather – I was to follow Maurice Smelt there when he was headhunted and wooed away from CPV – was famous for saying to the poets who applied to him for jobs, 'Ah yes, poetry. A good training for copywriting.'

By the time I left advertising – or it rolled over and threw me out, firing me for greed, ingratitude, frivolity and declining to work on cigarette accounts, or whichever loomed largest in their group mind – I had concluded that an advertising agency was the world in microcosm. At the bottom the proletariat, the cleaners, tea-ladies, typists and messenger boys, buzzing up and down in the lifts, busy about nothing: mysterious directives seeped down from the top floor, which seethed with conspiracy, and layered in between were the managerial classes: the aspiring grades of executives: the priesthood could be found in research, baffling in their wisdom: the technological classes in production, and sustaining the whole, of course, the 'creatives' – the writers and artists, on the whole unreliable and often drunk or absent, whose power was that they didn't care, who sometimes came up with the goods and sometimes didn't, but without whom nothing could happen at all, and who drove the rest mad.

Management would have done without the creatives if it possibly could, and let us know it. We were how they made money, and how they wasted it too. We got things wrong. We would propose campaigns which cost millions and sold nothing and lost clients. The first thing they did when the computer era began was to create a program which would obviate the need for copywriters – just fill in the name of the product and proceed as instructed, clicking on the adjectives most appropriate. It didn't work, of course. We humans did it better, just not all the time.

The strategies needed for survival inside an agency were pretty much the same as the ones outside, and it was in advertising that I developed a range of what are now called people skills which were to stand me in good stead. Regard one enemy as too many, a thousand friends as not enough. Say something nice before you say something nasty. Always praise before you blame. Deliver the good news first, then the bad. If there's any blame floating around, take it, even though it's nothing to do with you: others will be grateful that you carry the burden. Realize that today's scapegoat is tomorrow's hero, and vice versa. People hear what they want and expect to hear, not what is said. Never defend yourself: agree with your critics, it takes the wind out of their sails.

When a rogue art director turns out to be taking porno stills in the studio you have booked, do not join in. Find another studio and say nothing. But that was later, that was well into the Sixties, when sexual liberation ran wild. Everyone was at it, but you'd done all that. Orgies in Wardour Street? Forget it.

Lessons from advertising: realize that words on the page are always embattled. When it comes to work you deliver, pre-pare to fight but appear to be flexible: capitulate over small matters, so the large go through unchallenged: let the guilt of the victorious work on your behalf. The visually-minded would like to ease you off the page altogether: in a perfect world they would want a script with no dialogue, an ad with no copy. Every inch of picture is worth a thousand words, they'll say. They're wrong: they're just the looking kind, not the reading and the listening kind, who're just as numerous as they. Typographers will want to drive you off the page to make room for more space. Long paragraphs and small print? Forget it. Who wants to read if reading's difficult? They're right. Poets confine themselves to the middle of the page.

Juggling

But the office was always a piece of cake, compared to home. '*Unzip a banana!*' I wrote and there was little Nicolas all over London, the banana boy. I felt as if I were selling him. We kept our eyes lowered, both of us, and were glad when the posters disappeared from the hoardings, whilst buying a new bicycle. Morality, once you have children, seems to amount to pretty much what you can afford. And the good times, for such they were, didn't last long, or at any rate were well diluted by trouble.

Jane tried to throw herself from the window of Lexham Gardens: voices had told her it was the right thing to do. I went with her in the ambulance to Friern Barnet Mental Hospital, a place of long cream and green corridors, cell bars and clanking keys. We were to go to many such, in the future, though the age of the chemical cosh was dawning, and the bars and the keys got fewer as a whole new range of psychiatric drugs confined the disturbed inside their own heads. The bars and locks and clangings were worse for the visitors but better for the patients.

The director of *Titanic* and *Aliens*, James Cameron, I notice, has a love/hatred of corridors. He's forever filming in them, demonstrating the way they trap you, while luring you forward. They go on forever into the distance, and from time to time produce convulsions and disturbances, bug-eyed monsters or tides of seawater rushing down mahogany or metallic walls, and then you have to turn and run the way you came. Perhaps it's no more than primal memories of the passage through the birth canal, but I know what he feels.

In the old mental asylums the corridors were lined with chairs, in which sat depressives and paranoiacs, or anyone still prepared to recognize a chair as a chair. The depressives stared determinedly into space, the paranoiacs watched after you, with the body language of hostility, about to spring and jump. They played their bit parts well, they had a great sense of theatre. So had Jane. I was never sure she was sincere about her mental state. I used to hope and believe she was making it up, earning herself a well-deserved rest, having us all on. But this was the first and worst time: I went into the hospital with her and we stood, an ambulance driver in attendance, the cream and green corridor stretching before us, and waited, and then walking towards us out of the long distance, clanking keys getting near, came Matron and a male nurse. I handed my sister into their care and I walked away. I had deserted her. But someone had to go back and collect her children and look after them. The ambulance had gone. It took me hours to get back home.

By the morning I had four children, not just one, a pattern which was to continue for years, on and off. They were none of them ever naughty: they were too intelligent, and like myself as a child, too aware of the precariousness of life to rock any boats. Personally I love to see a wilful, naughty child: now there's luxury indeed. But they all grew up to be well-balanced, serious and witty persons, family people – happy, even – so between us, Jane, Margaret and me, we didn't do it too badly.

We were moving on to the Sixties out of the Fifties, age of the downers, into the hallucinogenic era. An account executive at CPV came back from lunch white as a sheet and said, 'I've jumped the gun to paradise, I'll pay the price for this.' He'd taken stuff called LSD, he said, inspired by Huxley's book, and sure enough, it had opened the gates of paradise, but hell as well. It was the first I'd heard of it.

And far from the last. Too many paid too high a price for a soupcon of mind-bending. LSD was stronger then: London was soon full of acid casualties, good friends with burned-out brains who'd go round in a perpetual state of puzzlement, traumatized by colours and shapes they'd never conceived of. Soon there was psychedelia on every shopping bag, every record sleeve, of course, and the brain took more easily to it – which merely meant those who wanted to be out of it took more of it.

Jane came out of hospital cheerful and positive, and went to live with the children in Newport, Essex, a pretty little village two stops down the railway line from Saffron Walden, in a cottage she rented from Winifred. Guido came and went. He had decided he wanted to join the church, and was about to start training as a vicar and had been accepted on the course. But then the plan fell through: he came across a Bishop at Liverpool Street station, who was dressed in his gaiters and other finery, and was overwhelmed by an urge to confess to

331

him, and told him that he was married and had children, and hadn't said so on his application forms. The bishop said he was sorry, but they could not now accept him for ordination. Sometimes it is better not to tell the truth, as Professor Knox had explained to me in what now seemed far-off days.

I fell out of love with Pers quite suddenly and without reason other than that I had wasted too much time in tears. As soon as I wanted him less than he wanted me, he decided to divorce his wife and marry me but I would not. And then he was in the same state of distress as I had been. It was hopeless.

Stepping Over the Cook

I was working by now as assistant to a consultant called Mary Gowing on the egg account. She was not young, single, and probably lesbian, though no one would have spoken about such a thing, and we certainly never did. She had worked for the Ministry of Food during and after the Second World War, writing wartime cookery books, as my grandfather Edgar had in World War I. He had written 'Eat Less Bread' – she had written 'Eat More Eggs', and now, well into peacetime, continued to do so. She knew everything there was to know about nutrition, housewifery, and about eggs.

She was a power in the agency, talked to clients and her bosses as if they were children, and was amazingly kind to me, I thought. It did not occur to me, at that time, that I had any special talent for writing. The knack was to state the obvious in the most simple way possible: the problem was others so often wouldn't let you. They were more preoccupied with their dignity than their profit. Back at CPV I'd wanted to say 'Vodka makes you drunker, quicker' but they wouldn't let me: now I wasn't allowed to name a new scent simply 'Yes'. Though someone recently quoted to me a slogan of mine which apparently Stanhope Shelton had enthused about, and was simple enough: 'Now you can pay for your central heating out of your housekeeping'. Was that brilliant? It didn't seem to me to be so then, or now: just obvious. But the client bought more space. Advertising agencies make their money on commission, buying space on the client's behalf. Their interests overlapped with those of the client, but were not identical. No one seemed quite to realize that, other than top management.

Mary Gowing lived on one of the first organic farms, outside London. She and her companion, a lady farmer, had spent ten years making the land free from artificial fertilizers and so forth. Mary looked out of the window one day and saw the old farmhand spreading artificial fertilizer on the ground. When challenged he said he was sorry for them, nothing grew without Fisons' stuff, he was doing them a good turn, and he was helping them out; they should be grateful. He'd been doing it for months. I was on the Fisons account at the time. I expect he had read one of my headlines – 'With Fisons green gets greener' – or some such slogan and had believed it. People did. One day I was late in for work and was called to Shelton's office. I thought he might be going to reproach me for my habitual lateness but he told me that Mary had died of a heart attack the previous night and would I take over the egg account as a temporary measure. This was Tuesday and the presentation was on Thursday. The show had to go on, no doubt about it.

I had a cleaning lady when I lived in Somerset, a Mrs Flower. She told me all about stepping over the cook. It was how you got promoted in the land of *Upstairs Downstairs*. Working conditions were bad, too much strain, too much heat, too much rich food, and cooks often drank the cooking sherry. So it was not unheard of for a good cook to have a heart attack and die during the course of a banquet. If she did so, the kitchen maid would step over her and take charge of the pots and pans, before other staff so much as dragged the body away and covered it with a tablecloth. The show must go on. This seemed to me what I had done. I had stepped over the cook. I still miss her. I wasn't bad at egg advertising but I didn't have the kind of holy simplicity she managed. And the egg farmers were getting restless, and the eggs were getting staler. And big independent producers did not see why they should have to pay dues to the Egg Marketing Board . . . and the account was in danger . . .

Stanhope Shelton had the bright idea of promoting the interests of our client the Metal Box Company – who provided the tin for the cans which contained the convenience foods of the day, in the days when fish fingers and frozen peas were still but a gleam in some entrepreneur's eye – by encouraging the use of canned foods in home cookery. To this end we were to take out weekly advertisements in the form of what looked like cookery columns. My face was to be there, smiling, looking wholesome, and beneath it the headline *Fay Bateman Says*, together with some useful recipes of my devising which involved the use of tinned food. For example: how to make a soufflé out of a can of concentrated chicken soup and six eggs. How to casserole the pork joint with baked beans and tinned tomatoes. I knew what was wanted in Acton, and Acton was our market.

Promotion meant more money. I was told by a fellow-worker (male) that I shouldn't accept it: the higher-paid jobs should be left to men, who had families to support. I protested that I too had a family to support, but he did not believe me. He could not conceive of a world in which women worked for anything but pin-money, or in which single women had children. Ten years later I was to have a meeting with an Inland Revenue inspector (female) who said to me 'but you're married: you work for pin-money', and when I said that I was the family breadwinner she too could not comprehend that either. People tend to believe that their own situation is universal. I hated to think how minuscule her salary must be.

I was just twenty-nine, my name was Fay Bateman, I was a copy group head, I was out of love with Pers, Nicolas was seven and going to school on his own, and I went to a party at the Empsons' in Hampstead, for which I got off the 31 bus in Adelaide Road, walked up the hill, and there met Ron Weldon; and that was that for thirty years.

Doubt and Destiny

Newly born, I had stayed at the family home at 120 Adelaide Road for a mere three weeks, for so short a period it barely counted. But the legend of it stayed with me, from what my mother and later my grandmother were to tell me. And here I was again, some thirty years on, on top of a bus as it passed Swiss Cottage and turned into Adelaide Road, on a moonlit night, making a decision that was to change my life. The date was 21 September, 1961. I don't forget it.

It was such a trivial decision, too, in the great scheme of things – was I going to stay on this bus or get off, go to a party in Hampstead, given by some people I didn't know, or not? I got off the bus, I went, and like someone in a romantic novel, met my destiny. But I so nearly didn't. Of course I don't 'believe' in astrology, numerology, palmistry, divination, or necromancy of any kind, but it is sometimes hard, in matters of love, not to. And it seems insulting to the universe to deny the possibility, if not the probability, of anything at all. If infinity is as they describe it, all things are not just possible but in the end certain: there can only be universes in which the 'destiny' of lovers is true, and universes in which it isn't. Easy and pleasant enough to slide from one parallel universe to the next and believe in 'destiny', and almost impossible, for lovers, not to. And how clearly the moments of epiphany are etched into the memory.

I was wearing, I have no doubt, what I always wore to parties: a black T-shirt, a cheap belt, a full skirt, stockings with ladders, safety pins to keep my bra together and as high heels as would pass my mother without comment. I loved the clatter they made down six flights of stairs though I don't suppose the other tenants did. My hair would be in the springy bird's-nest cloud around the face fashionable at the time. My kohled eyes, for once, were not red from crying over my hopeless love affair. I would have been reading a book or a magazine on the bus, probably science fiction.

Doubt set in just before Swiss Cottage. Why was I going to this party? I was partnerless and nearly thirty. I was not even going with a girlfriend. It would be embarrassing, I'd know no one there, nothing would *happen*. I would go home in the same state or worse for wear by cheap red wine. (By *happening*, of course, I meant meeting the man of my dreams. The trouble was I had met him, or so I thought – a handsome Dane, blond, intelligent and talented, but just so seldom *there*.) I would not go, I would stay on this bus until it got to Chalk Farm and from thence I would take the Tube home.

I did not listen to the voices of doubt, though I recall them as being extremely forceful, and probably right. I got off the bus in Adelaide Road at the stop nearest 120, walked back to Swiss Cottage, and up between the great houses of Fitzjohns Avenue, and cut over to Rosslyn Hill and Studio House, where the Empsons lived. Clip-clop all the way in high heels. Soon I was talking to the handsomest and tallest man in the room, as was my wont, and then saw his rather shorter, stockier, more interesting-seeming friend. He looked at me, I looked at him. His name was Ron Weldon. A few exchanges established us as both from dysfunctional backgrounds – like always calls to like – and that was that. Love at first sight. He wore jeans and a duffel coat: he was an artist. He had a Zapata moustache. I could not see what his mouth was like. Those moustaches were as much disguises as today's dark glasses ever were.

We walked home together in the early hours, over Primrose Hill, and down to his house in Chalcot Crescent. I took off my shoes. My feet could not endure any more. 'Keep looking on the ground,' he said. 'You never know what you might find.' And he bent down and picked a five-pound note from the gutter. I thought this was miraculous. I knew fate was on our side, and that I would marry him. It seemed to me that he knew so much and I knew so little. There was a full moon. Life, at least for brief patches, can get very like a Mills and Boon romance.

Of course you have to believe in destiny; that everything is sheer chance is an intolerable notion. That this future, this child, this job, this self as writer, is all because you decided to get off a bus and go to a party? Of course women, and men too, consult the stars to find out where destiny lies. I had no doubt at all at the time, or later, that meeting Ron was 'meant to be'. I daresay my grandparents Edgar and Frieda, meeting for the first time in 1897, felt the same about themselves, and I expect that Edgar, being the man he was, wanting to control even destiny itself, laid out a progressed horoscope to see what would happen next. That marriage lasted for thirty-four years. Mine with Ron was to last thirty-one. My mother's with Frank was a short six years. Were we to know the future, would any of us, in love, have doubted fate, or acted differently? I don't think so.

And I still like to remember exactly where I was on the bus (top deck, left-hand side) as it travelled up from West Hampstead to Swiss Cottage, just before it gets to Adelaide Road, when I felt destiny breathe down my neck. Just as sealed into my memory is the view out of the window, at a point between Westbury and Castle Cary stations on the train out of Paddington, when thirty years later I was to feel destiny doing the same again, and when least expected. Breathing down my neck, after a period of nothing happening, and nothing happening, except an all-pervasive melancholy, an uneasy sense of entropy. A winter's night, again a moon, a glittering landscape; 21 December, 1991, the winter solstice.

This time the voices didn't suggest escape: they were all excitement, thrill. Something is about to *happen*: every minute that passes brings it nearer. Absurd! My mother can read the *I Ching*, the Chinese Book of Oracles, and tell you who's going to win the Grand National. Whether she has the gift of prophecy, or is just good at judging form, take your pick. And as for the matter of Adelaide Road, that is no amazing coincidence; that is where the 31 bus *goes*.

Love at First Sight

If I am to look at this coldly, and leave out love at first sight, that kind of thing, I suspect that what happened was that Ron's and my mutual needs balanced themselves out to produce an equation more than satisfactory to both of us. Both of us, in the other's eyes, had plus and minus points and the plus very much outweighed the minus. Sexual attraction is evident within seconds, the rest within minutes of an initial conversation.

He was educated, well-read, artistic, bohemian, owned his own house, and was not currently married. He had come to the party with another woman so he was not any kind of reject. He was six years older than I was which was how it ought to be. He could teach me things I didn't know, about wine, art, music, politics and food. He had an eleven-year-old daughter who lived with him so he was a responsible parent. And isn't there something about him that reminds me of my father, whom one day I must get round to properly mourning? I've never yet had the time. And also a quality that reminded me of my mother: he knew what I was thinking and he occupied as of right the moral high ground, though his was concerned with artistic rather than moral sensibilities. Those were the pluses.

There were minuses too, there were bound to be. He had already been ten years in psychoanalysis, on which he had spent a large legacy, now just about run out: he had been married twice before, and I would have to share him with a daughter. He had a Fine Arts degree from Camberwell but didn't have a job, and though there was an easel in his bedroom and a fine smell of oil paint he was in the midst of a painter's block. He currently earned a living by painting and decorating.

As for me, I think he saw me thus. She was educated but not too bright, so far as could be observed. She was well-read, easy-natured, six years younger than he was, a good earner, albeit in advertising, had a child of her own, and so would be responsive to his. A port-and-lemon good-time girl, relatively unsophisticated, so he could teach her wine, music, politics. She spoke softly, moved softly, did not irritate overmuch, would cook and clean and look after his house, while not moving his things, and was no sort of rival. He would not teach her about art: if you didn't know instinctively you didn't deserve to know.

On the other hand she knew nothing about psychoanalysis, had a cloth ear, threw on her clothes, any old clothes, scarcely combed her hair, and worked in advertising in a very public kind of way, one hard to overlook. She had her photo in the paper every week, under a headline saying '*Fay Bateman Says*' in a half-page ad posing as a proper column, followed by a lot of silly domestic chat and recipes for terrible meals. How can I explain this to my friends, all of whom eat fresh food and avoid canned food on principle? Explain that she is writing this polluting junk on behalf of her employers? What kind of excuse is that? That a living must be earned somehow is no justification for rotting the fabric of society. And surely the only way a woman can have got to this position is if not exactly by sleeping her way to the top, at any rate by lying down rather easily when anyone suggested it?

But who cares, I said of him, and who cares, he said of me, it was love at first sight and there was no time for second thoughts. He assumed of me, as I assumed of him, that now we had met the person we had waited for all our lives, it was all we would either of us ever need. We were made for each other, we thought, and our lives would flourish so long as we were together. And so they did, for longer than we deserved, and for longer than is granted to most, and for that I must be grateful.

We had three children, conceived and born in love, rowed terribly, lived apart from time to time, came back together, and when eventually he was sixty-seven and scarcely in his right mind, and I was sixty-one, and believed I was in mine (as one does) we went too far. And we divorced and he died, and I thought the world would end. But it's amazing how it doesn't: or how much of him is part of me, if only by osmosis, and how we continue together. Nevertheless, the person who now loves and lives again, though still known on book jackets as Weldon, is on her doorbell Fox, and manages to hark back to include Birkinshaw, as if Weldon was just another interlude. Davies and Bateman were included in Weldon. Birkinshaw and Fay Bateman are included in Fox.

Many a therapist, looking at this sorry history, would say that what she describes is not love, it is neurotic dependency, but what do they know? The modern age has little under-standing of the phenomenon of love, and I daresay I played

341

my part in making sure it does not, since so much of the downside went into the fiction Weldon contrived, truer than truth, through the course of the marriage. She wrote a short story called *The Man with No Eyes*, which describes a family rent by a kind of blind elemental force, at the mercy of ancient demons, which summed much of it up. No wonder her husband tried to stop her writing in the early days of the marriage, forbade the use of the typewriter in the house, since the tap tap tapping annoyed him. He knew what was to come. Fox has lapsed into the third persoon again, but only temporarily. In the end Weldon must take the lion's share of the life, and it is cowardice for Fox to try to slip out from under.

At Sea

Meanwhile, in the autumn of 1961, a couple of weeks after I met Ron, Pers was due back from Malaga, or whichever of the little Mediterranean ports I will always associate with my earlier tear-drenched self. He phoned me to ask me to meet him in Christchurch, to crew with him on the cross-channel yacht race to Cherbourg. I had never crewed for anyone ever, let alone set sail. I was scared of the sea. After the voyage on the *Rangitoto* and the navy-blue waves of separation, who wouldn't be? But I went down to meet him, out of guilt and confusion, and we set off, the full manly crew, five of them, I think, Pers and I.

It seemed to me a very big boat. It became obvious a few miles out to sea that we were not going to win, or be anywhere near the lead, so we started the engine, and cruised leisurely into Cherbourg for the annual dinner – lobsters and champagne – before catching the midnight tide back home to Portsmouth. How they drank, these sailors – except, for once, Pers: sailing boats was the one responsibility he took seriously; forget the rest. You drank for the shore: stayed sober for the sea. He was a Viking trapped in an ad man's suit.

At midnight the crew staggered back to the boat to catch the tide, and set out to sea with raucous good cheer, and then they all passed out on their bunks, leaving Pers and me, sober, to get us home. A wind had got up and a choppy sea, and now a fog closed in – and we were going through the busiest shipping lanes in the world and couldn't see a thing. Pers leaped about from spar to spar in the dark, furling sails, meeting dire emergencies as they arose, telling me to take the tiller. What a hero! But what did I know about tillers? I have a brain deficiency when it comes to mirror images. It was why I never got into J. Walter Thompson – I couldn't do mirror images. I failed copy test after copy test. Much to my chagrin. Unfit! It didn't seem reasonable to me that when I moved the tiller to the right the boat went to the left: you can teach yourself, but under pressure the knowledge goes. And now I was under pressure. Indeed, I thought we would die.

Pers yelled to me over the storm that it was okay if you saw a red and green light coming towards you, but if they merged into one you were on a collision course, get out of the way. And all around all I could see were single lights coming towards me from all directions, and dark hulls slithering by, while Pers yelled and leapt. We got back to port alive and fell into an exhausted sleep, and eventually the rest of the crew woke and said they knew Pers could sail anything single-handed. I felt very proud of him but at noon I told him I loved another and fled. He took an overdose of sleeping pills, but was saved, and left advertising and stopped drinking, and married happily and went to live in Christchurch as a sailing man. He died not long ago and his wife let me know, so he must have spoken of me sometimes.

I moved into 3 Chalcot Crescent permanently the next day, with Nicolas, and lay for a week in bed in a state of acute depression; the world somehow whited out, and voices muffled, as if I was back in my childhood limbo and there had been a bad snowstorm. I should by rights have been happy: as it was I left undone those things that ought to have been done and couldn't even get to work. But perhaps I knew I was in a safe haven at last, and so all the traumas of the past, the things done which should not have been done, crept up on me now that there was time and space for my mind to repair itself. I heard someone in the house across the gardens at the back, in Rothwell Street, crying for help, or think I did, and did nothing about it. I could not make myself lift my head from my pillow. Ron said that if I didn't go into psychoanalysis he wouldn't marry me, so I said I would. Anything, even that. On my return from Cherbourg we had begun to talk about marriage. Marriage is what happens when one at least of the partners doesn't want the other to get away. It was unfortunate that we were both married to others, so the conversations were about how to get formally unmarried so as to start again properly.

Safe is safe but safe is not necessarily permanent: perhaps the cries for help from across the way were myself calling to myself, which is why they are so firmly lodged in my memory.

For now I come to think of it the cries came from the very house in Rothwell Street which fifteen years later I was to rent when 3 Chalcot Crescent was sold, and I was to move from house to house, a poor lost thing again, trying to find a dwelling which Ron liked sufficiently to move back in with me and our children. No wonder, if this is the case, I did not hear: no wonder I had whited out the world. I was whiting out common sense.

Prudence says one thing, desire says another, and I'd rather go with desire any time. But true love does leave one in very humiliating situations. By and large I am going for the myself-in-the-future talking to myself-in-the-past theory of voices heard but not responded to, because one's head is determinedly under the pillow.

Moving In

Rothwell Street was not a patch on Chalcot Crescent, that's for sure. Rothwell was short and straight, Chalcot had the prettiest curve. Chalcot was perfect. The crescent of tall narrow houses with matching porticoes had been built in the 1830s in the Georgian style. We had the second house along on the sunny side of the street. In the morning you looked out of the French windows of the first floor and there was Primrose Hill, green and glossy. At night you could hear the lions roaring in the zoo.

At that time the area was just about emerging from slumhood. The houses were shabby and unpainted, rented not owned.

Whole families would live in a single room. In the summer, front doors were left open and tenants sat on the steps and drank. The area, too near Euston for its own good, was known as the coal blow and had the highest bronchitis rate in Europe. Coal dust from the railway marshalling yards blew over and covered everything with black particulate soot. But the trains were being electrified, the air was becoming clean again, and the hill was returning to what it had been when the houses were built – intended for the new professional classes – elegantly proportioned, with a kitchen basement and a couple of attic rooms for the servants. Ron was the first of the owner-occupiers.

It was a matter of amazement to me to watch the poor disappear as the middle classes moved in. The gentrification process took a mere five years. Houses would be sold by the slum landlords, either cleared of tenants, at the new high prices, or with 'sitting tenants' in them, too well protected by the tenancy laws to evict, too stubborn to be bought out, or too brave to be threatened out. Then the new owners would have to undertake to house these refusees until they died, so the older they were, the higher the price asked. These creeping old people, sometimes glimpsed making their way through the newly decorated house to some back room, were treated rather as pets. For a time simply everyone had one.

'How are you today, Mr Jones?' would be the courteous question.
'Well enough, thank you,' came the reply, with the dark addition, 'more's the pity for you.'

Ron was very sociable. As the neighbours changed, the parties had to get quieter. The front door had to be painted. We had a tenant too, though not a sitting one. She was Ethel de Keyser, a white South African supporter of the ANC. My, how she raised funds. She was charming and persuasive and very busy. She had a little Mini and would leave the house at night in her nightdress and drive over to be with her lover, an African politician. The basement area where she lived was almost wholly underground. It must have been horrible. These days the council would declare it unfit for human habitation. There was a coalhole in the pavement in front of each house where the coalman, black with soot, could empty his sacks of coal, inches in front of Ethel's window, for us to haul upstairs to feed the Pither stove. Once the servants would have done that kind of thing.

But it was not yet time for the servants to move back in, not yet. By the Nineties the artists, writers and musicians had been eased out and the bankers, editors and dot com people had moved in, and a servant or two with them. The Crescent will always be just a hint racy, and the times when the drunken painters would throw bottles from balcony to balcony across the street as the drink ran out in one household, to be helped out by another, still quivers in the air. Otherwise the Crescent is back to normal, lived in by the kind of people it was meant for in the first place, the houses prettily painted, with architect-designed interiors, conservatories added, ground cut away to give the basement areas proper light, and nannies in plenty, albeit with well developed leg muscles from running up and down so many stairs.

In the days before I was run over by the writing steamroller, and could give my husband proper attention, we were amazingly happy. His daughter Karen was not: she wanted him for herself and who could blame her? I was a bad stepmother;

not that I was cruel, on the contrary, I doubt that I ever spoke a single cross word to her, but I wanted to be a better mother to her than her own, always a great mistake. With my current crop of stepchildren, three boys, I am much better, rarely speaking unless spoken to, and adopting a policy of emotional free trade and laissez-faire.

Karen, never a one for school, ran off the day Dan was born (in 1963) to be with her mother, then in Peru. She has been in and out of my life ever since, and having quite calmed down now, three admirable children later, is a marriage guidance counsellor and social worker in Bristol and looks pretty good to me.

A Career is Born

The Sixties had dawned. There was high employment. 'The job' had little by little turned into a career. The Beatles were singing up in the Cavern in Liverpool. Eve Smith, art director on the milk account at Ogilvie and Mather, went up to see them and came back raving and said she had to sign them up, but the general consensus was their hair was too long, they weren't right for a family campaign. The sun seemed always to be shining. I'd get the tube to Charing Cross station in the morning and walk down through the gardens in front of the Savoy to Waterloo Bridge and Brettenham House to work. Sometimes I would fall into step with Jonathan Gathorn Hardy, not yet a novelist, still a copywriter. He was very clever and lordly: I asked him once why the sole of his shoe was tied on with a piece of string to stop it flapping. Could he not afford to have it mended? (Those were the days when shoes were mended, not thrown away and replaced.) He said yes, just about, but it was his hope that Stanhope Shelton would notice, and give him a rise.

But I was worldly wise by then, and said, no, the newer your shoes, the less you looked as if you needed money, the more likely you were to acquire it. We agreed that it was terrible what life and time taught you. Jonny wrote an excellent novel called *The Office*, and later a book about nannies, which was a great hit, and he continues to write non-fiction, which makes money, and the kind of magical, elliptical novels which don't, being out of fashion. I have no doubt they will be acknowledged for what they are, with time, but we'll all be dead by then. Still, it's some comfort.

I was made copy group head. That meant more money, and that I got to sit at the desk next to the window. Edwin Brock the poet sat behind me, and behind him David Wevill, then married to Assia, who was later to die by her own hand, and take her child with her, because Ted Hughes was unkind. David was very handsome and very grand: and he and Assia, with her brooding sultry beauty, made a kind of glorious poetic pair that for a time rivalled the Ted Hughes and Sylvia Plath conjunction, Ted with his craggy northern looks, and Sylvia, all lanky American grace. When either pair entered rooms heads turned, and a kind of glow came in with them.

David was upset at having to make his living, if only temporarily, and perforce, writing copy. The rest of us were hardened to it. I think that now he is a professor of English at Austin, Texas, and will not mind if I say he was not very good at writing copy when a young man. He might even think it was to his credit. Edwin and I did his work for him, and put his initials on the top of our submissions, and I would countersign, and so we kept him going while he went off to the pub. I don't think he was at all grateful. He would look at what he was meant to have written with an expression of astonishment on his perfect, handsome face, and then at us, in bewilderment. How could such collections of words be wanted or needed by anyone in the world?

But he was a good poet, and we knew it was our duty to do what we could in the name of art. He was not as good as Brock, known as the Policeman Poet. Edwin was to stay in advertising after all of us had left: he worked for the *Financial Times*, quite brilliantly, and became a rather good potter too. A man of many parts, a stoical, sensible person with the sad, friendly intensity of being which comes from knowing more about the world than is necessary, as ex-policemen do, and he was often crossed in love.

David Wevill had met Assia on the ship coming over from Canada – I have a memory that she was on her way over to marry someone else – and they left the ship in love and married soon after. They lived for a while in Belsize Park Gardens, and then, looking for a new place to live, knocked on the Hughes' door, at 3 Chalcot Square. (I knew the Hugheses mostly from delivering their letters when they came to us at the Crescent by mistake.) Like recognizing like, they became friends, though they never took the flat.

The Wevills went to stay with the Hugheses in Devon for the weekend. Assia told me the reason she took up with Ted was because she felt insulted when Sylvia, then with two small children, asked her to peel the potatoes for lunch. Assia was always sensitive to anyone she thought treated her like a servant: she would bridle if you asked her to lend a hand, so one never did. She tended to be a 'how dare she', 'how dare he' kind of person, a tendency an Israeli background always encourages. So to be revenged she went down the garden where Ted, later to be Poet Laureate, was seeing to the beans, and flirted with him. And that's how it started. And then it became serious, said Assia, and soon there was no more Wevill marriage, and then, and then –

The Ted–Sylvia–Assia saga, which ended with such tragedy nearly forty years ago – Ted took up with Assia and made her pregnant and Sylvia killed herself, and five years later Assia was to kill herself and her child, out of guilt from which Ted declined to save her – was I think one of those seminal

351

events which brought forth the fruit of Seventies feminism. That such talented women should die for what – for love? Because that's what they died of, not depression, let alone 'born to suicide' as is so often said of Sylvia.

How could it happen, today's young women ask, in bewilderment? How could women see their lives only in terms of being loved or not loved by a man? The times were against them, so the times had to change. And so they did.

Change

The early Sixties were opulent, frivolous pre-feminist days. Bateman-cum-Weldon, in the changeover patch from one to another, is so busy she hardly knows what she's doing. She has arrived where she thinks she ought to be. Once or twice a week she flops down on her psychoanalyst's couch and has a little rest, and a rather tormenting little weep. All around her is change, the old order being swept away.

How suddenly the fashions changed. Skirts shot up, hair frothed around the face in a springy birds's-nest: look down on your shoes and they were green with satin bows, not the brown and black of the old days. Language loosened up: students took to Marxism, it became the thing to speak with the accents of the people: the young wore jeans in homage to the poor, the future was seen to lie with the workers. The schools stopped teaching by rote, and decided grammar was not important. Carrier bags were made of bright plastic not brown paper, and were everywhere, as people shopped for the fun of it; on the TV rockets aimed for the moon, curved, drooped and fell in a cloud of hot air.

This strange creature Bateman Before Weldon lives and speaks to the future in a gasp of event and activity. She has hardly time to get one sentence out before another takes over. Psychoanalysis does not 'cure' her of anything in particular, but it enables her, as she explains herself non-stop for the fifty-minute hour, to separate thought out from feeling, and turn both into a coherent narrative. She learns the value of finishing her sentences and composing them with grace. Otherwise it is torment: she dreads the sessions. She is trying to do something unnatural, as she realizes later: that is, to change herself to suit a patriarchal society, when she would be better employed changing society to suit herself. She is meant to overcome her penis envy, which is apparently at the root of her discontent.

Many of her women friends, in this pre-feminist phase, are in analysis, just as many now are in therapy. I think analysis was healthier: Freud-based, it suggested one had no one to blame but oneself, whilst acknowledging one was born flawed: psychotherapy, Jung-based, lets the patient off the hook, offering tea and sympathy, casting round for others to take the blame, as to why the one born perfect should have ended up in such a state. In the Sixties these examinations of the self took place against an arid background of almost universal emotional illiteracy: today we wallow in such seas of empathy it can be hard to keep afloat. Deluge replaces drought. The more we understand each other the harder it seems for us to cleave to one another for any length of time.

353

Both Ron and I went to see our analysts twice a week so really there was no need to speak to each other. Many years into Ron's analysis I called his, Mrs Warburg, in a fury to say I thought this was absurd. He never talked to me because he talked to her, and it had been going on for twenty-three years, was there never to be an end to it? She said, benignly, 'My dear, one day he will stop seeing me and then you will be sorry.' I was, too. My Miss Rowlands hardly spoke at all. She used to knit, I'll swear she did, though I would lie on a couch with my head to the wall so I couldn't see her, but I would hear the needles going click click click. But when my sister died, she cried, and I forgave her a lot for that. 'She was like a walnut withered in its shell,' Miss Rowlands said.

I thought Jane had had more of a life than that: and loved and lost and had children and wrote poetry, and sure, occasionally went mad, but was well acquainted with God: I think she was more like a rose which fell off its stem in a storm, instead of waiting to grow old and blowsy and drift away like the rest of us. She lies in the churchyard at Newport: the church is on a little hill, you can see it from the train from Liverpool Street to Cambridge, the station after Audley End, which used to be the junction for Saffron Walden. Perhaps it was Jane we heard weeping in the corridors of the haunted house on Market Hill, and ourselves for her.

Clutter

But how the material world bore in upon us at Chalcot Crescent. It became apparent the first morning I was there, when the heavy Victorian curtains were released from their corded tie and light streamed in upon the brass bed which was the epicentre of the house. Wherever you looked there was an object standing between you and the larger view: something old and battered, which with a bit of restoration could be made beautiful again, and even possibly valuable: a Jacobean chest with only one foot, a dresser without handles, a porcelain shepherdess without her crook, a grandfather clock with one hand, a soup tureen with only three legs: a shell carved by a seaman in the Napoleonic wars, faded rugs upon the floor, lost landscapes on the walls.

Just as my mother thought we were here on this earth to scavenge scraps of spirit left after the Fall, so Ron believed it was our function to rescue the lost material glories of the past. To rescue did not mean to restore, so much as to appreciate. What was broken was better than what was mended, being still all possibility, what was old and mended was better than what was new and perfect. What was new, what was made by machine, not hand, made of plastic, not wood, what was clean in line or form, was of today, and what was of today was worthless. New things were not needed in the house, let alone welcomed, though gradually of course convenience won over principle. It took thirty years, but in the end we had a washing machine, dryer, toaster, dishwasher, television, video, central heating, microwave, power steering, and stereo, like anyone else, though not yet a CD player. Digital sound was anathema.

Nicolas and Karen and myself learned to move among objects without knocking anything, moving anything, changing anything. There was no way I could impose my will upon the house I now lived in, any more than I had any say in a house in which my mother lived. And all this was even before Ron abandoned art and became an antique dealer. Mind you, clutter was the fashion of the time, still reflecting a world rapidly passing, in which wives and maids were there to dust and polish. Minimalism is a sensible response to too much to do, and too little time to do it in.

It was my normal female task to see to the domestic running of the house, the child-care, and do the shopping, the cooking and the laundry, as well as going out to work. I did not resent it, but took these duties for granted. The general assumption was that if a woman worked it was not to interfere with the household's comfort or leisure in any way. No matter how the household might depend upon her income, her working outside the home was seen as a kind of wilful, self-indulgent act: her true role was as a home-maker. A man who did housework or cooked, likewise, was despised. Male and female, we all busily gender role-played, in a way that seems extraordinary today. Ron refused to have a washing machine in the house – he did not like the sound of domestic machinery, and argued that there was no room for one. So twice a week after work I would haul my bags of washing to the launderette and put it through their machines. Nor did Ron like the sound of a typewriter in the house. Their use was embargoed. I had to take to writing by hand. His ideal woman, he once said, only half joking, was barefoot, pregnant, at the sink and up to her elbows in soapy water. A Saskia to his Rembrandt.

I wrote a dismal play once called *Shopping*, in which a woman lies dying on a hospital bed, with a little cluster of guests around her. They are called Shopping, Washing, Cleaning, Dusting, Cooking, and Socks. They reproach her for her lack of love, for ignoring them, giving the others too much time. They bicker among themselves. Socks is missing, but eventually turns up, bitter, faded and twisted, to deal the final death-blow. Between them they finish her off. The story is an historical document of a time now gone.

And I wrote a ghost story once in which the washing basket is found to be full of socks twisted and stretched out of shape and tied together to make a pile of writhing serpents. People want to know how autobiographical fiction is. It is and it isn't. If you have had three husbands and many sons socks count – though they seldom add up. What looms large in the life – as do these little scraps of fabric which fade and change from wash to wash, and shrink at different rates but always shrink, and if they start white and smooth, end up bobbled and grey – does tend to emerge in the fiction.

I learned to cook: extravagant, murderous cooking out of Elizabeth David. Recipes from all the world, spices and herbs from everywhere: the ingredients had finally arrived: olive oil, garlic, mushrooms, avocados, aubergines, if in doubt add cream and brandy, to make up for decades of plain roast lamb and steamed cod. I would work out dinner party menus in the morning, shop in the lunch-hour, plan the logistics in

357

the afternoon and put them into practice when I got back home. I became so proficient I could have a four-course dinner prepared in an hour, and put the children to bed, and deal with the day's emergencies, and welcome guests in a state of tranquillity.

My mother the while had taken on Jane's children and lived with them in the country, in the small town of Newport, Essex, by the courtesy of the State, and with help from myself. They lived frugally, which suited my mother, but contentedly, and thrived at the local grammar school. The cousins holidayed together, albeit in tents. The Welfare State did well by them: it had changed in ten years from the censorious and grudging safety net for the poor and indigent, which Jane met when the children were little and she tried to find relief from anxiety – how do we live? how do we eat? – into something far more positive. Too late for Jane, but not for her children. The State, too, provided me with an education without protest or argument, and I am grateful to it. I paid my taxes ungrudgingly. I do not think it does as well for its young citizens today.

Making Good

I typed out invoices for Ron's building and decorating work on his turn-of-the-century machine. 'To making good:' I'd write, '£20.' I loved the phrase 'making good'. After so much doing the opposite, here we were, doing just that. I did worry about his lady customers. They had so much time on their hands, so many of these women. They were so beautiful, they wore furs and silks and had high heels: they made films and wrote books and he had been in the custom of responding to their advances. Well, why not? But not now, surely. He had me.

He packed away his easel and his paints. The bedroom stopped smelling like an artist's studio, of oil paint, linseed oil and turpentine. I thought that was a shame. He said that no one could be an artist and a family man as well. I tried to persuade him that that was not true. I could not be responsible for this. I cited Rembrandt and Rubens but failed to convince him. Perhaps they were too orderly and northern as painters to count: he had a southern disposition. He was more a Van Gogh and Gauguin man. I once lost him in a market in the South of France; wherever I looked there were more of him, dark, stocky, sultry. Picassos all. I gave him the complete letters of Van Gogh and he wept as he read them. To him the choice was clear. The great artist, like the great religious leader, is the one who walks away from family ties, and perhaps for men this is true. He had decided that he would not, could not, walk away. The easel went up to the attic, to be brought down twenty-five years later.

Ron's father was a Weldon of the paper pattern factory: his grandfather was a Sainsbury of the grocer family: both Jewish immigrants into the East End around the turn of the century. His mother was a young lady from Scotland, who had married her first husband in St James Mayfair, a Mr Fairbanks, gone to India, and returned to run off with Ron's father, the black sheep of the by then wealthy Weldon family. He had not married her but they had lived as man and wife in a large house by the golf course in Bournemouth. He was a golfing man. When Ron was eleven and his brother nine their father had run off with a barmaid, abandoning wife and sons to genteel poverty, maintained in the large house by a family trust.

Ron had been sent to prep school, and then to a naval ship for the training of young officers. His experiences there had been much like Colyn's in the orphanage: he had had a nervous breakdown and been sent home to be privately tutored. The tutor was an ardent socialist, who had given him principles foreign to the rest of the family, and which were to last him for the rest of his life. When he was sixteen he ran a jazz club in Bournemouth, much to his mother's disgust. At eighteen he was conscripted into the army. He was selected for officer training, but the troops under his command simply jumped in the river instead of abseiling across on his command so he remained in the ranks. They did this, or so Ron claimed, because they wanted him as one of them.

He was put in a military band instead and played trumpet. He reported coming back to barracks late in the morning, still drunk, and would jazz up reveille to the great delight of the men if not the officers. He never got to the front line in Burma because his name began with a W, and was over a page which no one ever bothered to turn: everyone else went off and was killed, but he was spared. (This is the only advantage of being at the end of the alphabet of which I have ever heard. I speak as one who went from B on to D back to B and then leapt to W. Those at the beginning of the alphabet win more elections, get left off hotel reservation lists less and sell more books proportionately than those at the end. A for Archer means lean and stretch, W for Weldon means scrabble on the floor in the dust in the bottom right-hand corner of bookstore and library.)

After the war ended, however, Ron was set to work clearing rivers of dead bodies: he had nightmares about it until the end of his life: he would describe them to me, latterly, with a fair degree of sadism mixed up with the need to talk. That is what I mean when I say evil does not end: it just gets handed on.

Ron had been married twice, first to Karen's mother Barbara when he came back from the wars and became a student at Bournemouth Art College, and she was waiting for him, the sweetheart he had left behind. But he returned a different man. He and Barbara married in haste and too young, and soon divorced. Then he married a young painter called Cynthia Pell, who went very mad. I wrote a muted and I hope disguised description of the end of this marriage, as I imagined it, though I never knew, in a story called 'Through a Dustbin, Darkly'. Like my poor Aunt Faith, Cynthia lived for the rest of her life in an asylum.

Her paintings have since been collected and exhibited and are very well thought of, if distressing in their vision of humanity. But again, I think the horrid visions of the mad have as much to do with hating the rest of the world and wanting to punish it for being cheerful. She killed herself in the end by cutting her own throat. She came to visit me once, when my second son Daniel was a few months old, and told me I was crass, and insensitive, and had stopped Ron painting, and took the baby from my arms and threw him across the room. Then she left. She was dark with flushed cheeks, and stunning-looking. She was wearing very shiny clompy black shoes. Dan landed on a sofa and didn't even cry, just looked surprised. Ron said he'd see to it and the incident was never mentioned again. He didn't like to talk about Cynthia: he had too many horrors in his life. If he visited her he did not tell me. I hope he did. The marriage was full of things which we never mentioned.

Fay Weldon

1963. I am pregnant: we are both delighted. Together we have our second chance. We got off to dicey beginnings but it's going to be okay. The world opens up before us, full of new things and special delights. The world nearly comes to an end, actually, with the Cuba crisis, but we are reprieved. The quasar is discovered, the very first pictures are back from Venus, a Russian woman goes into space, the Christine Keeler scandal erupts, Martin Luther King has a dream, and Ronald Biggs robs a train. Harold Wilson is about to become Prime Minister, and I get bigger and bigger.

I can't stop work: we need the money. I will never be able to stop work: we will always need the money, but that's okay. No one moves me off the egg account or bothers to replace Mary Gowing as my senior. I am pretty much in charge round here. That's fine by me. People do what I say because I so seldom tell them to do anything. Things move ahead smoothly. We now have our own TV department: we don't farm production out to specialist agencies. It's done in-house.

It's not a very steady or stable department: people keep moving or being fired. Often there's only me to do the whole thing myself. Write the egg commercial, send out the film crews (lots of money swilling about: if I so much as write

362

'arctic' to describe the night in a script the whole crew is likely to take off to the North Pole to film: they'd prefer it if I wrote tropical, and often ask me to. I do my best to oblige. It is part of the writer's duty to provide employment.) They come back from wherever with the film, hand it over to me, I run it through the Moviola, edit, cut, dub, put on the music, I do the lot. I have to, because there's no one else to do it, and there's a transmission date coming up, and no one seems to know much about that either.

Pling plong, pling plong, mother-love music over mother – love that breakfast egg! *Crack* goes the spoon on the smooth curved shell. Caption: *'Go to Work on an Egg!'* So long as you don't notice it's technology, and think too much about how women allegedly can't do this kind of thing, it's all quite easy. I take the finished reels round myself in a taxi, without so much as an in-house screening. The more unobserved you are, I realize, the better the finished results. It's other people's doubts that hamper you.

My friend Julian Abercrombie down the corridor, who smokes a pipe but is definitely female and once had an affair with Dylan Thomas, writes a TV play. I marvel at this. Women don't write TV plays. They don't understand the technology. I realize that the only difference between a TV commercial and a TV play, is that the first is short and sells a product and the second is long and sells an idea. If you can do one you can do the other.

I was not yet Weldon – I was still Bateman – until five weeks before Dan was born, when both our divorces came through. In those days a private detective had to come and inspect the bed for signs of adulterous sexual activity: both of us

363

consented to be the guilty party. No one asked us for any money and we asked for none.

When the detective came to inspect the sheets it was a woman, which surprised me. Odd the things that women can do if they have to, though it's not the job I would choose. Our decrees absolute turn up in the post. Now we can get married. It's the middle of June. The baby's due in a couple of weeks. We go to the Camden Registry Office: Hetta Empson is there: I can't remember who else. It's a quiet wedding because people still tend to get married before they get pregnant, and I am very pregnant indeed. I can't remember what I wore: I expect it was some kind of voluminous silk caftan. We go to a Chinese restaurant after the ceremony and I can't manage the chopsticks. I have a lot to learn.

Ron puts half the house in my name. Now that's really something. The house and the things in it are his life. It's not yet customary for houses to be in joint ownership. Women can't even take out mortgages: very few own property.

I stay home to wait for the baby. My name is Weldon now, properly, Mrs Weldon: Birkinshaw, Davies and Bateman are behind me, I have moved into another phase. I wait and wait for the baby to come. It doesn't. It is very hot. June moves into July. I can hardly stand up. I have to do something with my time. I write a TV play. If Julian can do it so can I. It is about a man, of course – plays are, at that time – but the women have all the best lines. I called it *A Catching Complaint*.

'Unhappiness is a catching complaint,' I write. 'And misfortune is an insult to the fortunate. So let's peck them to death, the sad ones. They can't help it, but they ought to help it.' I can quote from it because I have a yellowed press cutting here beside me, found in an old photo album. Unlike novels, TV plays are as transitory as the present. No sooner here than it's gone. But the play starred Russell Godfrey, Diana Fairfax, Priscilla Morgan, Hilda Baker and Tessa Wyatt, the very best the times could offer.

I write by hand and get a friend to type the play out because of the embargo on typing in the house. The sun streams in on the table on the first floor of 3 Chalcot Crescent: Nicolas is happy and loves his school: Karen is being mysterious about her mother, who is back from Lima to kidnap her (Ron's description) or rescue her (Barbara's): the baby has stopped kicking and fallen quite quiet, which they do when they've decided it's time to be born.

I put the play into an envelope: I feel the same awe of it as I did of the story I wrote about a railway station when I was eleven, and about Pompeii when I was fifteen. I know it has an existence outside myself: I simply deliver it, as a midwife delivers a baby. It is 18 July, 1963. I call the doctor who is startled to find I haven't given birth yet and says I really have to go into hospital to have the baby induced, *now*. It's been too long.

I go to the hospital in a taxi: I can't get hold of Ron who's meant to be decorating a house in Gloucester Crescent in Camden Town – I think it was Jonathan Miller's – and has left me his number in case I go into labour, but they say he has not come back from lunch. This is a bit worrying because his painting partner is his best friend's girlfriend, blonde, a proper artist's moll, and I am now counted as a wife, and she is unhappy, but I am in no state to worry. I know he loves me.

Karen seems to be secretly packing, but I can't go into that now. I get the taxi to stop on the way to University College Hospital where my father trained, and where I am to have the baby, put *A Catching Complaint* through the letterbox on the corner of Regent's Park Road and Primrose Hill Road, where later I was to kill poor disagreeable Angie in *The Hearts and Lives of Men*, and three violent hours later Daniel has burst flailing into the world.

And I am now thoroughly Weldon, locked in by motherhood, steam-rollered. What I do from now on, all that early stuff digested and out of the way, is write, and let living take a minor role.